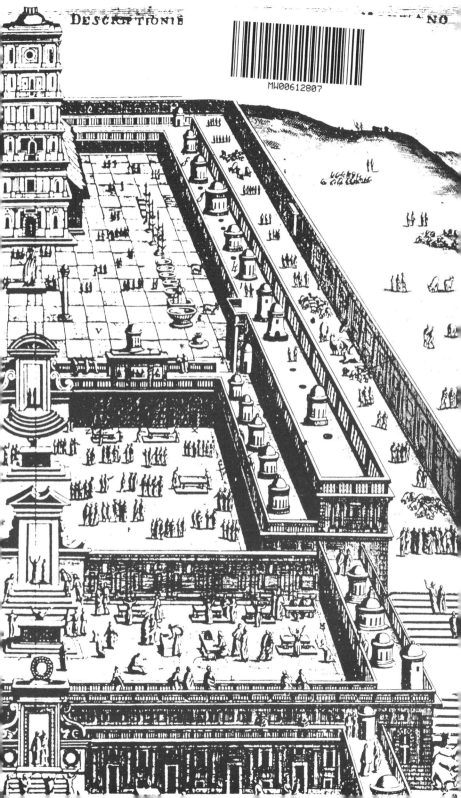

JERUSALEM

The Holy City in Literature

Jerusalem the Golden

Seventeenth-century engraving

JERUSALEM

THE HOLY CITY IN LITERATURE

Edited with introductory notes by
Miron Grindea

Preface by Graham Greene

KAHN & AVERILL, LONDON
with ADAM INTERNATIONAL REVIEW, LONDON

First published in 1968 by
Adam International Review

Reprinted as a hardcover in 1981 by
Kahn & Averill
9 Harrington Road, London SW7 3ES

Reprinted in 1996 by
Kahn & Averill and
Adam International Review

British Library Cataloguing in Publication Data

Jerusalem: the Holy City in literature.—2nd ed.
I. Jerusalem in literature
I. Grindea, Miron
809'.933256944   PN6071.J/

ISBN 0-900707-65-8

Printed in Great Britain by
The Cromwell Press Ltd, Melksham, Wiltshire

CONTENTS

PREFACE

Jerusalem, with a population a little bit larger than Leicester, is probably the most beautiful city in the world, and the preservation of this beauty is perhaps the only good fruit of the British Mandate. One of the most moving passages in Miron Grindea's far-ranging anthology of Jewish, Moslem and Christian literature, where Gibbon rubs shoulders with 16th Century Joseph Ha-Cohen and 10th Century Chasdai Iba Shaprut with Benjamin Disraeli, is a passage from Sir Ronald Storr's *Orientations* where he describes the restorations, the repairs and the preservation work done under his direction as High Commissioner: "Persons of wider experience and more facile emotions have often come there to pray and gone away to mock. For me Jerusalem stood and stands alone among the cities of the world...in a sense that I cannot explain there is no promotion after Jerusalem."

Those who come to pray and go away to mock are seeking the wrong Jerusalem. They expect, I think, to find peace there - the peace of a church, even of a museum. But Jerusalem was founded by a warrior king, it was the death-place of Christ who foretold that he would bring not peace but a sword, and it was the legendary scene of the Ascension of Mohammed who was hardly a peacemaker. The worst fate that a sick imagination could invent for Jerusalem would be for it to become a kind of Middle Eastern Geneva, her security guaranteed by the United Nations and a peaceful way of life supervised under the benevolent eye of a Dr. Kurt Waldheim. But that, thank God, can never be. Jerusalem's existence will always seem temporary and precarious as if she stood in the eye of a cyclone. She is the great survivor of the world.

Perhaps that is what has drawn Miron Grindea to make this anthology in celebration of its survival. He founded his magazine *Adam* in the midst of the greatest massacre the world has yet known and he has fought over forty years to keep it alive with some of the obstinacy of those old trees in the Garden of Gethesame that are more ancient, so it is said, than Hadrian's Wall.

Who knows better than he that hope always alternates with despair and how the beauty of Jerusalem does not depend on her peace?

July 1981   Graham Greene

CITY OF GRIEF AND HOPE

To the memory of my parents
— who dreamed of Jerusalem

The idea of this anthology came to us one Christmas Day when, in blazing sunshine, we first saw Jerusalem. Only the night before, in Rome in a downpour, we were among many thousands gathered for Midnight Mass at St. Peter's. Soon afterwards, in a storm-tossed, angry aircraft, we had accomplished in less than six hours the physical link between the two shrines: a journey that in former times took pilgrims months, sometimes years of travel on foot, horseback or in small boats over hostile seas and mountains, until Sion the dream became Zion the incredible sight.

When we arrived, there were still bullets whistling above and throughout the place, in the name of the recent 'unholy war'; a brooding desolation and an exhausted tension prevailed where the Holy City had been grotesquely and ruthlessly cut in two. It was not a sense of premonition, nor any particular prophetic anticipation, and certainly not a desire to make literary use of contemporary tragedy, that forced this particular subject upon us. It sprang rather from an emotional experience: finding ourselves in the *Civitas Dei* which, throughout the ages, has been a radiant and inexhaustible inspiration to writers, poets and mystics.

History from time to time seems to ridicule mankind, though in the case of Jerusalem it took thousands of years to fulfil the whole cycle of irony. Amidst the inevitable scholarly controversies as to the *precise* date, Jerusalem, a few years ago, released an unusual invitation throughout the world to a celebration unique in history: the three thousandth anniversary of God's City. Not of its mysterious birth, lost in legendary antiquity, but of the event that made it the metropolis of monotheistic religion—King David's conquest of Mount Zion.

The long dramatic sweep of history that lies between this event and the international disputes raging round the centre of three world religions, may perhaps be glimpsed in our selection of

5

prose and poetry. The image of the past is ever present with the various civilizations which have in turn settled there, mingling against a fantastic background of downfalls and rebuildings. Never at rest—in constant contradiction to the traditional interpretations of its name: *peace*. The city falls only to rise again after scores of destructions, each with its accompaniment of pestilence and famine. Assyrians, Babylonians, Egyptians, Romans, Moslems, Crusaders, modern armies have battered its gates, in defiance of Israel's claim: 'We will not fear, though the earth be removed, and though the mountains be carried into the heart of the sea. God is in the midst of this city, she shall not be shaken.' During centuries of warfare and strife, the level of the streets has risen higher and higher, to the despair of archaeologists trying to achieve concordance between the Biblical narrative and the findings of the spade.

The Holy City has been the subject of innumerable books of pious learning, as well as of inflammatory argument. It was natural that a literary record such as ours should try to avoid paraphrasing these serious feats of scholarship, skirt the traps of theological controversy and turn away from the deep involvement of religious dogma. Ours has been the more modest yet fascinating aim of tracing and assembling some of the most significant passages in literature, from Biblical times to the present day, when the Holy City has once more become a pawn in the universal game of political chess. There can of course be no illusions about the shortcomings and omissions of so vast an undertaking. To treat adequately a subject at once so noble and contentious would require a lifetime of research and far greater space. Several selections of Hebrew texts relating to Jerusalem have been published during the last fifty years or so, but of Christian and Arabic texts many have remained isolated or for the most part inaccessible in manuscripts or ancient editions. With all its limitations and omissions, it may be claimed, that this is the first Jerusalem anthology drawn from world literature.

It is surprising that even in England and the United States, love for the Holy Land, and for Jerusalem in particular, has with few exceptions been subordinated either to theology or, in the last hundred years, to history and archaeology. The present selection may bring into brighter focus how travellers, poets and visionaries have reacted to the image of the heavenly and earthly capital of the spirit: 'the rock of ages' which has endured, by virtue of its dramatic surroundings and the faith of those who have built and rebuilt it.

While refraining from taking sides in any of the controversies that hedge the subject, we have had the joy of travelling through innumerable avenues of poetry and prose, sacred and profane, magnificent or frivolous, eccentric or commonplace. Nothing of course has been so revealing as the journey through the Bible, which in the context of our exploration has been regarded, first and foremost, as literature of the highest order, and whose light, in Cardinal Newman's words, is 'like the body of Heaven in its clearness; its variants like the bottom of the sea; its variety like the scenes of nature.' However, we have assumed the Bible to be a thoroughly explored territory, hence the relatively small number of Biblical quotations. Our aim has been rather to concentrate on other sources, some well known but most of them relatively obscure; the limits of this anthology allowed little room for comment; it is hoped, though, that the introductory notes and the bibliography will further the interests of all those involved in literary history.

The extracts are arranged in ten sections, as they bear upon the varied history, the landscape and the spirit of Jerusalem. In each of these sections, the strict chronological order has often been interrupted to make room for what we consider to be of greater interest in the sequence of episodes recorded by ancient and modern writers. Many of the prose extracts and even some of the poems have had to be abridged. Similarly, the notes preceding each section present no more than a summary introduction to one particular aspect of this intensely human story still fraught with violent arguments.

Through this maze of antagonisms we have tried our best to steer a course as non-partisan as possible, except in the unavoidably 'heretic' partisanship that is implied when doing a work in which personal choice is both required and justified. This is a literary portrait of the holiest and most blood-stained city on earth—the 'city of the world's tears'—perhaps a key to the sublime idea of a future Jerusalem. The voyage has been richly rewarding in itself and for the spoils with which it has enabled us to return.

PART ONE The Story of Jerusalem

I Origins : David and Solomon

Father and Son

*King David and King Solomon
Led merry, merry lives,
With many, many lady friends
And many, many wives;
But when old age crept over them
With many, many qualms,
King Solomon wrote the Proverbs
And King David wrote the Psalms.*

James Ball Naylor

*Le roi courbe la tête et s'endort sur sa harpe.
Et la mort, doucement, murmure en elle-même:
Il faut l'envelopper dans son dernier poème.*

Itsik Manger: Le roi David,
translated by J. Milbauer, 1936

*Solomon wrote first the Song of Songs, then
Proverbs, then Ecclesiastes. When young, we
compose songs; when older, we make senten-
tious remarks; and when old, we speak of the
vanity of things.*

Canticles Rabbah (Midrash)

A name and a city, conspicuously and obsessively associated with modern Jerusalem, emerge through almost four thousand years of historical evidence. As with many oriental cities, the origins of Jerusalem fade into the mists of legend and antiquity. It may have been a populated dwelling long before the conquest of Canaan by the Israelites. According to Ezekiel, the place was of mixed origin. 'Thus said the Lord God unto Jerusalem : Thy birth and thy nativity is of the land of Canaan : thy father was an Amorite, and thy mother a Hittite.' Pottery discovered in a Canaanite tomb near Jerusalem suggests that it was already a reality by the year 3000 B.C. If so, the city may not after all owe its foundation to Melchisedek, the priest-king of Salem and a contemporary of Abraham. Recent discoveries show that, in the days of the Patriarchs, there existed a shrine of the God El at the city of Salem or Thalem. From still later times, a fire-blackened bas-relief in the British Museum represents the assault of *Ur-salammu*, probably by Sennacherib.

The Hebrew saga tells of 'Melchisedek, the priest of the most high God.' The 'most high' expresses a fitting relationship between the Hebrew conception of god and the location of the mountain city; the Divinity is thus from the beginning the protective image of the dwelling. Even within a modest range of the various and, alas, still warring etymologies, the similarity between *Yerushalem* and *Shalem* appears as tempting as the union of priest-king during the reign of David and afterwards.

According to the Midrash, God did not wish to 'upset' either Abraham (who called the city *Yir'eh*), or Shem (who called it *Shalem*), so he resorted to a compromise and called it by both names. But Uru-shalem seems a better interpretation of the Aramaic *Yerushlem*, the Syrian *Urishlem*, the old Hebrew *Yerushalayim* and the Assyrian *Urusalim*. The English spelling Jerusalem is used in many modern languages—derived from the AV of 1611 (*Jerusalem* in the Old Testament and *Hierusalem* in the New Testament)—and is no doubt nearest to the Hebrew Yerushalem. It appears as *Salem, Hierusalem* and *Hierosolyma, Solyma* (in most cases as a poetic abbreviation) or *Ierosolyma* (under the Crusaders and in many writings of the Fathers of the Church), in the Syriac version as *Urislem*, finally as *Sion* or *Zion* in many of the poems and prose descriptions included in this anthology.

After the city's destruction by Hadrian (A.D. 135–136) and until the time of Constantine, the very name of Jerusalem disappears from official use (except in Hebrew writings) and makes room for Hadrian's *Aelia Capitolina* or for *Kapitolias* at the time of Ptolemy. As such it passes even into Arabic as *Ailia* or *Iliya*, but Arabs will sometime use *Urisalam, Urishalam, Uraslam, Bait al-Maqdis, el-Maqaddas* (the Holy House), or more frequently and up to the present day, *El-Quds* ('the sanctuary'). In Arabic poetry it is occasionally referred to as *el-balât* (the Court). The idea of 'vision of peace' is also admitted, but scholars still quarrel over its true meaning.

For their poetical and devotional beauty a few other names should also be mentioned. In Isaiah, though apparently nowhere else, Jerusalem is called *Ariel* ('the hearth of God's home'). The same prophet does not hesitate to call it Sodom on account of its wickedness. Then it appears as 'Daughter of my people', 'The city of righteousness', and 'Virgin daughter of Sion'; whereas in the Psalms Jerusalem is 'The City of God' or 'of our God', or 'of the Great King'. During the first exile Jerusalem becomes simply 'The

City', and by implication the place where Jahveh will cause His Name to dwell. This leads to Nehemiah's 'Holy City' (*Ir ha-qodesh*) which also occurs in Matt. iv and Rev. xi. The *shelshalim* (coins) issued during the First Jewish Revolt (A.D. 66–70) carry the words *Yerushalaim Qedoshah* (Jerusalem the Holy). It is interesting that Herodotus, who visited Palestine, calls Jerusalem 'the great city of Cadytis', probably a derivation from the Syriac *Kadithi* and the Hebrew *Qedoshah*, both signifying 'The Holy'.

Then Ezekiel countered all these affectionate names by using the words 'Bloody city' because so many prophets and messengers of God had been killed within its walls; but in general the city is holy because 'the Lord chose it out of all the tribes of Israel to place his name there'. (Deut. xii. 5). According to the Talmud, 'three objects are called by the name of the Holy One, blessed be He: these are, the Righteous, the Messiah, and Jerusalem. The Messiah because it is written, "And this is his name whereby he shall be called, the Lord our Righteousness" (Jeremiah), Jerusalem, because it is written, "And the name of the city from that day shall be, 'Shamah, the Lord is there'".' It also appears in the Talmud as Beth-Olamim, 'the house of ages'.

As *Urusalim* it appears in the cuneiform inscriptions on the famous Babylonian Tell el-Amarna Letters, discovered in Egypt in 1887. At least four of the tablets throw definite light on this historical detail, and afford a precious glimpse of the city which, like other Canaanite dwellings, had to pay tribute to the Pharaohs. The prefect, or governor, of Urusalim complained to his sovereign about the audacity of the *Habiri*, who were laying siege to the city, and demanded prompt relief. 'Why do you love the Habiri and hate the regent?' he asks the king (Letter 286). The following passage is even more explicit:

> Let the king care for his land
> The land of the king will be lost. All of it
> will be taken from me; there is enmity to me . . .
> But now
> The Habiri are taking
> the cities of the king . . .
> After they have taken Rubuda,
> they seek now to take Urusalim . . .
> Shall we then let Urusalim go?
> I am very humbly thy servant.

(Letter 288)

Any connection between these Habiri and the ancient Hebrews remains a matter of speculation. The Old Testament, however, relates that when the Hebrews, led by Joshua, entered the Promised Land, Jerusalem was the capital city of the Jebusite country and it was then named after their common ancestor, Jebus, the grandson of Ham. (Jebus, Jebusi and the Jebusite, as names of the city, appear in the Authorized Version.) 'Joshua killed the Jebusite King' (x. 1–27); however, in spite of the loss of their king, the Jebusites put up a stout fight and Jerusalem remained unconquered, even during the fairly long period of the Judges and also during the reign of Saul (1038–1011 B.C.). Not till the might and skill of David smote them were the Jebusites dislodged. Despite a series of merciless destructions, modern archaeologists believe the original wall to have been identified, and even the Jebusite water tunnel and shaft by which David penetrated the city.

From Biblical times the city is mentioned as possessing exceptional strategic importance because of its rocky plateau and the two promontories divided by the valley of Kidron (Roman *Tyropoeon*). The 'stronghold of Zion' becomes the 'City of David' (Samuel II) and the capital of the Hebrew nation. The real story of Jerusalem begins with David, king of Judah and of Israel. In his effort to win peace and unity for his people, David chose this lonely site, belonging neither to a northern nor to a southern tribe. The city is difficult of access and especially *high*, with a *wide view towards heaven*. It is true, the Samaritans never forgave David for transferring the holiness of Mount Gerizim to the Sanctuary of Mount Moriah, which they called *Bet Maktash* (the house of shame), but this was a minor flaw in a great act of statesmanship, that created the first and only capital of the Hebrew nation. More than thirty centuries ago, she began its tormented and sublime progression as the dwelling destined to become sacred to three world religions.

DAVID

As founder of the Jewish Dynasty, and the first king of a truly united Israel, David holds a unique position in the history of both the Jewish people and of Jerusalem, his capital. During his reign, the kingdom of Israel and its fame and glory expanded to their furthest limits, with boundaries stretching from the Valley of the

Lebanon to the River of Egypt, from the Arabian Desert to the Mediterranean. And the city of Jerusalem gained a symbolic and historical meaning which has never diminished.

Initially, Jerusalem was not David's capital. The young king reigned from Hebron for seven and a half years, until he felt ready to assault Jerusalem and establish his rule over the whole of Israel. When he did, he took the apparently unassailable city by a brilliant military stratagem, which has furnished commentators and archaeologists with endless controversy as to its *bellum topographicum*.

The momentousness of this achievement, and the colossal importance of David's historical role, echoes throughout the Bible's vivid unfolding of his story. Significantly, there are three versions of his entry into public life. The first singles out the artistic gifts of the young poet-musician who was called into the presence of Saul to assuage his despair. In the second, David comes forth from the obscurity of a shepherd's life as the hero who freed his people from the menace of the giant Goliath. (It was this story that much early Christian art chose for its depictions of David, and it made him a symbol of liberty in 15th-century Florence and a symbol of heroism still today.) The third version relates how God sent Samuel to Jesse to find the new king of Israel. When none of Jesse's sons appeared to be God's choice, the prophet at last asked for the youngest, whom his father had not considered. 'Now he was ruddy, and had beautiful eyes and was handsome. And the Lord said, "Arise, anoint him, for this is he".'

And so the rest of the epic story follows. We hear of the early adventures, his proverbial friendship with Saul's son Jonathan, his troubles with the jealous Saul, his hazardous life as a refugee, then his successes as leader of his own army. Yet for all these details we cannot be sure of his real name. The recent excavations of Mari on the Euphrates—also known as Tell el Hariri—have disclosed that *davidum* is a military title: it has been suggested that David, whose original name might have been Elhanan (II Samuel xxi. 9), adopted the title of military marshal as the name by which he wanted to be known.

His fame in succeeding centuries rested a great deal more on, for instance, his re-creation of the city of Jerusalem. 'And David dwelt in the stronghold, and called it the City of David.' David's greatness and that of his city grew apace. He brought carpenters and stone-cutters from Tyre to build the royal palace; he introduced a central government with forms of administration that he borrowed perhaps from Egypt, perhaps via the Phœnicians. No longer was he a simple 'chief of the people' as Saul had been. He was a king, with a political organization and a well-regulated administration that survived in a modified form until the destruction of Israel.

But to make Jerusalem the centre of Israel's world demanded more. So David brought the ark to the city—a symbol of the presence of God in the midst of his people that probably dated back to the nomadic period. Its removal from Cariathiarin to the summit of Mount Moriah in Jerusalem was celebrated by a great religious festival. 'And David and all the house of Israel played before the Lord on all manner of instruments and of fir wood, even on harps, and on psalteries, and on timbrels, and on cornets, and on cymbals' (II Samuel). He was anxious to construct a more worthy house for the ark, which was originally placed in a tent. He, David, confined himself to collecting materials, and later instructed Solomon in their use for the temple. Before that, though, he had organized the Levites as singers and dancers in honour of the Ark.

Conqueror and administrator, a man of wild passions and troubled conscience, poet, musician and dancer, David is remembered in history and legend as the ideal of kingship and prototype of the expected Messiah. His life has been placed between 1012 and 972 B.C., chronologically almost midway between Abraham and Jesus. He was the founder of a dynasty that reigned in Jerusalem for four centuries, until its destruction by Nebuchadnezzar—a dynasty that came to be associated with messianic hopes which shaped the Jewish religion and extended into the New Testament. The prophets clearly believed that David's house would last forever; yet they were never blind to the complexity of David, immensely human in his faults, so magnificently analysed by the prophet Nathan in what is surely one of the finest psychological portraits in world literature. Legends and folklore, too, have gathered about his name. One states that David was destined to live only three hours, but Adam offered him seventy of his own one thousand years. In Muslim lore he is Da'ud, the Kalif of Allah, a Hebrew Orpheus; in the *Kashf al-mandjub*, an early work of Sufism, paraphrasing the prophet Amos concerning David's musicianship, we are told that at the sound of his voice wild beasts left their lairs, water ceased to flow and men and women followed him into the desert to die there in ecstasy.

David as kingly musician has captured the imaginations of artists throughout history—as in the many representations in Christian art of David with crown and harp (for instance in the stained glass at Chartres). Even Voltaire, to whom the Scriptures were pretexts for jesting, when he re-read Psalm 51, he was so affected by it that he threw down his pen in disgust. David may not have written the Psalms, but it was he who gathered them together—into what Wordsworth once called 'the spiritual epitome of history'.

Other writers have not always served David well. Too often they have preferred to isolate an unsavoury incident or aspect, treating it as best they could. So the story of David and Bathsheba, murder, passion, repentance and all, has attracted many: it has been dramatised as a 'comedi' by the Nuremberg Meistersinger Hans Sachs; by George Peele, in a clumsy pre-Shakespearean formula; and in rather more courtly fashion by Antoine de Montchrestien in France. In more modern times, neither J. M. Barrie, in his last play, *The boy David* (1936), nor D. H. Lawrence in one of his early dramatic efforts could lay much claim to successful treatment of David's character.

Complaining about the spiritual emptiness of so much church sculpture, Goethe suggested David as one of twelve Biblical figures who should make rewarding subjects. (Perhaps the sculptures by Donatelli, Verrocchio and Michelangelo prompted this idea.) Goethe's comment on David's complexity applies as much to the writer as to other artists—that only 'the artist of genius may succeed in representing all in one—the son of a shepherd, the adventurer, the hero, the king and the lover . . .'

The basic concept behind these remarks is secular, for Goethe fails to mention David's constant sense of responsibility before God! 'He that ruleth over men must be just, ruling in the fear of God.' Above all, comes the awareness of his incalculable importance in history, and in the history of the great and sacred city.

SOLOMON

If David represents statesmanship, poetic fervour and unusual courage to confess his transgressions, Solomon (971–932 B.C.) is a bewildering mixture of wisdom and swarming concubinage. The author of this part of the Biblical narrative is anxious to show that indulgence in sensuality preceded the first downfall of the Holy City. Jerusalem could not for long be the home of debauchery on the scale of that of the Persian or Egyptian kings. But at the

same time Solomon is thought to be the author of *Shir Hashirim,
The Song of Songs*, surely the most beautiful love poem in world
literature.

Endless are the legends woven around his meeting with the
Queen of Sheba. The king and his beautiful guest stand together
at the portals of Chartres, and appear in many versions of the
legends of the origin of the Cross. Solomon is also an outstanding
figure in Moslem folklore. Here, as Suleiman, he is regarded as one
of the great rulers of Islam, and is frequently mentioned in the
Koran as a true apostle of Allah. His fabled powers included
control of the winds, knowledge of the speech of animals, and
command over djinns, who are his servants. Later Moslem legends
magnified the rabbinical tales, and Solomon was credited with
rule over a universal kingdom, and power over both good and evil
djinns. The seal of Solomon, in the form of a six-pointed star, came
to be commonly carried as a charm. Legends abound in the Arab
world—the king sheltered from the heat under a canopy made by
all the birds, or the sun standing still while he was saying his
evening prayers. Apart from wisdom, prowess in building brought
Solomon fame both in legend and in fact.

The Biblical accounts of the reigns of David and Solomon have
an epic simplicity and faith in the future never recovered again in
the long history of the destruction and reconstruction of the holy
city. Later, prophets rather than kings stand out as the important
figures, and the Temple built by these early kings remains a more
unifying symbol of the city than do the reigns of their successors in
divided kingdoms. All accounts agree that wealth poured into
Jerusalem. Among Solomon's achievements the most glorious
was, of course, the Temple, unsurpassed in splendour in the whole
history of the city. Universally famous it has disappeared under the
ruins of five later cities built one on top of another; but it is at
least known that Solomon's masterpiece enshrined all the objects
of worship, the Ark, the shewbread, the candlesticks, and naturally
the 'Holy of Holies'. It became the heart of the nation, and
rabbinical tradition sanctified its site, Mount Moriah, as the place
where God created Adam.

And yet this luxurious 'foundation' of silver and gold, of brass
and cedarwood, which adorned the Jerusalem of Solomon's time,
led to downfall. The Temple was challenged by the king's adoption
of the pagan cults of his many foreign wives. Maybe the abstract
worship of the invisible, unknowable Jahweh, the God whose Holy

of Holies was a place of darkness, yet the dwelling place of the light of the world, of whom no graven image might be made, could not satisfy the people of the surrounding countries who had to pay taxes for the riches of the sanctuary and the royal harem. The king was constantly involved in conjugal troubles as his father had been (which reminds us of Mark Twain's *Huckleberry Finn*, whose hero doesn't think 'Sollermun de wises' man dat ever liv'' with all those wives: '. . . would a wise man want to live in de mids' er sich a blim-blammin' all de time? No—'deed he wouldn't.') At his death, the kingdom of Israel was divided, leaving Jerusalem merely the threatened capital of only one of its two parts, Judah.

B

THE SONG OF THE NIGHT

As David in his youthful days was tending his flocks on Bethlehem's plains, the spirit of the Lord came upon him, and his senses were opened that he might comprehend the songs of the night.

The heavens proclaimed the glory of God; the glittering stars all formed one chorus. Their harmonious melody resounded on earth, and the sweet fullness of their voices vibrated to its uttermost bounds.

'Light is the countenance of the Eternal,' sang the setting sun. 'I am the hem of his garment,' responded the rosy tint of twilight.

The clouds gathered and said, 'We are his nocturnal tent,' and the waters of the cloud, and the hollow voices of the thunders, joined in the lofty chorus. 'The voice of the Eternal is upon the waters; the God of glory thundereth; the Lord upon many waters.'

'He did fly upon my wings,' whispered the wind, and the silent air replied, 'I am the breath of God, the aspiration of his benign presence.'

'We hear the songs of praise,' said the parched earth; 'all around is praise, I alone am silent and mute!' And the falling dew replied, 'I will nourish thee, so that thou shalt be refreshed and rejoice, and thy infants shall bloom like the young rose.'

'Joyfully we bloom,' replied the refreshed meadows. The full ears of corn waved as they sang, 'We are the blessing of God, the hosts of God against famine.'

'We bless you from above,' said the moon; 'We bless you,' responded the stars; and the grasshopper chirped, 'Me too He blesses in the pearly dew-drop.'

'He quenched my thirst,' said the roe; 'and refreshed me,' continued the stag; 'and grants us our food,' said the beasts of the forest, 'and clothes my lambs,' gratefully sang the sheep.

'He heard me,' croaked the raven, 'when I was forsaken and alone.' 'He heard me,' said the wild goat of the rocks, 'when my time came and I calved.'

And the turtle-dove cooed, and the swallow and all the birds joined their song: 'We have found our nests, our houses, we dwell on the altar of the Lord, and sleep under the shadow of his wing, in tranquillity and peace.'

'And peace,' replied the night, and echo prolonged the sound, when chanticleer awoke the dawn and crowed, 'Open the portals, the gates of the world! The King of glory approacheth! Awake! Arise! Ye sons of men, give praises and thanks to the Lord, for the King of glory cometh.'

. . .

The sun arose and David awoke from his melodious rapture. But as long as he lived, the strains of creation's harmony remained in his soul, and daily he recalled them from the strings of his harp.

Talmudic Legend

Josephus (37–105)

DAVID'S CAPTURE OF JERUSALEM, THE ROYAL CITY

Now the Jebusites, who were the inhabitants of Jerusalem, and were by extraction Canaanites, shut their gates, and placed the blind, and the lame, and all their maimed persons, upon the wall, in way of derision of the king; and said, that the very lame themselves would hinder his entrance into it. This they did out of contempt of his power, and as depending on the strength of their walls. David was hereby enraged, and began the siege of Jerusalem, and employed his utmost diligence and alacrity therein, as intending, by the taking of this place, to demonstrate his power, and to intimidate all others that might be of the like (evil) disposition towards him: so he took the lower city by force, but the citadel held out still; whence it was that the king, knowing that the proposal of dignities and rewards would encourage the soldiers to greater actions, promised that he who should first go over the ditches that were beneath the citadel, and should ascend to the citadel itself and take it, should have the command of the entire people conferred upon him. So they all were ambitious to ascend, and thought no pains too great in order to ascend thither, out of their desire of the chief command. However, Joab, the son of Zeruiah, anticipated the rest; and as soon as he got up to the citadel, cried out to the king, and claimed the chief command.

When David had cast the Jebusites out of the citadel, he also rebuilt Jerusalem, and named it, *The City of David*, and abode there all the time of his reign: but for the time that he reigned over the tribe of Judah only in Hebron, it was seven years and six months. Now when he had chosen Jerusalem to be his royal city, his affairs did more and more prosper, by the providence of God, who took care that they should improve and be augmented. Hiram also, the king of the Tyrians, sent ambassadors to him, and made a league of mutual friendship and assistance with him. He also sent him presents, cedar-trees, and mechanics, and men skilful in building and architecture, that they might build him a royal palace at Jerusalem. Now David made buildings round about the lower city; he

19

also joined the citadel to it, and made it one body; and when he had encompassed all with walls, he appointed Joab to take care of them. It was David, therefore, who first cast the Jebusites out of Jerusalem, and called it by his own name, *The City of David*.

Antiquities of the Jews, Book VII, Chapter III

Dante (1265–1321)

THE RETURN OF THE ARK

There in the self-same marble were engraved
The cart and kine, drawing the sacred ark,
That from unbidden office awes mankind.
Before it came much people, and the whole
Parted in seven quires. One sense cried 'Nay',
Another, 'Yes, they sing'. Like doubt arose
Betwixt the eye and smell, from the curl'd fume
Of incense breathing up the well-wrought toil,
Preceding the blest vessel, onward came
With light dance leaping, girt in humble guise,
Israel's sweet harper; in that hap he seem'd
Less and yet more, than kingly. Opposite
At a great palace, from the lattice forth
Look'd Michal, like a lady full of scorn
And sorrow.

Purgatorio, x. 50–64

Translated by Henry Francis Cary, 1812

Antoine de Montchrestien (1575–1621)

DIEU DE MON SALUT

Seigneur ie te connois le Dieu de mon salut:
Vien bien tost me lauer du crime d'homicide;
Et lors iusque au Ciel où ta grandeur réside,
Ie pousserai ma voix & le son de mon Luth.

Car ainsi que le coeur tu m'ouuvriras la bouche;
Et ma langue suiuant le uol de mon penser,
S'en ira ta louange aux peuples anoncer,
D'où leue le soleil iusqu'en l'onde où il couche.

Tu ne désires point, O seigneur immortel,
Une grasse victime offerte en sacrifice:
Si par un tel moyen on te rendoit propice,
I'en eusse mille-fois arrozé ton autel.

Celuy qui uent t'offrir vne hostie agréable
Qu'il t'apporte son coeur contrit & désolé,
Du dormir de peché par ta grace esueillé
Bien-heureux en toy seul, wen luy seul misérable

O Dieu uen tes faveurs espandre sur Sion;
Ses fondemens sacrés à jamais fortifie:
De ta sainte Cité les saints mures édifie,
Comme elle se promet de ton affection.

David ou l'Adultère, 1601

Abraham Cowley (1618-1667)

DAVID

I sing the man who Judah's sceptre bore
In that right hand which held the crook before;
Who from heft poet, heft of kings did grow,
The two chief gifts Heav'n could on man bestow.
Much danger first, much toil, he did sustain,
Whilst Saul and Hell crops'd his strong fate in vain;
Nor did his crown less painful work afford
Less exercise his patience or his sword;
So long her conq'ror Fortune's spite pursu'd
Till with unwearied virtue he subdu'd
All homebred malice and all foreign boasts;
Their strength was armies, his the hord of Hosts.

Davideis, a sacred poem of the
troubles of David, in four books, 1653

THE STORY OF DAVID AND BERSEBA

To a pleasant new tune

When David in Ierusalem,
   as royal king and did rule & raigne,
Behold what hap'ned unto him,
   that afterward procur'd his paine.

On the top of all his Princely Place,
   a gallant prospect there had he,
From whence hee might when't pleas'd his Grace,
   many a gallant Garden see.

It chanced so upon a day,
   the king went forth to take the ayre,
All in the pleasant moneth of May,
   from whence he spide a Lady faire.

Her beauty was more excellent
   and brighter than the morning Sunne,
By which the king incontinent,
   was to her favour quickly wonne.

He stood within a pleasant Bower,
   all naked for to watch her there,
Her body like a Lilly Flower,
   was covered with her golden haire.

The King was wounded with her love,
   and what she was he did enquire,
He could not his affection move,
   he had to her such great desire.

She is Uriah's wife, quoth they,
   a captaine of your Princely Traine,
That in your Warres is now away,
   and she doth all alone remaine.

Then said the King, Bring her to me,
    for with her love my heart is slaine:
The prince of beauty sure is she
    for whom I doe great griefe sustaine.

The Servants they did soone prepare,
    to doe the message of the King,
And Berseba the Lady faire,
    unto the Court did quickly bring.

The King rejoyced at her sight,
    and won her love, and lay her by,
Till they in sport had spent the night,
    and that the Sun has risen high.

The King his leave most kindly tooke
    of the faire Lady at the last:
And homeward then she cast her looke,
    till that three moneth were gone & past.

And then in Berseba so faire,
    she found her former health exilde,
By certaine tokens that she saw,
    the King had gotten her with childe.

Then to the King she made her mone,
    and told him how the case did stand:
The King sent for her Husband home,
    to cloake the matter out of hand.

When from the Camp Uriah came,
    the King receiv'd him courteously,
Demanding how all things did frame
    concerning of the Enemy.

Uriah shew his Highnesse all
    the accident of warlike strife,
Then said the King, this night you shall
    keep company with your owne wife.

The Arke of God (Uriah said)
    with Iudah's Folk, and Israel,
Keepe in the Field, and not a man
    within the house where they doe dwell.

Then should I take my ease, quoth he,
   in beds of Downe with my faire wife?
O King, he said, that must not be,
   so long as I enjoy my life.

Then did the King a Letter frame,
   to Ioab Generall of the Post,
And by Uriah sent the same,
   but certainely his life it cost.

And when the King for certaine knew
   Uriah thus had murdered beene,
Faire Berseba to Court he drew,
   and made of her his royall Queene.

Then God that saw his wicked deed,
   was angry at King David's sinne:
The Prophet Nathan then with speed,
   came thus complaining unto him.

O David, ponder what I say,
   a great abuse I shall thee tell;
For thou that rul'st in equity,
   shouldst see the people ruled wel.

Two men within the City dwell,
   the one is rich, the other poore:
The rich in Cattell doth excell,
   the other nothing hath in store.

Saving one silly little Sheepe
   which yong he did with money buy:
With his owne bread he did it feed,
   amongst his Children tenderly.

The rich man had a stranger came
   unto his house that lov'd him deare,
The poore mans Sheepe therefore he tooke,
   and thereof made his friend good cheere.

Because that he his owne would save,
   he us'd the man thus cruelly:
Then by the Lord the King did sweare,
   the rich man for that fault should die.

Thou art the man, the Prophet said,
   the Princely crowne God gave to thee:
The Lord's wives thou thine owne has made,
   and many more of faire beauty.

Why hast thou so defilde thy life,
   and slaine Uriah with the sword,
And taken home his wedded Wife,
   regarding not God's holy Word?

Therefore, behold thus said the Lord,
   great warres upon thy house shall be,
Because thou hast my Lawes abhord,
   much ill be sure Ile raise on thee,

Ile take thy wives before thy face,
   and give them to thy neighbour's use:
And thou thereby shalt have disgrace,
   for men shall laugh at thine abuse.

Then David cried out pittiously,
   fore have I sinned against the Lord,
Have mercy God therefore on me,
   let not my prayers be abhor'd.

But as the Prophet told to him,
   so did it after chance indeed,
For God did greatly plague his sinns,
   as in the Bible you may read.

The scourge of sinne thus you may see,
   for murther and adultery.
Lord grant that we may warned be,
   such crying sinnes to shun and flie.

Finis

Printed at London for I. Wright, dwelling in
Gilt-spurre street, neere New-gate, 1567

Lord Byron (1788–1824)

THE HARP THE MONARCH MINSTREL SWEPT

The harp the monarch minstrel swept,
The King of men, the loved of heaven,
Which Music hallow'd while she wept
O'er tones her heart of hearts had given,
Redoubled be her tears, its chords are riven!
It soften'd men of iron mould,
It gave them virtues not their own;
No ear so dull, no soul so cold,
That felt not, fired not to the tone,
Till David's lyre grew mightier than his throne!

It told the triumphs of our king,
It wafted glory to our God;
It made our gladden'd valleys ring,
The cedars bow, the mountains nod;
Its sound aspired to heaven and there abode!
Since then, though heard on earth no more,
Devotion and her daughter Love
Still bid the bursting spirit soar
To sounds that seem as from above,
In dreams that day's broad light cannot remove.

Hebrew Melodies, 1815

Alphonse de Lamartine (1790–1869)

THE KING OF LYRIC POETRY

This is Sion! the palace, the tomb of David! the seat of his inspiration and of his joys, of his life and his repose! A spot doubly sacred to me, who have so often felt my heart touched, and my thoughts enraptured by the sweet singer of Israel! the first poet of sentiment! the king of lyrics. Never have human fibres vibrated to harmonies so deep, so penetrating, so solemn. Never has the imagination of a poet been raised so high, never has a poet sung so true. Never has the soul of man expanded itself before man, and before God, in tones and sentiments so tender, so sympathetic, and so heartfelt!

The most secret murmurs of the human heart found their voice, and their note, on the lips and the harp of this minstrel! And if we revert to the remote period when such chants were first echoed on earth; if we consider that at the same period the lyric poetry of the most cultivated nations sang only of wine, love, war, and the victories of the Muses, or of the coursers at the Elesian games, we dwell with profound astonishment on the mystic accents of the prophet-king, who addresses God the Creator, as friend talks to friend; comprehends and adores His wonders, admires His judgments, implores His mercies, and seems to be an anticipatory echo of the evangelic poetry, repeating the mild accents of Christ before they had been heard. Prophet or not, according as he may be contemplated by the philosopher or the Christian, neither of them can deny the poet-king an inspiration bestowed on no other man! Read Horace or Pindar after a psalm: for my part I cannot!

I, the feeble poet of an age of silence and decay, had I resided at Jerusalem, I should have selected, for my residence and abiding place, precisely the spot which David chose for his at Sion. Here is the most beautiful view in all Judea, Palestine, or Galilee. To the left lies Jerusalem with its Temple and its edifices, over which the eyes of the king or of the poet might rove at large without his being seen from thence. Before him, fertile gardens descending in steep declivities, lead to the bed of that torrent, in the roar and foam of which he delighted. Lower down, the valley opens and extends itself; fig trees, pomegranates, and olive trees overshadow it. On one of those rocks suspended over the rolling tide; in one of those sonorous grottos refreshed by the breeze and by the murmur of the waters; or at the foot of a terebinthus, ancestor of that which shelters me, the divine poet doubtless awaited those inspirations which he so melodiously poured forth! And why will they not also visit me, that I might recount in song the griefs of my heart, and of the hearts of all men, in these days of perplexity, even as he sang of his hopes in an era of youth and of faith? Song, alas! no longer lives in the heart of man, for despair sings not! And until some new beam shall descend upon the obscurity of our times, terrestrial lyres will remain mute, and mankind will pass in silence from one abyss of doubt to another, having neither loved, nor prayed, nor sang.

A Pilgrimage to the Holy Land, London, 1832–33

John Henry Newman (1801–1890)

DAVID NUMBERING THE PEOPLE

'I am in a great stait—Let us fall now into the hand of the Lord.'

If e'er I fall beneath Thy Rod,
As through life's snares I go,
Save me from David's lot, O God!
And choose Thyself the woe.

How should I face Thy Plagues?—which scare,
And Haunt, and stun, until
The heart or sinks in mute despair,
Or names a random ill.

If else—then guide in David's path,
Who chose the holier pain;
Satan and man are tools of wrath,
An Angel's scourge is gain.

Verses on various occasions, 1868

THE DEDICATION OF THE TEMPLE

And Solomon placed himself before the altar of the Lord in the presence of all the congregation of Israel, and spread forth his hands towards heaven;

And he said, O Lord, the God of Israel, there is no God like thee, in the heavens above, and on the earth beneath, thou who keepest the covenant and the kindness for thy servants that walk before thee with all their heart;

Who has kept for thy servant David my father what thou hadst promised him; and thou spokest with thy mouth, and hast fulfilled it with thy hand, as it is this day;

And now, O Lord, the God of Israel, keep for thy servant David, my father, what thou hast spoken concerning him, saying, There shall never fail Thee a man in my sight who sitteth on the throne of Israel; if thy children but take heed of their way, to walk before me as thou hast walked before me.

28

And now, O God of Israel, I pray thee, let thy word be verified, which thou hast spoken unto thy servant David my father.

For in truth will God then dwell on the earth: behold, the heavens and the heavens of heavens cannot contain thee: how much less then his house that I have built!

Yet will thou turn thy regard unto the prayer of thy servant, and to his supplication, O Lord my God, to listen unto the entreaty and unto the prayer which thy servant prayeth before thee today;

That thy eyes may be open toward this house, night and day, toward the place of which thou hast said, My name shall be there, that thou mayest listen unto the prayer which thy servant shall pray at this place,

And listen thou to the supplication of thy servant and of thy people Israel, which they will pray at this place; and oh, do thou hear in heaven thy dwelling-place; and hear, and forgive.

If any man trespass against his neighbour, and an oath be laid upon him to cause him to swear, and the oath come before thy altar in this house:

Then do thou hear in heaven, and act, and judge thy servants, by condemning the wicked, to bring his way upon his head; and by justifying the righteous, to give him according to his righteousness.

When thy people Israel are struck down before the enemy, because they have sinned against thee, and they return then to thee and confess thy name, and pray, and make supplication unto thee in this house:

Then do thou hear in heaven, and forgive the sin of the people Israel, and cause them to return unto the land which thou hast given unto their fathers.

When the heavens be shut up, and there be no rain, because they have sinned against thee; and they pray towards this place, and confess thy name, and turn from their sin, because thou hast afflicted them:

Then do thou hear in heaven, and forgive the sin of thy servants and of thy people Israel; for thou will teach them the good way wherein they should walk; and give then rain upon thy land, which thou hast given to thy people for an inheritance.

Kings viii. 22, 62

Reginald Heber (1783-1826)

BUILDING THE TEMPLE

'There was neither hammer nor axe nor any tool of iron heard in the house, while it was in building.' (I Kings v. 1–7).

Then towered the palace, then in awful state
The temple reared its everlasting gate;
No workman's steel, no pond'rous axes rung:
Like some tall palm the noiseless fabric sprung.
Majestic silence! Then the harp awoke,
The cymbal clanged, the deep-voiced trumpet spoke,
And Salem spread her suppliant arms abroad,
Viewed the descending flame, and blessed the present God.

Poetical Works, 1845

THE TEN WONDERS

Ten wonders were wrought for our fathers in the Temple:
No woman miscarried through the smell of the flesh of the Hallowed
  Things.
And no flesh of the Hallowed Things ever turned putrid;
And no fly was seen in the shambles;
And the High Priest never suffered pollution on the Day of Atonement;
And the rains never quenched the fire of the wood-pile (on the Altar);
And no wind prevailed over the pillar of smoke;
And never was a defect found in the Omer or in the Loaves or in the
  Shrewbread;
And the people stood pressed together yet bowed themselves with ease;
And never did serpent or scorpion do harm in Jerusalem;
And no man said to his fellow this place is too cramped for me that
  I should lodge in Jerusalem.

Pirqe Aboth. v. 5 (*The Mishna*)

George Herbert (1593–1633)

SION

Lord, with what glorie wast Thou serv'd of old,
When Solomon's temple stood and flourished!
  Where most things were of purest gold,
  The wood was all embellished
With flowers and carvings mysticall and rare;
All show'd the builders crav'd the seer's care.

Yet all this glorie, all this pomp and state,
Did not affect Thee much, was not Thy aim:
  Something there was that sow'd debate;
  Wherefore Thou quit'st Thy ancient claim,
And now Thy architecture meets with sinne,
For all Thy frame and fabrick is within.

There Thou art struggling with a peevish heart,
Which sometimes crosseth Thee, Thou sometimes it;
  The fight is hard on either part:
  Great God doth fight, He doth submit.
All Solomon's sea of brasse and world of stone
Is not so deare to Thee as one good grone.

And truly brasse and stones are heavie things—
Tombes for the dead, not temples fit for Thee;
  But grones are quick, and full of wings,
  And all their motions upward be;
And ever as they mount like larks they sing;
The note is sad, yet musick for a king.

The Temple, 1634

Heinrich Heine (1797–1856)

SALOMO

Dumb are the trumpets, cymbals, drums and shawms to-night,
The angel shapes engirdled with the sword,
About the royal tent keep watch and word,
Six thousand to the left, six thousand to the right.

They guard the King from evil dreams, from death.
Behold! a frown across his brow they view:
Then all at once, like glimmering flames steel-blue,
Twelve thousand brandished swords leap from their sheath.

But back into their scabbards drop the swords
Of the angelic host! the midnight pain
Hath vanished, the King's brow is smooth again;
And hark! the royal sleeper's murmured words:

'O Shulamite! the lord of all these lands am I,
This empire is the heritage I bring,
For I am Judah's king, and Israel's king;
But if thou love me not, I languish and I die.'

Translated from the German by Emma Lazarus

Matthew Prior (1664–1721)

THE JOY WAS PAST

... Artists and plans relieved my solemn hours;
I founded palaces, and planted bowers.
Birds, fishes, beasts of each exotic kind,
I to the limits of my court confined.
To trees transferred I gave a second birth,
And bid a foreign shade grace Judah's earth.
Fish-ponds were made, where former forests grew,
And hills were levelled to extend the view.
Rivers diverted from their native course,
And bound with chains of artificial force,
From large cascades in pleasing tumult rolled,
Or rose through figured stone, or breathing gold.
From farthest Africa's tormented womb
The marble brought, erects the spacious dome;
Or forms the pillars' long extended rows,
On which the planted grove, and pensile garden grows.

The workmen here obeyed the master's call,
To gild the turret, and to paint the wall;
To mark the pavement there with various stone,
And on the jasper steps to rear the throne.
The spreading cedar that an age had stood,
Supreme of trees, and mistress of the wood,
Cut down and carved, my shining roof adorns,
And Lebanon his ruined honour mourns.

A thousand artists show their cunning power,
To raise the wonders of the ivory tower.
A thousand maidens ply the purple loom,
To weave the bed, and deck the regal room;
Till Tyre confesses her exhausted store,
That on her coast the Murex is no more;
Till from the Parian isle, and Libya's coast,
The mountains grieve their hopes of marble lost;
And India's woods return their just complaint,
Their brood decayed, and want of Elephant.

My full design with vast expense achieved
I came, beheld, admired, reflected, grieved;
I chid the folly of my thoughtless haste,
For, the work perfected, the joy was past.

Solomon on the vanity of the world, Book II: Pleasure, 1718

John Keble (1792–1866)

THE WATCH BY NIGHT

'And Uriah said unto David, the ark and Israel, and Judah, abide in tents, and my lord Joab, and the servants of my lord, are encamped in the open fields, shall I then go into mine house, to eat and to drink? As thou livest, and as thy soul livest, I will not do this thing.' II Samuel xi. 11.

The Ark of God is in the field,
Like clouds around the alien armies sweep,
Each by his spear, beneath his shield,
In cold and dew the anointed warriors sleep.

And can it be thou liest awake,
Sworn watchman, tossing on thy couch of down?
And doth thy recreant heart not ache
To hear the sentries round the leaguered town?

Oh dream no more of quiet life,
Care finds the careless out, more wise to vow
Thine heart entire to Faith's pure strife,
So peace will come thou knowest not when or how.

The Christian Year, London, 1827

II The fortunes of the city

Thus saith Jehovah, behold, I will extend peace to her like a river.

Isaiah lxvi. 12

*Signs on earth and signs on high
Prophesied thy destiny.*

Tennyson: The Fall of Jerusalem

The history of Jerusalem and of Israel changes remarkably in tone after the days of optimism and proud prosperity associated with David and Solomon. When Solomon died, the northern tribes separated; Jerusalem became the capital only of Judah and Benjamin. Prophet after prophet denounced the sins of Jerusalem proclaiming divine vengeance on the city—and yet retaining faith in its future restoration. King after king either feared or defied the prophetic warnings. Yet the decline had begun. In the reign of Rehoboam, Solomon's son, the capital city was plundered by Shishak, Pharaoh of Egypt. From then on Philistines, Assyrians, Babylonians and Arabs would involve it in continual warfare and alien domination. No longer was Jerusalem described with pride as resplendent with gold, silver and cedarwood. The northern kingdom fell in 721; Judah's decline reached its depths when Nebuchadnezzar swept into it in 587 B.C.

Jerusalem the city became a ruin, deserted by all except a few poor inhabitants scratching out their survival among the debris, but Jerusalem the symbol continued to be treasured by all the exiles in Babylon. A reprieve came in 538 when Cyrus of Persia allowed the captives to rebuild the city. From their seventy years' captivity the Jews returned fortified with a renewed culture and a renewed determination. The rebuilding of the capital was strengthened by the symbolic value it had gained during the exile: resistance, hope and love had centred on it. 'How doth the city sit solitary, that was full of people! . . . How is she become tributary!'

But though rebuilt, the city had not regained independence: it continued as a counter in the mighty struggles between great empires. Events in Jerusalem depended entirely on the policy of each successive occupying power. Religious tolerance or intolerance produced obedience or defiance. Throughout this chaotic time of war and misery, the Temple remained more than ever the

35

focus of racial and religious unity, representing the attitude and the fate of the people in and around the Holy City. So the rebuilding of Jerusalem and the Temple coincided with the religious codification achieved by the leaders of the returning Jews—as in Josiah's reform of 621 that proclaimed Jerusalem as the sole shrine for sacrifice and worship; or as in the editing by Ezra of the Pentateuch, a far-reaching event for the whole civilized world. But at the same time new domination, new grief, awaited the city.

In 332 B.C. it fell peaceably to Alexander the Great, during his sweeping away of the Persian power that reshaped the ancient East. Josephus writes that the young Greek emperor was so impressed by the high priest Jaddeus, who asked him to spare the Holy City, that he entered the Temple and sat overawed through the service. But the Hellenistic empires that succeeded Alexander were not so generous: the city found itself in the middle of the destructive rivalry between the Ptolemies of Egypt and the Seleucids of Syria. A momentous outcome of this clash occurred in the reign of Ptolemy II Philadephus, when seventy-two Jerusalem scholars were invited to Alexandria to translate the Hebrew Scriptures into Greek (Septuaginta). This Hebrew-Greek symbiosis was to become one of the great influences of Western civilization. Unfortunately, the reign of Antiochus Epiphanes brought a new desecration of the Temple. He entered the Holy of Holies and sacrificed a sow on the altar, and sprinkled a broth made from its flesh all over the building.

In 168 B.C. Epiphanes, was defeated by the Jewish patriot Judas Maccabaeus. The revolt of the Maccabees established the Hasmonean kings and gave one more short breathing space of independence to the city. 'Jerusalem the Holy' was inscribed on the coins of the time, while other coins commemorated the 'freeing of Zion'. Again, the Temple appeared as the national and religious centre when Judas rededicated it in 165 B.C. and instituted the eight-day Feast of Lights. But then, one hundred and five years later, the rivalries of Syrian rulers drew the intervention of Rome. In 63 B.C., Pompey came with his armies to end the civil war and at the same time to annex Jerusalem to the Roman Empire. He besieged the city for three months and finally took it on a Sabbath—after massacring twelve thousand Jews.

Herod ('by birth an Idumean, by profession a Jew, by necessity a Roman, by culture and by choice a Greek') became Roman Governor in 40 B.C. and started rebuilding the city, adorning it with a theatre and gymnasium, but also soiling it with the cruelties for which his name has become a byword. Anxious not to exasperate Jewish susceptibilities too far, Herod enlarged the Temple; but at the same time he introduced within its precincts signs of Greek mythology that failed to please his subjects. The 'Solomon's Stables', still visible today, are believed to be the remains of Herod's underground masonry when he rebuilt the Temple. Despite Herod's vast architectural programme, his unpopularity with the natives who resisted hellenization continued. Feeling the approach of his death, he enclosed the most eminent Jews in the hippodrome with orders for their execution at the time of his death, so that Jerusalem should thus be forced to mourn at his passing away. Herod's reign of terror lasted thirty-eight years and ended in 4 B.C., the supposed date of the birth of Jesus.

Thus the Jerusalem that formed a background to the life of Christ was a provincial city in the Roman Empire which stretched from the Caucasus to the Atlantic, from Central Europe to the Saharan deserts. The Empire was an autocracy, governed by Augustus, the former republican triumvir who had translated himself to godhood. But at least Rome's official religion was tolerant: the Empire's syncretistic tendencies meant that all beliefs were acceptable as long as allegiance to the State was formally declared. In the Near East, too, Roman hegemony meant that the wars of two millennia were finally over. Soon the East would conquer its conquerors through the proselytising secret society of the first Christians, while, in its turn, Christianity was to become the State religion.

Pontius Pilate was the fifth procurator, to be shortly followed by Herod Agrippa ruling as king and tetrarch. The oppression of the Jews following the trial of Jesus widened, and people revolted in A.D. 66. (In the same year, the Christian community of Jerusalem left the holy city and began its process of expansion throughout the world.) Once again, Jerusalem faced destruction. In A.D. 67 Nero sent Vespasian and his son Titus to suppress the revolt. Two years later, Vespasian became emperor, and urged his son to intensify the siege against the indomitable rebels. Josephus Flavius, at that time a general in the rebel army resisting the Romans, has left invaluable accounts of the resistance: Eleazar and his supporters held the inner wall of the Temple, John of Gishala the doors and other passages, while Simon and his faction maintained despotic control in the high city and parts of the lower city.

The defence was heroic, but doomed. In A.D. 70 Titus was beaten off at Gib'ath Saul, but moved on to Mount Scopus and thence to the Mount of Olives. Surrounding the city, he blocked the water supply and laid waste to the countryside (from which can be traced the present barrenness of the outskirts of Jerusalem).

Famine struck the city, and at last it fell to the Romans, who burned the Temple and massacred the Jews. Pockets of resistance still remained; the patient Romans laid siege to them, as at Massada, where Eleazar held the nearly impregnable hilltop until A.D. 73—and where its defenders finally took their own lives rather than surrender to the conqueror. Only with the excavations at Massada recently completed by an archaeologist of vision, Yigal Yadin (son of the equally great Sukenik, who deciphered the Dead Sea Scrolls), has the whole story of this fantastic resistance come to life.

The Great Revolt ended with (according to Josephus) more than one hundred thousand Jews killed (though Tacitus puts the figure at six hundred thousand). The rest were sold into captivity. And just as Maccabean coins had commemorated the freed Jerusalem, so now Roman coins appeared with the inscription: *Judaea Capta*, and the images of a weeping woman, symbol of the country, and a captive Jew.

When Hadrian visited the city in A.D. 130–131 he found it completely destroyed except for a few houses and a Christian church on Mount Zion. When he announced his plan to build a completely new pagan city, another Jewish revolt—under Simon Barkochba (the Son of the Star, no doubt an allusion to Balaam's prophecy, Num. 1)—achieved one more brief period of freedom. But Roman power overcame that resistance too, and the troops completed the destruction of Jerusalem more fiercely even than in A.D. 70—ploughing over the Temple area and the city with salt. The very name of Jerusalem disappeared, replaced by that of *Aelia Capitolina*. It marked the final severance of Jews and Christians. A new city of relentlessly straight streets emerged, lined with columns. Two statues of Hadrian stood near the new temple built on the site of the Holy Sepulchre. Pagan temples were erected on Calvary itself to Jupiter Capitolinus and Venus.

Within this Roman city, from which Jews were excluded under penalty of death, the new Christian Jerusalem began to grow. The Roman authorities did everything to desecrate the ground where the Temple once stood, but since Christians were allowed to enter the city, Jerusalem gradually became a focus of building, residence, and worship. Then the conversion of the Roman Empire to Christianity gave added stimulus and power to pilgrimages and, naturally, to the new Christian cult of the Holy City. Origen, the 'iron man' and author of six thousand works, settled in Jerusalem in 228 and composed a scholarly edition of the Old Testament. In the writings of this learned church father there is the first reference to an organized library in the Holy City, established by the Bishop of Alexandria.

Helena, mother of Constantine (the first Emperor after the division of the Empire), is traditionally credited with the discovery of the Cross during her visit to Jerusalem in 320. Religious art depicts the discovery, while legends elaborate the story. The Cross of Christ is said to have been distinguished from others found with it, by the miraculous cures it wrought; one of its nails is believed to have been thrown by Helena into the Adriatic to quell a storm. The early Christian writer Eusebius does not mention this discovery, but writes of two magnificent churches erected by Constantine on the supposed sites of the crucifixion and resurrection. These were sought, identified, and then adorned by new churches that were to become famous shrines.

As Jerusalem became a rising Christian centre, Jews came to be allowed (according to the Bordeaux Pilgrim) to re-enter their old city once a year to visit the site of the Temple 'and bewail their fate'. Under Julian the Apostate, Jews were encouraged to return in greater numbers; but then Valentinian resumed the harsh Roman policy. Soon, with the second division of the Empire, in 379, Jerusalem fell under the hegemony of Constantinople. (At this time Jerome, living in a cell at Bethlehem, was working on his translation of the Old and New Testament, the Vulgate.) The growing importance of Jerusalem is shown by its promotion from a Bishopric to a Patriarchate, which included Palestine (Prima, Secunda and Tertia) at the Council of Chaldecon in 451. Although hermits and monks had been coming to live in Jerusalem since the third century, the first monastery is supposed to have been founded in the fifth century.

But once again, the changing world and its power struggles entered to shatter this period of stability. The Persians drove the Christian Romans from Syria and Palestine, and in A.D. 614 Chosroes was at the gates of the City. The splendid new churches were destroyed, and another Jerusalem lay in ruins. But the

Christian Empire fought back, and Persia withdrew from the Byzantine lands. The victorious Emperor Heraclius entered the city as a pilgrim, barefoot and poorly clad, to restore the relic of the Holy Cross to the Sepulchre. (In A.D. 633 the relic was sent to Constantinople.)

But then the Roman power, in its turn, withdrew—in the face of the Arab forces that had by then routed the Persians. So for yet another race and religion, Jerusalem became a holy city, because of the famous 'night journey' of Mohammed from Sinai to Bethlehem and then to Jerusalem. Originally, in Mohammed's mind, Jerusalem was to be the first sacred city of the Moslem world—but he afterwards gave Mecca and Medina pride of place. Yet, revering Jerusalem for its links with the prophets whom he considered his predecessors, Mohammed chose Jerusalem for his 'ascent to Heaven'. The beautiful Dome of the Rock (Kubbat al-Sakhra) rose in A.D. 688 on the site of the old Temple—and Jerusalem acquired a new name, el-Quds, 'the Sanctuary'.

Mohammed enjoined tolerance towards Jews and Christians—and certainly the first caliph, Omar, treated the Christians with unusual forbearance—though the Jews, left without a centre of worship, seem to have met with less consideration. On the whole, however, throughout eleven centuries of Islamic rule, the affinities of the three faiths were better recognized in Moslem lands than, for instance, in Christian Spain. Certainly in Jerusalem—despite extortionate taxes, confiscation of some lesser holy places, corruption and other abuses common to almost all regimes—Jews and Christians, not being 'idolators,' enjoyed a certain amount of protection.

However, peace was hardly Jerusalem's fortune, for it fell to Egypt in A.D. 969, and then to the Seljuks in A.D. 1072. Henceforward bigotry and atrocity darkened the epoch of the Crusades. Between 1099 and 1187 the Crusaders built a second Christian city; then Saladin took over Jerusalem, and for fifty-six blood-drenched years Christian rule alternated with Moslem. A new peril appeared in 1244, when the Mongolian hordes swept down. Finally, 1516 saw the establishment of Ottoman rule, under Saladin Selim I, whose successor Suleiman 'the Magnificent' (a title borne by few other rulers save Lorenzo de Medicis) built, in 1542, the present walls. He beautified the city, adding to the Dome of the Rock its faience tiles, marble slabs, and the windows we can see and admire to this day; he also improved the water supply and restored the Tower of David.

For Christians, Ottoman rule was not too harsh. The Church had resigned itself to regard Jerusalem as a place of pilgrimage—Greek Orthodox and Catholics (mostly Franciscans) shared the primacy while most of the ancient sects had altars in the Church of the Holy Sepulchre and elsewhere, and convents of all shades of belief were to be seen. For the Jews, however, despite the relative lack of intolerance found in Europe, life was harder: extortion and persecutions were by no means uncommon. In 1625 the Governor, Muhammad Farukh, made such demands upon the Jewish Community that the people fled to rocks and caves, especially when the *cadi* of Jerusalem joined in the oppression.

The stagnation of Turkish rule persisted until the Napoleonic invasion in 1798. Napoleon's strategic plan was to restore Palestine to the Jews—'je soulève et j'arme toute la Syrie', he wrote; 'Je renverse l'Empire turc; je fonde dans l'Orient un nouvel et grand empire qui fixera ma place dans la postérité'. But strangely the French general soon abandoned the idea, perhaps because of the Battle of the Pyramids. There followed a period of unrest: revolts against Turkey, invasion and capture by Muhammad Ali of Egypt, and an uprising, in 1834, by the *fellahín*. Eventually, in 1840, the Great Powers thought fit to restore the Turks in Palestine. This restoration, centralized and containing certain reforms to impress pilgrims and tourists, led to the age of modern progress in Jerusalem.

In 1827 an American Mission was set up, followed four years later by a British Mission. The seat of the Orthodox Patriarch was moved from Constantinople, while in 1847 the Latin Patriarchate was renewed. Finally, in 1849, the founding of the Jerusalem Literary and Scientific Society paved the way for the great Palestine Exploration Fund, created in 1865. Two years later Captain Charles Warren inaugurated his epoch-making excavations of the old city, which are today continued by the British School of Archaeology and the Israel Exploration Society.

Jewish enterprise was most notable during the second half of the nineteenth century. Sir Moses Montefiore's movement for a 'return to the land' coincided with a series of buildings in the New City in 1860. Comparable emancipation came for the Christians when, in 1885, the Cross was carried through the streets for the first time since the Crusades. Three years later the *Haram ash-Sherif* Mosque (on the site of the old Temple) was opened to visitors (but not to Jews) for the first time. Economic improvements were also effected. The increase in population—from ten thousand in 1800 to nearly one hundred thousand in 1914, two thirds of whom were Jewish—both encouraged and demanded railways, external trade, skilled workmanship, modern banking, hospitals and schools. It would be out of place to list here these institutions or movements in their rich diversity; even so, it is obvious that no other Eastern city was so socially progressive as was Jerusalem.

In November 1917, Allenby conquered the city. The Balfour Declaration in 1917, implementing the Zionism proposed by Theodor Herzl in 1896, led to the creation, in 1919, of a British Mandate over Palestine. It is difficult, and probably unnecessary, to chronicle in detail the unusually tragic story of the last twenty years. Suffice it to say that, on 14th May 1948, with the British Mandate finally ended, Palestine (or the newly proclaimed state of Israel) was invaded simultaneously by the armies of Egypt, Syria, Lebanon, Saudi-Arabia, Iraq and Transjordan. The Israelis defended themselves heroically and successfully. After a strange war, interrupted at intervals by cease-fire orders imposed by the United Nations, Israel emerged in control of the greater part of Palestine, and armistice agreements were signed with the Arab countries in the spring of the following year.

Throughout this period Jerusalem was the centre of hostilities. For months before the termination of the Mandate, a bloody guerrilla war was being fought within the city between Jews and Arabs. Quarter was embattled against quarter, street against street, with the accompanying horrors of bomb explosions and massacres in which hundreds of lives were lost on both sides. This phase culminated in the total siege of the Jewish parts of Jerusalem from 14th May to 11th June 1948. All roads were blocked, food, water and electricity were cut off, and the city was bombarded night and day by the artillery of the British-officered Arab Legion. After a long and dramatic resistance the University building on Mount Scopus and the ancient Jewish quarter around the Wailing Wall in the Old City were cut off. But the main Jewish settlement in the modern city stood firm. Poorly armed and ill trained, recruited from citizens of both sexes and all ages, its defenders beat off direct attacks and kept the essential services going throughout the siege. Meanwhile a secret road through the Judean hills had been constructed, and when, after a four-weeks' truce, the fighting flared up again on 9th July, the garrison was re-equipped and passed over to the offensive.

Ten days later a truce was negotiated which, despite sporadic flare-ups, remained operative in its essentials up to the 'Six-Day War' of June 1967. This unique feat of strategy, which will command the puzzled attention of many future military historians, has already created its own mythology. Its literary aftermath, however, is bound to take some time to crystallize. But among its most stirring and far-reaching consequences is the fact that a nation debarred from its capital city in A.D. 70 was able to return in A.D. 1967, by its own historical courage, to reclaim the holy city for future generations.

THE BIRD WITH FOUR FEATHERS

When Nabugodonosor, fers in fight,	(fierce)
Ierusalem had thought to wynne;	
And so he dede with mayn & might,	(strength, virtue)
And brent the temples that were er Inne;	(burnt)
And all the gold that he there founde	
He Toke with him and hom gan ryde;	
Him thought ther schold no thing withstonde,	
His herte was set so heigh In Pryde;	
Till the king of myghtes most	
Browght him there that lowest was,	
And caught him from his real oost,	(host, army)
And drof him to a wildernesse;	
And there he lyued with erbe & rote,	
Walking euer on foot' on honde,	(hand)
Till god of mercy dede him bote,	(remedy, profit)
And his prison out of bonde:	
Thanne seide this kyng thise wordes, Iwis:	(indeed)
'Al thing be, lord, at thi powste,	(power)
Mercy I crie; I haue do mys—	(mice)
Parce mici domine!'	

Fragment from a fourteenth-century lyric—MS. Bodley 596

GOD'S ARROW

When the guilt of the Israelites grew too great for the forbearance of the Most High, and they refused to listen to the words and warnings of Jeremiah, the prophet left Jerusalem and travelled to the land of Benjamin. While he was in the holy city, and prayed for mercy on it, it was spared; but while he sojourned in the land of Benjamin, Nebuchadnezzar laid waste the land of Israel, plundered the holy Temple, robbed it of its ornaments, and gave it a prey to the devouring flames. By the hands of Nebuzaradan did Nebuchadnezzar send (while he himself remained in Riblah) to destroy Jerusalem.

When the city had been captured, he marched with the princes and officers into the Temple, and called out mockingly to the God of Israel,

'And art Thou the great God before whom the world trembles, and are here in Thy city and Thy Temple!'

On one of the walls he found the mark of an arrow's head, as though somebody had been killed or hit near by, and he asked, 'Who was killed here?'

'Zachariah, the son of Yehoyadah, the high priest,' answered the people; 'he rebuked us incessantly on account of our transgressions, and we tired of his words and put him to death.'

The followers of Nebuchadnezzar massacred the inhabitants of Jerusalem, the priests and the people, old and young, women, and children who were attending school, even babies in the cradle. The feast of blood at last shocked even the leader of the hostile heathens, who ordered a stay of this wholesale murder. He then removed all the vessels of gold and silver from the Temple, and sent them by his ships to Babel, after which he set the Temple on fire.

The high priest donned his robe and ephod, and saying, 'Now that the Temple is destroyed, no priest is needed to officiate,' threw himself into the flames and was consumed. While the other priests who were still alive witnessed this action, they took their harps and musical instruments and followed the example of the high priest. Those of the people whom the soldiers had not killed were bound in iron chains, burdened with the spoils of the victors, and carried into captivity. Jeremiah the prophet returned to Jerusalem and accompanied his unfortunate brethren, who went out almost naked. When they reached a place called Bet Kuro, Jeremiah obtained better clothing for them. And he spoke to Nebuchadnezzar and the Chaldeans, and said, 'Think not that of your own strength you were able to overcome the people chosen of the Lord; 'tis their iniquities which have condemned them to this sorrow.'

Thus the people journeyed on with crying and moaning until they reached the rivers of Babylon. Then Nebuchadnezzar said to them, 'Sing, ye people—play for me—sing the songs ye were wont to sing before your great Lord in Jerusalem.'

In answer to this command, the Levites hung their harps upon the willow trees near the banks of the river, as it is written, 'Upon the willows in her midst had we hung up our harps'. Then they said, 'If we had but performed the will of God and sung His praises devoutly, we should not have been delivered into thy hands. Now, how can we sing before thee the prayers and hymns that belong only to the One Eternal God?' as it is said, 'How should we sing the song of the Lord on the soil of the stranger?'

Then said the officers of the captors, 'These men are men of death; they refuse to obey the order of the king; let them die.'

But forth stepped Pelatya, the son of Yehoyadah, and thus he addressed Nebuchadnezzar:

'Behold, if a flock is delivered into the hands of a shepherd, and a wolf steals a lamb from the flock, tell me, who is responsible to the owner of the lost animal?'

'Surely the shepherd,' replied Nebuchadnezzar.

'Then listen to thine own words,' replied Pelatya. 'God has given Israel into thy hands; to Him art thou responsible for those who are slain.'

The king ordered the chains to be removed from the captives, and they were not put to death.

Talmudic Legend

Isaac Rosenberg (1890–1918)

THE BURNING OF THE TEMPLE

Fierce wrath of Solomon,
Where sleepest thou? O see,
The fabric which thou won
Earth and ocean to give thee
O look at the red skies.

Or hath the sun plunged down?
What is this molten gold—
These thundering fires blown
Through heaven, where the smoke rolled?
Again the great king dies.

His dreams go out in smoke
His days he let not pass
And sculptured here are broke,
Are charred as the burnt grass,
Gone as his mouth's last sighs.

Sir Philip Sidney (1554–1586)

PSALM LXXXVII

Founded upon the hills of holiness
God's city stands: who more love beareth
To gates of Sion high in lowliness,
Than all the towns that Judah reareth.
  City of God, in God's decree,
  What noble things are said of thee!

I will, saith he, henceforth be numbered
Egypt and Babel with my knowers;
That Palestine and Tyre, which combered
The Fathers, with the after-goers,
Shall join: see Aethiope from whence
They born shall be, as born from hence.

Yea this, men shall of Sion signify:
To him, and him it gave first breathing;
Which highest God shall highly dignify,
Eternal stay to it bequeathing.
Jehovah this account shall make,
When he of his shall muster take.

That he, and he who ever named be,
Shall be as borne in Sion named:
In Sion shall my music framed be,
Of lute and voice most sweetly framed:
I will saith he to Sion bring
Of my fresh fountains ev'ry spring.

The Psalms of David, translated into verse by Sir Philip Sidney
and finished by his sister, The Countess of Pembroke (1555–1621)

T. S. Eliot (1888–1965)

NEHEMIAH

There are those who would build the Temple,
And those who prefer that the Temple should not be built.
In the days of Nehemiah the Prophet
There was no exception to the general rule.
In Shushan the palace, in the month Nisan,
He served the wine to the king Artaxerxes,
And he grieved for the broken city, Jerusalem;
And the King gave him leave to depart
That he might rebuild the city.
So he went, with a few, to Jerusalem,
And there, by the dragon's well, by the dung gate,
By the fountain gate, by the king's pool,
Jerusalem lay waste, consumed with fire;
No place for a beast to pass.
There were enemies without to destroy him,
And spies and self-seekers within,
When he and his men laid their hands to rebuilding the wall.
So they built as men must build
With the sword in one hand and the trowel in the other.

The Rock, Chorus IV

W. B. Yeats (1865–1939)

SOLOMON TO SHEBA

Sang Solomon to Sheba,
And kissed her dusky face,
'All day long from mid-day
We have talked in the one place,
All day long from shadowless noon
We have gone round and round
In the narrow theme of love
Like an old horse in a pound.'

To Solomon sang Sheba,
Planted on his knees,
'If you had broached a matter
That might the learned please,
You had before the sun had thrown
Our shadows on the ground
Discovered that my thoughts, not it,
Are but a narrow pound.'

Sang Solomon to Sheba,
And kissed her Arab eyes,
'There's not a man or woman
Born under the skies
Dare match in learning with us two,
And all day long we have found
There's not a thing but love can make
The world a narrow pound.'

The Collected Poems, 1939

Gaon Achai Shabcha (died 762)

WHY DID THE TEMPLES FALL?

It is forbidden for an Israelite to hate his neighbour; for it is written:
'Thou shalt not hate thy brother in thine heart.' (Lev. xix. 17.) And we
find that it was the hatred of the brothers for Joseph which brought our
ancestors into the slavery of Egypt. Our Rabbis have taught: 'Thou shalt
not hate thy brother.' Perhaps by this might be understood: 'Thou shalt
not wound him, thou shalt not quarrel with him, thou shalt commit no
outrage against him.' It is for this reason that the prophet adds: 'Thou
shalt not hate thy brother *in thine heart*,' in order to make clear that it is
not permitted to carry hatred toward anyone within one's self, even if no
outward expression is given to it. As to the punishment which is foreseen
for unjustified hatred, it is equal to that which is imposed for the three
capital crimes, which are: idolatry, luxury and murder. Why did the
first Temple fall? Because of idolatry, luxury and murder. And why did
the second Temple fall, since we know that in its time the Torah was
observed, good works were practised, and the commandments were
respected? It fell because of the unjustified hatreds which reigned then,
from which it may be concluded that unjustified hatred is a sin as heavy
as idolatry, luxury and murder.

The Talmud

49

Tacitus (55-120)

ROME'S ANGER

When peace dawned once more on Italy, the anxieties of foreign war returned, and the anger of Rome was intensified by the remembrance that the Jews alone had not submitted to her sway. Titus pitched his camp before the walls of Jerusalem and displayed his legions in battle array. The Jews marshalled their lines close in under the very ramparts . . . Our cavalry supported by some light auxiliary foot was sent forward against them and encountered them with no decisive result . . . The Romans then prepared to storm the city. Indeed it seemed beneath their dignity to await the effect of famine on the foe, and they clamoured for the perils of the fray, some of them under the inspiration of courage, but the majority through mere savagery and greed for booty . . . The city, which occupied a commanding natural position, had been strengthened by vast works of defence . . . the towers when favoured by high ground were raised to an altitude of sixty feet each, while on the slopes they reached as much as one hundred and twenty feet; within the fortifications a second line of defence surrounded the palace, and on a jutting crag stood the tower of Antony . . .

The Temple resembled a citadel, and had its own fortifications, which had been rendered superior to all the rest by the labour spent on their construction . . . Their numbers were increased by a vast influx of the dregs of the inhabitants of the other cities that had been destroyed, for the most obstinate of the rebels had taken refuge in Jerusalem, and the spirit of faction was consequently all the more rampant there . . . a vast supply of corn was burnt. . . .

We have heard that the number of the besieged, of every age, and including both sexes, were six hundred thousand. All the able-bodied men bore arms, and a number of the rest, far above the usual average in a population, were brave enough to do the same. Men and women were equally determined, and they plainly showed that, if they were forced to abandon their homes, they would dread life far more than death itself. Such were the city and the race, when the strength of their position prohibited either an assault or any attempt at surprise, which Caesar Titus resolved to attack by a system of raised mounds and pent houses.

History, II, 10-13, translated from the Latin by C. Halm, 1883

Dio Cassius Cocceianus (c. 155–c. 235)

AS IT HAD BEEN FORETOLD

A war was kindled, and that no small one, nor short lived. For the Jews, being sore angered that Aliens should be settled in their own city (Hierosolyma), and that foreign rites should be established in it, kept quiet indeed so long as Hadrian was in Egypt and again in Syria, except in so far as they of design wrought less fitly the weapons commanded of them by the Romans, being themselves denied by the Romans leave to carry arms. But when Hadrian was far away, they rebelled openly.

Now they dared not face the Romans in pitched battle. But, seizing suitable places throughout their land, they fortified these with underground passages and walls, as places of refuge into which to flee when they were hard pressed and to have secret intercourse with one another, and they pierced holes in these passages for air and light.

At first the Romans held them of no account. But when now the whole of Judea was disturbed, and the Jews everywhere in every land were likewise troubled and conspired with the rebels and wrought much hurt to the Romans, both in secret and openly (many others also of alien folk joining with them for the sake of gain), and the whole world was moved thereat, then at last Hadrian sent against them his best generals of whom Julius Severus was foremost in command, being called from Britain of which he was governor.

But Severus risked not giving open battle against the enemy in any place, seeing their numbers and their fury. Therefore, cutting them off piecemeal by flying columns of greater strength under commanders of lower ranks, intercepting also and depriving them of supplies, he was able by this method, a slower one indeed, yet one less perilous, to wear them down and so to crush them utterly. Very few in fact survived. Of their forts the fifty strongest were razed to the ground. Fifty-eight myriads of men were slaughtered in skirmish and in battle. Of those who perished by famine and disease there is no one that can count the number.

Thus the whole of Judea became desert, as indeed had been foretold to the Jews before the war. For the tomb of Solomon, whom these folk celebrate in their sacred rites, fell of its own accord into fragments, and wolves and hyenas, many in number, roamed howling through their cities.

Many also of the Romans were slain in the war. Wherefore Hadrian, writing to the Senate, would not use the Emperor's wonted opening form of words, 'I and the army are well.'

Roman History, lxix

John Clare (1793–1864)

THE MAID OF JERUSALEM

Maid of Jerusalem, by the dead Sea,
I wandered all sorrowful thinking of thee—
Thy city in ruins; thy kingdom deplored,—
All fallen and lost by the Ottoman's sword.

I saw thee sit there in disconsolate sighs
Where the hall of thy fathers a ruined heap lies;
Thy fair fingers showed me the place where they trod,
In thy childhood when flourished the city of God.

The place where they fell and the scenes where they lie,
In the tomb of Silea. The tear in her eye
She stifled—transfix'd there, it grew like a pearl
Beneath the dark lash of the sweet Jewish girl.

Jerusalem is fallen: still thou art in bloom,
As fresh as the ivy round the lone tomb,
And fair as the lily of morning that waves
Its sweet-scented bells o'er the desolate graves.

When I think of Jerusalem in kingdoms yet free,
I shall think of its ruins and think upon thee,
Thou beautiful Jewess! Content thou mayest roam,
A bright spot in Eden still blooms as thy home.

Poems, 1820

Robert Southey (1774–1843)

FATE OF NATIONS

The individual culprit may sometimes
  Unpunished to his after-reckoning go:
Not thus collective man; for public crimes
  Draw on their proper punishment below,
When nations go astray, from age to age
The effects remain, a fatal heritage.

Bear witness, Egypt, thy huge monuments
Of priestly fraud and tyranny austere!
Bear witness then, whose only name presents
    All holy feelings to religion dear—
In earth's dark circlet once the precious gem
Of living light—O fallen Jerusalem!

Collected Works, 1838

Henry Wadsworth Longfellow (1807–1882)

JUDAS MACCABEUS

JUDAS

Who and what are ye, that with furtive steps
Steal in among our tents?

FUGITIVES
                                    O Maccabaeus,
Outcasts are we, and fugitives as thou art,
Jews of Jerusalem, that have escaped
From the polluted city, and from death.

JUDAS

None can escape from death. Say that ye come
To die for Israel, and ye are welcome.
What tidings bring ye?

FUGITIVES
                                    Tidings of despair.
The Temple is laid waste; the precious vessels,
Censers of gold, vials and veils and crowns,
And golden ornaments, and hidden treasures,
Have all been taken from it, and the Gentiles
With revelling and with riot fill its courts.

JUDAS

All this I knew before.

FUGITIVES   Upon the altar
Are things profane, things by the law forbidden;
Nor can we keep our Sabbaths or our Feasts,
But on the festival of Dionysus
Must walk in their processions, bearing ivy
To crown a drunken god.

JUDAS   This too I know,
But tell me of the Jews. How fare the Jews?

FUGITIVES

The coming of this mischief hath been sore
And grievous to the people. All the land
Is full of lamentation and of mourning.
The Princes and the Elders weep and wail;
The young men and the maidens are made feeble;
The beauty of the women hath been changed.

JUDAS

And are there none to die for Israel?
'Tis not enough to mourn. Breastplate and harness
Are better things than sackcloth. Let the women
Lament for Israel; the men should die.

FUGITIVES

Both men and women die; old men and young;
Old Eleazer died; and Máhala
With all her Seven Sons.

JUDAS   Antiochus,
At every step thou takest there is left
A bloody footprint in the street, by which
The avenging wrath of God will track thee out!
It is enough. Go to the sutler's tents:
Those of you who are men, put on such armour
As ye may find; those of you who are women,
Buckle that armour on; and for a watchword
Whisper, or cry aloud, 'The Help of God'.

                              Act III, Scene II, 1872

Chayim Nachman Bialik (1873–1934)

THE DESTRUCTION

The ministering angels assembled in their ritual choirs to say matins. They opened the windows of the sky and leaned out to see if the temple door was open and the cloud of incense rising.

They saw the Lord God of Hosts, the Ancient of Days, sitting on the ruins in the half-light of dawn. He had a mantle of smoke and a footstool of dust and ashes and mountains of grief on his head and his head was sunk between his hands. The exasperation of all the ages darkened his eyelids and in his eyes froze the great silence.

Even the lion of fire, which crouched on the altar day and night, had vanished except for one curl of its mane that flickered and went out in the quiet of the morning.

The ministering angels realized what God had done. They were very moved, and all the stars of the morning trembled with them. The angels covered their faces with their wings, they were afraid to look at sorrowing God. They went aside and wept in silence. The world's heart broke. God couldn't help himself, he leaped up and roared like a lion and beat his hands together and the Holy Ghost ascended from the ruins and went into hiding.

Book of Fire, translated from the Hebrew by Michael Harari

Samuel Taylor Coleridge (1772–1834)

JERUSALEM AS AN EPIC POEM

The destruction of Jerusalem is the only subject now remaining for an epic poem, a subject which, like Milton's Fall of Man should interest all Christendom, as the Homeric War of Troy interested all Greece. There would be difficulties as there are in all subjects; and they must be mitigated and thrown into the shade, as Milton has done with the numerous difficulties in the Paradise Lost.

But there would be a greater assemblage of grandeur and splendour than can now be found in any other theme. As for the old mythology, *incredulus odi*; and yet there must be a mythology, or a quasi-mythology, for an epic poem. Here there would be the completion of the prophecies —the termination of the first revealed rational religion under the violent

55

assault of Paganism, itself the immediate forerunner and condition of the spread of a revealed mundane religion; and then you would have the character of the Roman and the Jew, and the awfulness, the completeness, the justice. I schemed it at twenty-five; but, alas! *venturum expectat.*

Table Talk, April 28, 1832

*

I have already told you that in my opinion the destruction of Jerusalem is the only subject now left for an epic poem of the highest kind. Yet, with all its great capabilities, it has this one grand defect—that, whereas a poem, to be epic, must have a personal interest—in the destruction of Jerusalem no genius or skill could possibly preserve the interest for the hero from being merged in the interest for the event. The fact is, the event itself is too sublime and overwhelming.

In my judgment, an epic poem must either be national or mundane. Milton saw this, and with a judgment at least equal to his genius took a mundane theme—one common to all mankind. He ventures upon no poetic diction, no amplification, no pathos, no affection. He was very wise in adopting the strong anthromorphism of the Hebrew Scriptures at once. Compare the Paradise Lost with Klopstock's Messiah, and you will learn to appreciate Milton's judgment and skill quite as much as his genius.

Table Talk, September 4, 1833

Abraham Shlonski (b. 1900)

THE PLOT

Jerusalem is a hill city,
The hills are founded on gold and pinnacled with gold
For among them walked the men who saw God,
The priests magnificently walked,
Moonstruck with holiness.

Drift in the hills
And smell the scattered stones
Like the bones in Ezekiel's valley;
The incense of life will fill your nostrils,
You'll lose your head and prophesy:

'A stone and a stone make the wall of a house,
A house and a house make a glittering suburb
And so I build Jerusalem.'

Jerusalem is a hill city,
There are foreign villages in those hills,
Nests of the eagle in the clefts of the rock;
And Jerusalem is a dove.

Did they smell carrion,
The children of Kedar, gathering in their tribes?
The eagle is upon you, Jerusalem.
The viper is upon you, gazelle among nations.

Gazelle of Zion,
They plotted to fell your shining antlers.

Zalman Shneur (1886–1959)

THE REBUILDING

The cup of the ancient city walls
Is brimming with houses
And rectangular temples
Bubbling with domes.
The crowded stonework froths
And spills over in streets;
The froth is pink, grey and white:
It has covered the Hundred Measures,
It has risen to the Castle,
Glided over Rehavia
And reached the House of the Vine.
This boiling building-storm
Has never had a rest,
Clouds from the molten pitch,
Tourbillons of cement-dust.
The gravel is good as gold.
Stones churned in the mixers
Race like a petrol engine.
Along the straight roads
Run lorries blood-red
As the blood in the veins of the stone:
Camels and donkeys
Flow from morning till evening

Along hillocky zigzag ways,
Bringing food
To the throat of the power of the building of the city.
Soon the storm will involve
The green valley of Jehoshaphat[1]
That separates the living and the dead.

Yehuda Carni (1884–1949)

THE DEFENCES

Take me for rubble to stop up the wall:
Perhaps I shall expiate the guilt of my people
Who let the stone-work fall.

In the spirit I followed my people through fire and sea,
Through shouting and silence: now I'll enrich my body
By following bodily.

Cement me to all the Jerusalem stones:
At the coming of the Messiah
The wall will sing with my bones.

Jacob David Kamzon (b. 1889)

THE BREAKING OF THE BLOCKADE

The daughters of Zion
Kissed the wheels of lorries and armoured cars.
Muffled in praying shawls
The ancients cried
And hugged and kissed the soldiers
Who took the Jerusalem road.
Happy the eyes that saw the sight that never seer did see
In Jerusalem, city of prophets.

Translated from the Hebrew by Michael Harari

[1] A valley by Jerusalem where Jews, Christians and Moslems alike believe the Last Judgment will be held.

Walter Lever (b. 1909)

YEAR ONE OF THE APOCALYPSE

14 May 1948: It's hard to believe that my last entry was made less than a week ago. Then we were still conscious of belonging to the world and sharing its standards of measurement. Jerusalem was the capital of a little land named Palestine, occupying a minute portion of the map. (In my school atlas, there was only sufficient room to print the letters PAL. between the sea and the Jordan.)

When I look at my pocket-book, there's a smooth, blank sequence of numbered days running on through the rest of May and into the summer, ruled off in neat sections, as if the future were a ready-made suit, just waiting to be put on. Now all this is changed. There's no world left except this city, cut off in space, ringed round with enemies. There's no month of May, no year 1948: only day and night, with chances changing every hour and tomorrow as arbitrary as the particles of the quantum theory. We might be anywhere in history; at the ford of the Red Sea; or beyond history, in the Book of Revelations. No one would marvel if he saw a few hundred of our dead fighters step lightly out of the 'temporary burial ground' at Sanhedriah and stride off with their sten-guns to the front line a few hundred yards away. Indeed, they'd be most welcome.

The new era began early this morning. There was a ring at the door just as I was waking up. B. from our *emdah* stood on the step telling me that I was to go at once to Bait Vegan and report for duty.

'What's the news?' I asked him.

'The British are in the course of leaving. And Kfar Etzion has fallen. Also there's total mobilisation, and all of us are now full-time soldiers.'

At the road-block outside Bait Vegan, which marks our front line on this sector, they gave me a pickaxe and directed me towards the wadi, below the quarry. It reaches all round the southern outskirts as far as the Bethlehem road. I climbed down the rough slope. It was a morning of matchless beauty; the hills radiant; every wild flower between the rocks gem-like and unearthly. Over to the left was the long white skyline of Jerusalem. A terrific battle was raging there. I could hear the ceaseless rattle of automatic gunfire and the perpetual crash of bombs. The din mounted in an infernal crescendo: it seemed that the city could stand no more; that at any moment it would break into fragments.

Stripped to the waist, a number of men were hacking out a deep trench to serve as a tank-trap. We worked on steadily. About noon someone brought half a bucket of water down the hill from Bait Vegan and we passed it round, taking gulps from the brim.

Thursday, 10 June: Only now, when it's a matter of counting the hours until the guns go silent, do I begin to grasp what we have accomplished. We have stood out for twenty-seven days, with one single illusory break, against a bombardment that has steadily grown in intensity. We have repelled head-on assaults by two armies, supplied with almost every kind of modern weapon. We have subsisted in isolation, cut off from food and water, from fuel and electricity, from arms and ammunition. And we are unconquered. We stand; Jerusalem stands. How has it happened? . . .

We have witnessed no angels with fiery swords. We have not seen God's Right Arm uplifted. If that is what is meant by a miracle, then nothing untoward has come to pass. But then, who are we to say that of our own workaday selves we saved the city? Is it to be conceived that we common men have brought about this marvel?

Add up the sum-total of our abilities and resources. Reckon the number of times when this or that individual's action at a crucial moment decided the fate of Jerusalem. Work it out, if possible, on the negative side: the opportunities missed by the enemy, the little blunders and hesitations when nothing could have stopped him from breaking through. The multiplication of ordinary instances transforms quantity into quality, introduces an imponderable factor. Natural causes become supernatural direction; common men become agents of providence. Faith is the catalyst that turns biology into history, history into prophesy. With it, miracles are achieved; without it, even the calculable fails. Faith is not to be summoned up at will; nor does it appear by suppression of the critical faculty. The men through whom it functions, who experienced the miracle, are transformed: never again will they be the men they were.

Jerusalem is called liberty, 1951

Arthur Koestler (b. 1905)

BURMA ROAD

This morning I went shopping, and on the way back to the hotel ran into Alexis of the U.N. Commission, who was just going to inspect the famous new road to Jerusalem. I got into his car with the blue-and-white U.N.O. pennant, which from a distance looks like the Zionist flag.

This new life-line to Jerusalem is the biggest sensation of the war. It is called the Burma Road of Israel, was built in secret, and opened three days ago for military traffic. Haganah have been working on it for about three weeks. It starts at Hulda, which is inside Israel's boundaries and solidly held by the Israeli Army, and joins the old road at Bab el Wad from where onward to Jerusalem it runs through Jewish-controlled territory. The 'Burma Road' is thus a connecting link between the two separate chunks of Jewish Palestine. It was built across Arab territory, and in some stretches at a distance of less than two miles from Arab positions. All work was done at night, in darkness and silence, literally under the nose of the Arab army. Two nights before the truce came into effect the first convoy with supplies reached besieged Jerusalem.

The road became worse; in fact it could hardly be called a road at all. We bumped up and down slopes and wadis, the jeep swaying like a camel and sometimes leaning over at forty-five degrees. Then we came to the critical patch, about which we had been warned beforehand, a very steep incline of sand and loose rocks about a hundred yards long. It was only negotiable downhill in the direction of Jerusalem; on the return journey trucks, cars and even jeeps had to be pulled up the slope on ropes by a giant caterpillar bulldozer. As we went down the slope we were very nearly overturned, and Alexis performed an acrobatic jump out of the jeep and down the slope into a shrub of camel thistles. This we found the more damaging to the prestige of U.N.O. as the rest of us, ensconced in the back of the jeep, were unable to extricate ourselves. In the opposite direction an enormous bus was being hoisted up the slope by the bull-dozer. It was a fantastic sight. The front wheels of the bus were in the air, and the bulldozer looked like a giant terrier shaking and dragging along a giant rat by its teeth.

On the other side of this wadi the road improved. About two miles away we could see the monastery and police station of Latrun; the Arabs holding it were no doubt watching us through glasses and grinding their teeth. They couldn't shoot at us because of the truce; and if hostilities are resumed, Arab artillery may theoretically dominate the road, but to hit a moving target at night will still remain difficult for them.

We rejoined the old Tel Aviv-Jerusalem road at Bab el Wad. As only fifteen miles of excellent road lay between us and Jerusalem, we decided to let permits look after themselves and to drive on into the city. The number of civilians who had, by one means or another, got into Jerusalem since the beginning of the war could be counted on one's fingers.

In less than twenty minutes we passed the last check-post before the city, and after an absence of four years I saw my beloved Jerusalem again. We drove in through Jaffa Road, past the familiar landmarks: the ruins of the modern blocks in Ben Yehuda Street which British Mosleyites blew up in 1947; the wing chipped off the King David Hotel which the Jews blew up in 1946; and so on. That is the kind of landmark which gives the atmosphere of modern Jerusalem; the Old City in its immortal glory and beauty we were not allowed to see. Incidentally this is the first time since the destruction of the Temple that Jews have been prevented from worshipping at the giant stones of the Wailing Wall, last relic of Israel's ancient statehood.

Through devious routes, by-passing road blocks and miles of barbed wire which have turned Jerusalem into a new version of the labyrinth of Minos, we reached the Y.M.C.A. building, now the seat of the extra-territorial Red Cross mission. There we left Alexis to see his U.N. colleagues, and drove on to the house of Gershon Agronsky, editor of the *Palestine Post*. His wife Ethel gave us tea, one cup *per capita*—the Arabs have cut Jerusalem's water supply, and the ration per day is two gallons for all purposes—washing, cooking, drinking, laundry, and everything else. Normally at this time of year the Jewish Jerusalemite takes half a dozen showers a day and drinks at least a gallon of tea and lemonade.

We apologized for not having brought any supplies, as our visit was improvised, and asked what we should bring next time. Ethel said a lemon and a carrot; Gershon said cigarettes. They were hungry for food, hungrier for cigarettes, and hungriest for news. As so often under abnormal conditions of life, psychological needs seem to reverse the hierarchy of physiological needs.

While we were talking, Alexis came in slightly shaken: on his way from the Y.M.C.A. to the French consulate he had been shot at and narrowly missed by an Arab sniper from the old city. If this isn't a breach of the truce, I don't know what is; but we had to promise that the story would be off the record. Half of what goes on concerning this country is off the record anyway: the British arms deliveries to the Arabs and the desperate efforts of British diplomacy to keep them from collapsing and the war going; the Czech and French arms deliveries to the Jews; the fatuous pretence of the United Nations who know that the truce is broken every day in every way by all parties directly and indirectly concerned. The Holy Land is becoming a kind of ethical atom-pile whose poisoned radiations are spreading in all directions over the world.

The Israeli Government will either have to withdraw its original assent to the internationalisation of the capital and claim at least the new town for Israel, or the old prophecy will come true and, having forsaken Jerusalem, her right hand will forget its cunning. There is little doubt that they will choose the first course and in one form or another annex modern Jerusalem; and then international quarrelling, haggling and mediation will start all over again. No other town has caused such continuous waves of killing, rape and unholy misery over the centuries as this Holy city.

For those, however, who are inside it, matters appear much simpler;

constantly exposed to its radiations, they live in holy blindness. There is an old Jewish legend: when, after their long siege, the legions of Titus put fire to the Temple, the Priests threw the keys of Jerusalem high into the air and cried to God: 'Stretch out Thy hand, for Thou art now the guardian of these keys'. And in the midst of the flames a hand was seen reaching down from the sky; its fingers closed over the keys and took them. On May the Twentieth, 1948, when the Arab Legion began its attack on the Jews in the old city, among the many rumours of war there was one passed on among the old men, from bearded mouth to side-locked ear: the ancient keys of the city gates had been found by the Commander of Haganah, in the courtyard of the Hurva Synagogue. Thus the Lord, having sulked with the Jews since A.D. 71 had at last given Jerusalem back to them. *Promise and Fulfilment*, Palestine, 1917–1949

Arvid Mörne (1876–1946)

THE DISBELIEVER AT THE WAILING WALL

Jehovah, ever-watchful eye of heaven,
Look down on one whose anguished soul implores—
How much of thy stern vengeance must we bear,
And must unending be our punishment?
Look down, look down on mourning Israel!
Torment and woe Thy people have endured,
With bitter gall their cup of sorrow filled.
Answer, Jehovah, one whose soul knows doubt,
Suffers the empty pangs of disbelief.
That prophecy, those words of hope you laid
In mercy on the prophet's tongue, were these
Words of a song whose meaning is unknown,
A hollow chant sung by the wind and waves?
The table of the law, the Toran roll,
Were these but fancies made in childhood play,
And has our long obedience and faith
Led to the cross that stands on Golgotha?
Was not the star that over Bethlehem stood
Light of the light of your full countenance?
In dust, forgotten, lies Jerusalem.

Translated from the Finnish-Swedish by
Stig Appelgren and Michael Harari

Irvin Shaw (b. 1913)

THE APPROACH

Approach Jerusalem with caution; there are ghosts on the road. Climb the Judean hills from the sea and pass the burnt-out trucks of the ambushed convoys that went to the relief of the city many months ago. The dead have long since been removed and the rusting hulks are pushed to one side, but it is not hard to imagine the noise in the ravines, the sound of the machine guns and mortars, the cries of the wounded, the crackling of the flames. Violent men have violently died here, leaving their wrenched and blackened weapons as a reminder to the traveller that the city he is about to enter must not be taken lightly.

Or come to the city not through space but through time. Descend through the centuries to the torn streets and damaged walls and pass through ages of conflict, siege, plunder, massacre, torture, antagonism, constantly renewed, constantly refreshed with blood.

Jerusalem is a city of endless contention. It is a border city marking the frontier in time and space between military empires, religions, cultures. Here the old gods lost out to the One God, here Faith fought heresy and heresy became Faith; here the nomad clashed with the settler, the West with the Orient, the machine age with the feudal era. Every religion has suffered here and caused suffering to others.

At Latrum there is a Trappist monastery and one of the bitterest battles of the war was fought here when the Israeli forces had attacked the Arab Legion which was entrenched around this monastery. Now that peace has descended upon the region the monks are again silently tending their vines, undisturbed even by the noise of passing traffic. For the road from Tel Aviv past the monastery is no longer used. A loop through the hills was hastily bulldozed and paved by the Israeli Army, and you approach Jerusalem slowly and bumpily across back country on a track that has been grandiloquently named the Burma Road. Seen from afar, the city looks lost in almost medieval tranquillity, its stone buildings rose and beige coloured on the silvery olive hills, and the music of its church bells sounding clear and peaceful in the hazeless atmosphere.

For many years now, Jerusalem has been not one city but two, and the war served to make that demarcation more sharp. The Old City, behind its fortress walls, encloses a hive of narrow, winding streets, Oriental bazaars under looming archways, sacred stones, minarets, domed churches, synagogues, the holy memories and traditions of three faiths. Here reason stops and faith claims all.

The Old City is in Arab hands, and from the walls the sentries of the

Legion peer down across the battered and quiet no man's land to the Israeli-held new city. The new city, with its impressive apartment houses, its well-proportioned public buildings, combines the modern and the traditional in a just and spacious manner.

Spiritually, Jerusalem has a tendency to disappoint the pilgrim. As one of the men attached to the American consulate said 'They come here, full of religion, and they expect to undergo a great experience, a sort of vision in a thunderclap. Nothing of the kind happens and they're heartbroken.' When I had been in the Old City in 1943, the Church of the Holy Sepulchre, swathed in scaffolding to keep it intact after the damage suffered in the 1927 earthquake, was surrounded by chattering guides and salesmen of garish mementos, who served effectively to dampen all pious thoughts on the part of the English and American soldiers who were coming to the church on leave.

At the entrance to the narrow courtyard, along one side of which ran the Wailing Wall, the remnant of the Temple which is a shrine for orthodox Jews, a British sentry in a box kept, in those days, an incongruous vigil next to a telephone which rang again and again over the scene. Old women and old men who had come to Zion to die crept along the Wall touching it inch by inch, first with their finger-tips, then with their lips, giving a strange appearance of idolatry to their whispered prayers. And there is a more formal ceremony at the Wall, in which a leader chants in solo and a chorus responds. There are no Jews in the Old City now to conduct this sorrowful litany, but while there were, the guides, including self-appointed barefooted Arab children, while not interfering with the worshippers themselves, were lavish with capsule lectures to all tourists on the size, shape and supposed history of the Temple and often threw in a brisk two- or three-minute description of the past glories of the Jews and their present sufferings.

The Moslem position with regard to the shrines is a complicated one, since it includes all the holy spots of the other two religions, which Mohammed regarded as authentic but incomplete, revelations of the Word of God, to which he added his own final synthesis. Jerusalem at first was the city toward which Mohammed ordered his followers to bow in prayer, only later changing to Mecca.

Delicate, too, is the fact that there is an embarrassing excess of holy places, different sects claiming different locations as the locus of legendary and miraculous events. A rascally guide explained to me 'There are three kinds of holy places—dinkum (authentic), probable and picturesque.'

On the other hand, many men and women pass their lives in single-minded devotion within the city limits. God is worshipped here in a

E

bewildering variety of tongues and with an almost endless luxuriance of forms. Monks, nuns, and priests of all orders and nationalities stroll the streets and their chants and responses can be heard throughout the day from behind old walls. Ministers of the Protestant sects browse in the bookshops and the wild ecstatic cries of the Hasidic Jews and the rhythm of their dancing can be heard through the windows of the synagogues in which, through ecstasy, they attempt to approach God. Gaunt and bearded Talmudic scholars, their skin pale and stretched from long hours of studying the Law, move in their wide hats and long coats among the taxis, the buses, and the Army trucks, oblivious to politics, oblivious to war, oblivious, almost, to the twentieth century as they wander back through more than two thousand years of parables, rules for worship, argument on the nature of the Deity, the rambling discussion and counter-discussion of generations of rabbis.

Old forms survive side by side with the brusque innovations of the modern world. A stonemason working on repairing the damage to a war-torn office building takes two hours off, claps on a cap, and rushes to a rooftop, where, among seventy other couples, he is hastily married under the sky, this being the first day, except one, since Passover that his religion permits weddings to be solemnized. But the prosaic march of progress will, as it always does, in all countries, diminish the picturesque in favour of the practical.

The years lie heavily on Jerusalem. Holy city, blessed city, promised city, city where peace, charity and love have been most passionately preached, it peers back from an uncertain and bloodstained present to a riotous, bitter past. New grudges, streamlined and paid off in machine guns and high explosive, are piled on the incalculable old enmities that were paid off by the sword and battle-axe. The city balanced uneasily over a flaw of the human spirit, which, like a flaw in the earth, in its own time, shifts and quakes, bringing destruction to all who live above it. In Jerusalem men may store up joy for themselves in the world to come, but they walk the streets of this one under a brooding cloud. Peace, the carved stone letters say on the monuments; peace, chant the worshippers. But if men can have peace in Jerusalem, men can have peace anywhere on the planet.

Report on Israel, New York, 1950

III Twenty-five centuries of mourning

If I prefer not Jerusalem
Above my chief joy . . .

Pauvres filles de Sion,
Vos liesses sont passées,
La commune affliction
Les a toutes effacées.

Notre orgueilleuse Cité,
Qui les a cités de la terre
Passait en felicité,
N'est plus qu'un monceau de pierre.

Robert Garnier (*1544–1590*):
Les Juives, *1583*

In A.D. 363 the Emperor Julian the Apostate
ordered the restoration of the Temple, but the
work was interrupted by a cataclasm. Since
then no responsible Jew has advocated the
rebuilding of the Temple. The meat shortage
alone would make the ancient sacrifices im-
possible. There is a strong movement to divert
the national disposition for mourning into more
topical channels. A shrine has been erected
under the walls of the old city where the ashes
of Jews murdered by the Germans are un-
ceasingly venerated. It is probable that this
will take the place of the Wailing Wall in the
minds of the next generation.

Evelyn Waugh: The Holy Places, *1952*

Whenever anyone—prophet or deceiver—
throughout the two thousand years of exile
plucked the string, the entire soul of the
people was brought into vibration.

Stefan Zweig: The World of
Yesterday, *1941*

When Jerusalem and the Second Temple were destroyed, the
dream of returning to *the city* and rebuilding it became a symbol of
the larger dream of the Jews' actual return to the land of Israel.
In fact, after the destruction, the name of the holy place was often
used as a synonym for the whole of Israel. Often the dream seemed
close to reality, as when Julian the Apostate promised in A.D. 362
that when he returned from the Persian War he would rebuild the
Temple and rejoice there with the Jews. But he never returned

Still the Jews of the Diaspora clung to the dream. Many of their houses had one wall left unpainted to recall the story of Jerusalem, now trailing in the dust. And in their prayers three times a day the Jews faced east (as they still do) towards the Holy City. Small wonder if Jerusalem appears in Hebrew writings, both sacred and secular, as 'the light of the world'.

As Christianity forged further ahead in its attempt to win the world, Jerusalem became to the Church a divergent force. But for the Diaspora, still carrying within it the yearning for the lost city, it acted as a convergent force. The persistence of this Jewish longing, its unbroken spiritual continuity passed on from generation to generation accounts for the emotional character of much Hebrew literature. Laid low by countless conquerors and humiliations, Jerusalem is once more the capital of Israel. The mourning is over, the homecoming achieved, the dream realized. If in time past to Jew and to Christian the city was the centre of the world, she has now become the heart of a new historical adventure.

Adam Mickiewicz (1798–1855)

JERUSALEM, WARSAW, WATERLOO[1]

... We are bound up with the mourning of Israel who in every corner of the globe weep today for the desolation of Jerusalem.

We Poles must rouse similar feelings in ourselves when we remember the massacre in Prague and the capture of Warsaw. To the French it is Waterloo.

Come, let us bow down before the people of Israel, which has for eighteen centuries known how to keep alive its anguish as if the disaster had occurred only yesterday.

A letter from Susa, 458 B.C.

ARTAXERXES, KING OF PERSIA,
TO EZRA, THE PRIEST

And now I make a decree, set free all the people of Israel and their priests and the Levites, in my realm, that are minded of their own free will to go with thee to Jerusalem. Go! Forasmuch as thou art sent of the King and his seven counsellors, to inquire concerning Judah and Jerusalem, according to the law of thy God which is in thy hand; and to carry the silver and gold which the King and his counsellors have freely offered unto the God of Israel, whose habitation is in Jerusalem, and all the silver and gold that thou shalt find in all the province of Babylon, with the freewill offering of the people, and of the priests, offering willingly for the house of their God which is in Jerusalem; therefore thou shalt with all diligence buy with this money bullocks, rams, lambs with their meal offerings and their drink offerings, and shalt offer them upon the altar of the house of your God which is in Jerusalem.

---

[1] On the ninth of Ab, corresponding to 11 August 1845, Mickiewicz and some members of his group of Polish emigrés in Paris visited the Jewish Synagogue in the Rue Notre Dame de Nazareth where he made the above statement. After the reading of Lamentations in the synagogue Mickiewicz delivered from the altar a fiery exhortation in which he cried out that 'the most beautiful, the most glorious day in the life of a people is the day on which the whole people fasts'. And he consoled the Jewish congregation, and urged them not to lose hope, because the redemption was near, and (he said) 'we Poles will help you so that we shall all be delivered from dispersion'.

Julian the Apostate (331–363)

THE TWENTY-FIFTH EPISTLE

To the Community of Jews,

More oppressive for you in the past than the yoke of dependence was the circumstance that the new taxes were imposed upon you without previous notice, and you were compelled to furnish an enormous quantity of gold to the imperial treasury. Many of these hardships I myself noticed but I learned more from the tax rolls that were being preserved to your detriment, which I happened to light upon. I myself abolished a tax, which was about to be levied upon you, and thus put a stop to the impious attempt to bring infamy upon you; with my own hands did I commit to the flames the tax-rolls against you that I found in my archives, in order that no one might ever spread such a charge of impiety against you. The real author of these calumnies was not so much my ever-to-be-remembered brother Constantius, as those men who, barbarians in mind and atheists in heart, were entertained at his table. With my own hands have I seized these persons, and thrust them into the pit, so that not even the memory of their fall shall remain with us.

Desiring to extend yet further favours to you, I have exhorted my brother the venerable Patriarch Julio to put a stop to the collection of the so-called Spostole among you, and henceforth no one will be able to oppress your people by the collection of such imposts, so that everywhere throughout my kingdom you may be free from care; and thus enjoying freedom you may address still more fervent prayers for my empire to the Almighty, Creator of the Universe, who has deigned to crown me with his own undefiled right hand.

It seems to be the fact that those who lead lives full of anxiety are fettered in spirit, and do not dare to raise their hands in prayer. But those who are exempt from all cares, and rejoice with their welfare, are better able to direct their sincere prayers for the welfare of the Empire to the Mighty One, in whose power it lies to further the success of my reign, even according to my wishes.

Thus should you, in order that when I return safely from the Persian war, I may restore the Holy City of Jerusalem, and rebuild it at my own expense, even as you have for so many years desired it to be restored; and therein will I unite with you in giving praise to the Almighty.

The Works of the Emperor Julian, translated
from the Latin by W. C. Wright, 1913

MOTHER ZION IN MOURNING

The Prophet Jeremiah meets Mother Zion mourning for her exiled children. Jeremiah said: 'While going up to Jerusalem, I lifted up mine eyes, and saw a woman sitting on the top of a mountain, clad in black garments, her hair dishevelled; she was crying and asking who would comfort her, and I was crying and asking who would comfort me. I drew nigh unto her, and said: "If thou art a woman, speak to me; if thou art a ghost, depart from me." She replied: "Dost thou not know me? I am she who had seven children; their father went away to a city across the sea. A messenger came and said unto me: 'Thy husband died in the city across the sea'. While I went about weeping for him, another messenger came, and said unto me: 'The house fell upon the seven children, and killed them'. Now I know not for whom I should weep and for whom I should dishevel my hair." I said: "Thou art not better than my mother Zion, and yet she has become pasture for the beasts of the field". She answered and said unto me: "I am thy mother Zion, I am the mother of the seven, for thus it is written: 'She that hath borne seven languisheth.'"' Jeremiah then said unto her: 'Thy misfortune is like the misfortune of Job: Job's sons and daughters were taken away from him, and likewise thy sons and daughters were taken away from thee; I took away from Job his silver and gold, and from thee, too, did I take away thy silver and gold; I cast Job on the dunghill, and likewise thee did I make into a dunghill. And just as I returned and comforted Job, so shall I return and comfort thee; I doubled Job's sons and daughters, and thy sons and daughters shall I also double; I doubled Job's silver and gold, and unto thee shall I do likewise; I shook Job from the dunghill, and likewise concerning thee it is written: "Shake thyself from the dust; arise, and sit down, O Jerusalem". A mortal of flesh and blood built thee, a mortal of flesh and blood laid thee waste; but in the future I shall build thee, for thus it is written: "The Lord doth build up Jerusalem, He gathereth together the dispersed of Israel".'

The Midrash

PITY THY CITY

But let Thy pity be poured out, O Lord our God, on the just and the pious, and on the elders of the house of Israel, Thy people, and on the scribes that still remain, and on the strangers who are just, and on us. Give Thou good recompense to those that put their trust in Thy name, and let our portion be with them for ever, and we shall not be put to shame, for in Thee is our trust. Blessed art Thou, O Lord, the stay and comfort of the just.

And turn again in pity to Jerusalem, Thy city; make Thy dwelling-place therein, according to Thy promise. And build it soon, in our days, that it may endure for ever . . .

The Jewish Prayer Book
Shemoneh Esreh—The prayer of the eighteen benedictions

LEAD US WITH SONG TO ZION

. . . And by the hand of Thy servants the prophets Thou hast written: Ye that dwell on earth, all the inhabitants thereof, ye shall behold a standard lifted on the mountains, and ye shall hear a great trumpet, and they that were lost shall return from out of Assyria and they that were oppressed from out of Egypt, and they shall bow low before the Lord in the sacred mountain of Jerusalem. And it is said: And they shall see the Lord their God over them, and the lightning shall be His arrow, and He will blow a trumpet and ride on the whirlwinds of Temen. The Lord God of Hosts will shield them: Thy peace shall be like a shield over Thy people Israel.

God, our God and the God of our fathers, sound the great trumpet of our liberation, and lift up the standard to assemble our exiles, and draw together those that are scattered among the nations and those that are dispersed to the ends of the earth, and lead us with song to Zion, Thy city, lead us in ever-lasting joy to the house of Thy holiness, Jerusalem.

The Jewish Prayer Book, Prayer for the New Year

Amittai ben Shephatiah (10th Century)

LORD, SAVE US!

Lord, I remember, and am sore amazed
To see each city standing in her state,
And God's own city to the low grave razed;
Yet in all time we look to Thee and wait.

Send us Thy mercy, O Redeemer! Make,
O thou my soul, to Him thy mournful plaint;
And crave compassion for my people's sake;
Each head is weary and each heart is faint.

O Thou who hearest weeping, healest woe,
Our tears within Thy vase of crystal store;
Save us, and all Thy dread decrees forego,
For unto Thee our eyes turn evermore.

Translated from the Hebrew by Nina Salaman

Known in Hebrew as *Ez'krah Elohim V'e'hemayah*, a hymn sung on the Day of
Atonement.

Solomon Ibn Gabirol (1021–1070)

GOD AND ISRAEL

God:

Though bereaved and in mourning, why sit thus in tears?
Shall thy spirit surrender its hopes to its fears?
Though the end has been long and no light yet appears,
  Hope on, hapless one, a while longer.

I will send thee an angel My path to prepare,
On the brow of Mount Zion thy King to declare,
The Lord ever regnant shall reign again there,
  Thy King, O proclaim, comes to Zion.

Israel:

How long, O my God, shall I wait Thee in vain?
How long shall Thy people in exile remain?
Shall the sheep ever shorn never utter their pain
  But dumbly through all go on waiting?

God:

Have faith, hapless one, I will pardon and free,
Not always shalt thou be abhorrent to Me,
But be Mine e'en as I shall return unto thee,
  'Tis yet but a little space longer.

Israel:

How long till the turn of my fate shall draw near,
How long ere the sealed and the closed be made clear,
And the palace of strangers a roof shall appear?

God:

Hope on for a shelter and refuge.
With healing shall yet thy entreaties be graced,
As when Caphtor was crushed shalt thou triumph re-taste,
And the flowers cast off shall re-bloom in the waste,
    Hope on but a little space longer.

Selected Religious Poems, translated by Israel Zangwill

Jehudah Halevi (1080–1145)

ODE TO ZION

Art thou not, Zion, fain
To send forth greetings from thy sacred rock
Unto thy captive train,
Who greet thee as the remnants of thy flock?
Take Thou on every side,
East, west and south and north, their greetings multiplied.
Sadly he greets thee still,
The prisoner of hope who, day and night,
Sheds ceaseless tears, like dew on Hermon's hill.
Would that they fell upon thy mountain's height!

Perfect in beauty, Zion, how in thee
Do love and grace unite!
The souls of thy companions tenderly
Turn unto thee; thy joy was their delight,
And weeping they lament thy ruin now.

The Lord desires thee for His dwelling place
Eternally, and bless'd
Is he whom God has chosen for the grace
Within thy courts to rest.
Happy is he that watches, drawing near,
Until he sees thy glorious lights arise,
And over whom thy dawn breaks full and clear,
Set in the orient skies.
But happiest he, who, with exultant eyes,
The bliss of thy redeemed ones shall behold,
And see thy youth renewed as in the days of old.

Translated from the Hebrew by Alice Lucas

MY HEART IS IN THE EAST

My heart is in the east, and I in the uttermost west—
How can I find savour in food? How shall it be sweet to me?
How shall I render my vows and my bonds, while yet
Zion lieth beneath the fetter of Edom, and I in Arab chains?
A light thing would it seem to me to leave all the good things
    of Spain—
Seeing how precious in mine eyes it is to behold the dust of
    the desolate sanctuary.

Selected Poems of Jehudah Halevi, translated
from the Hebrew by Nina Salaman, 1894

Mose ben Nachman Ramban (1195–1270)

WEEPING OVER THE SIGHT

A mournful sight I have perceived in thee, Jersualem. Only one Jew is here, a dyer, persecuted, oppressed, and despised. At his house gather great and small when they can get *Minyan*.[1] They are wretched folk, without occupation and trade, consisting of a few pilgrims and beggars, though the fruit of the land is still magnificent and the harvests rich. Indeed it is still a blessed country, flowing with milk and honey . . .

Oh! I am a man who has seen affliction. I am banished from my table, removed far away from friend and kinsman, and too long is the distance for me to meet them again . . . I left my family. I forsook my house. And there with my sons and daughters, and with the sweet and dear children whom I have brought up on my knees, I left also my soul. My heart and my eyes will dwell with them for ever . . . But the loss of all this and of every other glory my eyes saw is compensated by having now the joy of being a day in thy courts, O Jerusalem, visiting the ruins of the Temple, and crying over the desolate sanctuary; where I am permitted to caress thy stones, to fondle thy dust, and to weep over thy ruins. I wept bitterly, but I found joy in my tears. I tore my garments, but I felt relieved by it.

Commentary to the Pentateuch, translated from
the Hebrew by Solomon Schechter, 1896

[1]*Minyan* (or *number*) is the Hebrew word for a congregation at of least ten adult males (i.e. over the age of thirteen) necessary in any public worship.

Jeremy Robson (b. 1939)

THE CRADLED CITY

I can only stare over the cradled city
And watch the rocks, the trees and the silent streams dream on.
I can only hear the urgent voices in the air
And the beautiful breathing of a million stars,
And sense love and music everywhere.
And nobody sees and nobody hears my tears
trickle on the sand—and disappear.

Jerusalem, 1960

Edmond Fleg (1870–1965)

FAITH AND HOPE

The wandering Jew comes to the wall
Passing between the stumbling generations
    of nations on the heel of nations
the Jew came to the place of Lamentations.

On the twelve Tribes by the Wall of Tears
    death drifted, veiling
the crippled captives of the stolen years
    with his shadow falling.

With naked hands they tore the granite,
    and the centuries with them
echoed their sorrow, murmuring in it,
    'O lost Jerusalem.'

The dead cities warn the cities of today
'Look on us, cities, as we dead look at you:
We were the corn, the sailing ship, the statue;
    We were the embattled armies, we have been
    the human soul of the machine.
Each of us sought to pluck the stars from heaven,
Men have forgotten us, but God has not forgiven.

To the future generations:
We bring the kindly soil of earth to be
the fixed foundation of the Sanctuary.
Carpenters of the dawn, we square the sky
to be the Temple-roof of the Most High.

The Dreamer:
Faith, Hope and Charity, each in their place
the chosen architects of strength and grace,
as though Beethoven wrote the score for them,
to music build the New Jerusalem.

Le Mur des Pleurs, translated from
the French by Humbert Wolfe

Matilde Serao (1856–1927)

AT THE WAILING WALL

Every Friday a procession of Christians, starting from the Praetorium, passes through the streets of Jerusalem, kneeling and praying at every one of the fourteen 'stations'. The markets are closed. The ancient Solima, the city of David and Solomon, is wrapped in silence. The Christians returning from the Via Dolorosa regain their hotels or the Franciscan convent, to rest after their exciting pilgrimage of the 'Way of the Cross'. Later in the afternoon they are reminded by their faithful guides that they should go and witness the most pathetic of sights, the 'Wailing of the Jews'. Every Friday the Jewish population, which throughout the rest of the week works so hard, which feeds so sparingly, sleeps so little, is so silent, obstinate, abandons business and trade to give vent to its pent-up feelings by weeping and wailing before the walls of its erstwhile time-honoured Temple. There is no stranger, sadder, or more moving sight on earth than this weekly 'Wailing of the Jews' of Jerusalem.

A wall! Not an ordinary wall, but a lofty, over-powering mass of Cyclopean brickwork: is all that now remains of the Temple of Solomon; of the Seat of the Mosaic Law; of that Temple whose grandeur and majesty fills the Scriptures. Only a wall—but so magnificent, so colossal, that the sonorous descriptions of it do not appear exaggerated; and the

77

eye raised to take in its height is quickly lowered, as if humbled by the spectacle of so much might and strength. The stones of which the wall of the Temple is made are long, wide, and thick, and are more like huge slabs, evenly placed one above the other, forming a sheer rock, square, polished, heavy and overwhelmingly strong. All else has been demolished: did not Jesus say that He could destroy the Temple and build it up again in three days? Nothing remains of its rich inlaid woods, ivories, and precious stones, which made it so bewilderingly bright and lovely: only this wall is left standing to show what the Temple must have been, and the power of the Hand which crumbled it to dust. These huge slabs alone bear witness to the past glory of Israel, and, in order that the curse might seem the more tragic, Fate has decreed that this wall, which testifies to the greatness of Moses and Solomon, to the pride and splendour of a nation, should now be the support of the left wing of the Mosque of Omar!

The Turks, during the reign of Omar, made use of the foundations of the Temple to build a magnificent mosque, the most important in Islam, after the one at Mecca, which contains the Prophet's tomb, and that of Medina. The wall, which was covered with costly woods, carbuncles, and emeralds, and inlaid work of gold and copper: the sacred wall which had witnessed the solemn rites of the Law of Moses has now become the prop of a mosque, whose only ornaments are straggling Mohammedan inscriptions and a series of blue and yellow tiles running along the great cornice of its interior. The wall looks on to a narrow, dirty alley, where its huge grey stones contrast strangely with the neighbouring small houses and squalid huts. The glory of Solomon has vanished; the greatness of the Jewish people is no more; that sacred wall which heard the Judaic prophecies and prayers, which was the ideal cradle of the Law, is now polluted by Mohammedans. The Jews who come every Friday to wail and weep, never enter the Mosque of Omar, which they hold in horror, for it is said that the Book of the Law was buried underneath the peristyle, and they fear to enter lest they might, inadvertently, tread it under their feet. They cannot, moreover, bear to see the Crescent shining over the place where the Ark of the Covenant once was venerated; or to see the *mirhab* on the sight of the Tabernacle. Every Friday, women, children, old men and young, set out for the narrow lane where King Solomon's mighty wall still endures. The women wear a kind of toque of silk or wool over their hair, and above it a light woollen shawl with a flowery pattern, in the folds of which they hide half their faces. The Russian and Polish Jews wear a fur cap; others, the French and English, a black silk cap; and some still wear the real old Hebrew *Zimarra*.

Along the houses opposite the wall of Solomon there are stones and benches upon which the old people and children sit, praying and reading their holy books. And all along the wall itself, with their foreheads pressed against it, is a crowd of women, their shawls thrown back from their heads, with shoulders bent, weeping in silence; and thus the cold, smooth wall gradually becomes saturated with tears. Two or three hundred people at a time, men and women, congregate there, remaining ten minutes or a quarter of an hour, sobbing silently. When they have finished their wail, two or three hundred other people take their places, beating their heads against the stone, praying and weeping; and as they do so they recite in a dismal monotone, a doleful yet touching litany.

The rabbi, or some other ancient, pious and fanatical servant of Israel says the first part of this dreary dirge, to which the mourning people make answer. And as the narrative of their misfortunes continues and all the fulness of the misery of the Jewish race, with no father-land, no nationality, and no king, is unrolled in one great lamentation, the wailing increases: since nothing now remains to Israel of her vanished glory and prosperity but these rocks, piled one upon the other to remind her that she was once the chosen people of God. To these poor souls this fragment of the wall of their Temple is a sort of huge sepulchre in which their nationality, their pride, and their history lies buried! Nothing remains to the Hebrews of their mystical inheritance but this poor remnant of a crumbling wall—and even this is no longer theirs, since it belongs to Mahomet!

Out here, in the cold open air, in a narrow, filthy alley, their feet in the mire, looking like so many whipped curs, they kiss these stones and weep over them in the presence of a crowd of unfeeling onlookers, Turks and Christians. They endeavour to stifle their sobs, but, none the less, the air is filled with the sound of their wailing and with the rhythm of their sighs. Phlegmatic English tourists watch them through their eyeglasses, and when I was last there an impertinent obstinate old lady, riding donkey-back, insisted upon inspecting the entire line, thereby greatly disturbing their piteous lament.

Strange and touching spectacle! Weeping is surely contagious, and in this dark alley tears seem bidden to flow almost involuntarily by the subtle hypnotic influence of Solomon's wall, where the Jews grieve over a real woe, whilst expiating the greatest of all crimes. They only find in religion a fresh source of sorrow; even as we discover therein our chief consolation! How can anyone deride them?

Nel Paese di Gesú,
translated from the Italian by Richard Davey, 1905

Llewelyn Powys (1884–1939)

THE DWARF'S PRAYER

The next morning we set out to visit the Dome of the Rock and the Achsa Mosque. It was Friday and we found that Christians were forbidden entrance to the ancient Temple area on that day. Presently as we sauntered through the narrow crowded alleys my eye lit upon the figure of a dwarf. This homuncule was bustling along the pavement with great purpose. He was dressed in a long black coat under the tail of which brown stockings were visible. His shoes were too big for him and as he walked he made a slipper-slop sound. I never saw his face, but as my eyes followed his humped shoulders disappearing in the distance I could not prevent myself speculating upon the background of his life. Where had he slept this last night? In what attic under a flat roof had he been dreaming while the waning moon had floated down the sky? Where was he off to now with all this hurry?

We came upon a vegetable market and stood to watch the venders. Many Arab girls in gay clothes were sitting near their baskets of garden produce. Their eyes were bright, their bangles shining. I saw them sell radishes of a very large size. Arab men in rough homespun garments stood about. They carried staffs in their hands. There was something imperious in their bearing. They seemed superior to the city life, as if they had come to Jerusalem from some far-off desert village with green date palms overtopping white mud walls. I came close to one of them and noticed the separate threads of his unmanufactured tunic. A curious smell came from him. It was like stale mare's milk mixed with the smoke of a camp fire. They looked at us with cold attention as hawks look at pigeons.

We went to visit the Wailing Wall, reaching it down a narrow winding lane, past some daubed hovels. Once we had rounded the last corner we were confronted by a memorable scene. The wall is far higher than I had imagined it to be—it is the very wall of the old Temple, built at its base of stupendous Herodian stones. They seemed to me bigger than any stones I had ever seen used for building. Enormous grey masses of obdurate matter upon whose broad backs had rested the burden of two thousand years!

That morning there were some fifty Jews assembled, each one of them crooning out his lamentations. They swayed backward and forward in front of the masonry in a kind of sexual ecstasy. They kissed the dumb blocks, they laid the palms of their hands flat against them. They howled like dogs against a shut door. Their furred gaberdines flapped. They pleaded. They sent up supplications. The problem of the dwarf was solved. Here was *his* journey's end. He let his frustrated spirit fly loose from his deformed body. This ceremony was his ceremony. Here he could take his share with his fellows on equal terms, could be at one with that row of fantastic frantic mourners. What memories these Jews have! Was there ever such a people? It is impossible to kill them, it is impossible to beat them away. The same emotion that troubled them in Babylon troubles them still.

A Pagan's Pilgrimage, 1931

Shmarya Levin (1867–1935)

MOURNING IN EXILE

The period lies between the seventeenth day of the month of Tammuz and the ninth day of the month of Ab. The time is midsummer. During that period it was our *duty* to be mournful. We had to be mournful even in *cheder*, and walk around with heads down and eyes fixed on the ground. We were not allowed to bathe as usual in the river Swisla. We were forbidden to eat meat—with the exception of the Holy Sabbath. With regard to this last law—the prohibition of meat—most of the Swislowitz Jews stood to gain in the heavenly account, for the majority of them never had a piece of meat even to look at during weekdays. Thus a privation which under ordinary circumstances was the result of their poverty could during this period be ascribed in heaven to their piety.

I remember the effect which the last Nine Days had upon me. I used to lose my usual joyfulness, at least at home. There was little change in my father's dark bearing, but my mother walked about the house, pale and subdued and more than once her cheeks showed signs of weeping. An atmosphere of real suffering and sadness surrounded her, and spread throughout the house.

My mother was the first to tell us about the horrors of the destruction of the Temple, and she laid the colours on thick. In her telling the story there was so much freshness, so much passion, and so much personal indignation, that the sense of time was wholly destroyed. It was as though she had taken part in the sufferings of our forefathers. It was not the history of a national destruction, but the recital of a personal disaster. She carried us from Swislowitz back to Jerusalem, up to the summit of the

81

Hill of the Sacred House, and she showed us the Temple in its glory, the Ark and the Cherubim and the Altar of brightest gold, the High Priest in the splendour of his robes, and the host of priests and Levites, with their gorgeous instruments—viols and harps and trumpets and drums.

Then came Shabbath Hazon (Sabbath of Isaiah's Vision), the Sabbath before the Black Fast, and it was truly a black Sabbath. On this one occasion the joy and contentment which the Jew is commanded to feel on the day of rest were overshadowed by the huge wings of our unforgettable disaster. A black curtain was drawn across the ark in our Synagogue, and all worshippers—including even the well-to-do citizens who always occupied the prominent seats by the eastern wall—came in humble, workaday attire. Judah, the president of the community, came almost in rags, with buttons missing on his coat, his shirt torn in front, and his earlocks hanging in neglect over his ears. Close to the cantor's desk, apart from the rest of the congregation, sat his older brother Ziskind, competing with Judah for the palm of desolation. But his thin face, instead of expressing wretchedness and sorrow, bore on it a cruel and angry look: I always thought that he belonged more to the triumphant army of Titus the wicked than to the fleeing hordes of the vanquished and ravaged Jews. In the right-hand corner, under the shadow of the Sacred Ark, sat the Rav himself, Rabbi Wolf, an old Jew who was both a scholar and a saint. From his wrinkled face shone piety and learning. He had put on no outward symbols of mourning, but when they called him up to read aloud from the Torah he walked with slow, quiet steps, like a man sunk deep in thought. And over all of us came the feeling: This is the bearing of a man who remains noble and dignified even in his deepest sorrow. And in later years, when I learned how the Elders of the Sanhedrin had followed in chains the gilded chariot of Titus the godless, I saw them walking with the same slow pace, the same silent sadness as old Rabbi Wolf.

*

A strange scene would occur that afternoon in the house. Neighbours and friends of my mother, all the wives of well-to-do Swislowitz Jews would come on their usual Sabbath visit. They wore clothes which were neither of the Sabbath nor yet of the weekdays, a compromise as it were between duty and pride. On the table, instead of the usual tea, there was nothing but the big leather Yiddish translation of Jeremiah . . . And my mother had not read far before there arose round the table not a weeping, but a sort of wailing, the wailing which goes up from a city given up to

82

the sword. It was as though all the cruelties and miseries of the Destruction were being enacted again in that room . . .

*

In the Synagogue we sat in stockinged feet, as one sits in the house of a mourner. The lamps were unlit. Instead they laid the desks flat, and fastened tallow candles on them. After evening prayer the congregation sat down upon the floor, the naked Ark stripped of its gilded curtain, the oppressive melody of the Lamentations—all these threw terror into my soul. Everyone and everything wept. The stifled sobs of the men were like a bass accompaniment to the shriller sound of weeping which came from the women's section. The naked Ark wept, and a weeping came from the shadowy walls. And the candles fastened into the overthrown stands wept tallow tears which ran over their sides.

Childhood in Exile, translated from the
Hebrew by Maurice Samuel

S. Y. Agnon (b. 1888)

HOW LONG, O LORD?

At the eve of new moon I walked to the Western Wall, as we in Jerusalem are accustomed to do, praying at the Wailing Wall at the rising of each moon.

Already most of the winter had passed, and spring blossoms had begun to appear. Up above, the heavens were pure, and the earth had put off her grief. The sun smiled in the sky; the City shone in its light. And we too rejoiced, despite the troubles that beset us; for these troubles were many and evil, and before we had reckoned with one, yet another came in its wake.

From Jaffa Gate as far as the Western Wall, men and women from all the communities of Jerusalem moved in a steady stream, together with those newcomers whom The Place had restored to their place, albeit their place had not yet been found. But in the open space before the Wall, at the booth of the Mandatory Police, sat the police of the Mandate whose function was to see that no one guarded the worshippers save only they. Those who had come to pray were herded together and driven to seek shelter close up against the stones of the Wall, some weeping and some as if dazed. And still we say, How Long, O Lord? How long?—For we have trodden the lowest stair of degradation, yet you tarry to redeem us.

I found a place for myself at the Wall, standing at times amongst the bewildered bystanders. I was amazed at the peoples of the world: as if it were not sufficient that they oppressed us in all lands, yet they must also oppress us in our home. As I stood there I was driven from my place by one of the police who carried a baton. This man was in a great rage, on account of some ailing old woman who had brought a stool with her to the Wall. The policeman took a flying kick, throwing the woman to the ground, and confiscated the stool: for she had infringed the law enacted by the legislators, which forbade worshippers to bring seats to the wall. And those who had come to pray saw this, yet held their peace: for how can right dispute against might? Then came forward that same old woman whom I knew, and looked the policeman straight in the eye. And the policeman averted his glance, and returned the stool to its owner.

*

. . . How can I describe Jerusalem? He who in His goodness daily renews the works of creation, perpetually renews His own City. New houses may not have been built, nor new trees planted; yet Jerusalem herself is ever new. I cannot explain the secret of her infinite variety. We must wait, all of us for those great sages who will one day enlighten us.

I came upon a man of learning, and he drew me to his house, where he set before me all his recent findings. We sat together in deep contentment, while I asked my questions, and he replied; or spoke of problems, which he resolved; or mentioned cloudy matters, which he made clear. How good it is, how satisfying, to sit at the feet of one of the learned men of Jerusalem, and to learn the Law from his lips! His home is simple, his furnishings austere, yet his wisdom ranges far, like the great hill ranges of Jerusalem which are seen from the windows. Bare are the hills of Jerusalem; no temples or palaces crown them. Since the time of our exile, nation after nation has come and laid them waste. But the hills spread their glory like banners to the sky; they are resplendent in ever-changing hues; and not least in glory is the Mount of Olives, which bears no forest of trees, but a forest of tombs of the righteous, who in life and in death gave their thoughts to the Land.

Translated from the Hebrew by Walter Lever

Yaakov Fichman (1881–1952)

ROCKS OF JERUSALEM

Since once you have told of the loveliness of Jerusalem, tell now of the loveliness of its rocks. There's a secret to these rocks, and there are moments when they seem to flutter with the full weight of their mass, like shrubs in the wind. Observe them then, listen to them, and you will notice that they too have movement and change. They too grow and wither unseen, none knowing the secret of their sealed lives. Each day slowly inscribes them with its indelible marks. Examine them and see how all the secret lines and magic touches have become transfixed in their wrinklings to the end of time. Yet there is something still held within, that even in petrification will not rest, and it is that which shakes your heart like organ keys when evening blows.

Out walking yesterday towards sunset, I chanced upon a crowd of rocks that attracted me like a sprouting wood. Each rock, struck by the cool mountain wind, seemed to invite me to touch it, to run my fingers over it. As I walked down the narrow trail between the crouching masses of stone, the echo of my footsteps rose wonderfully high in the evening stillness. I was taken by a desire to stand there for a long time, to listen, to pour out my complaint as in a temple.

My heart has always been with earth, saturated with that force which makes growth, that crumples the clods from whose open mouths young impatient sprouts and green shoots joyfully burst out. Even in this isolated parcel of a hill, what delight to see each clump of earth blushing gently among the naked Jerusalem rocks. But with sunset, the spirit of the taciturn giants seemed to take flight, and as the shadows deepened, the wind began to sing like a nocturnal forest lifting its palms into the dark and praying for growth.

Translated from the Hebrew by Ludwig Schwerin

Abraham Klein (b. 1909)

THE STILL SMALL VOICE

The candles splutter; and the kettle hums;
The heirloomed clock enumerates the tribes;
Upon the wine-stained table-cloth lie crumbs
Of matzoh whose wide scattering describes

85

Jews driven in far lands upon this earth.
The kettle hums; the candles splutter; and
Winds whispering from shutters tell re-birth
Of beauty rising in an eastern land,
Of paschal sheep driven in cloudy droves;
Of almond-blossoms colouring the breeze;
Of vineyards upon verdant terraces;
Of golden globes in orient orange-groves . . .
And those assembled at the table dream
Of small schemes that an April wind doth scheme,
And cry from out the sleep assailing them:
Jerusalem, next year! Next year, Jerusalem!

Babette Deutsch (b. 1895)

PSALM: 1933

By the rivers of Babylon
We sat down, we wept . . .

And the sun goes down, and the waters are dark. Whitely,
Like the fist of a dead man, or a fragment of bone,—
Curving over the river, against the windows,
Now the moon, like a stone carelessly thrown.

We sat down, we wept
When we remembered Zion . . .

We have bad memories. We read the papers,
Sitting on Riverside Drive, or anywhere,
Behind drawn blinds, under the lamps, frowning,
Turning the page again with a dry-eyed stare.

Upon the willows in the midst thereof
We hanged up our harps.

When Tara's walls were down, a broken harping
Sounded until the minstrel fell. Tune in on
Götterdämmerung tonight. There's static
Only when there is storm. But this is none.

For they that led us captive required of us songs,
And they that wasted us required of us mirth:
Sing us one of the songs of Zion.

The words are lost. Shall we sing 'Go down, Moses'?
We always liked that one. Or 'Weep no more,
My lady, for your old Kentucky home'?
There are good tunes in any Sullivan score.

How shall we sing the Lord's song
In a strange land?

And the sun goes down, and the waters are dark. Whitely,
Murmurous with her millions, a quivering gem,
Over the river, the city: New York, Paris, Berlin,
Puts out Jerusalem.

If I forget thee,
Let my right hand forget its cunning;
Let my tongue cleave to the roof of my mouth
If I prefer not Jerusalem above my chief joy.

Is she down, is she gone and forgotten?
So they trample a grave that is swept
Of even a stone for remembrance?
By the rivers of Babylon we sat down, we wept . . .

IV Jesus

*J'ai vu Jésus moi aussi. Il s'est démontré à moi
dans la beauté de la précision. Je l'aime: je le
tiens contre mon coeur et je le disputerai aux
autres, s'il le faut. Mettez l'idée pure, sage, et
juste de la Révolution dans la grande âme
religieuse de l'humanité. Ainsi soit-il.*

Henri Barbusse: Jésus, *1927*

*He is the outstanding personality of all time
. . . He became the Light of the world. Why
shouldn't I, a Jew, be proud of that?*

Sholem Asch: I had to
write these things, *1951*

Jésus prisonnier de son humanité.

François Mauriac: Vie de Jésus, *1936*

*Pope Fotis listened to the bell pealing gaily,
announcing that Christ was coming down on
earth to save the world . . . He shook his head
and heaved a sigh: 'In vain, my Christ, in
vain,' he muttered; 'two thousand years have
gone by and men crucify You still. When will
You be born, my Christ, and not be crucified
any more, but live among us for eternity?'*

Nikos Kazantzakis: Christ Recrucified, *a
novel translated by Jonathan Griffin,
London 1954*

*How sweet the name of Jesus sounds
In a believer's ear!*

John Newton: Olney Hymns, *1779*

*Give me back Jesus, he is my brother.
He will walk with me behind
The gray ghetto wall into the slaughter house.
The little children pricked with the
    death-bubble
Will come unto him.
Return to him the yellow badge.
Give me back Jesus.*

Marie Syrkin: To a Christian Friend

The Jerusalem of Jesus has been made familiar not only through
the Gospel narratives but through illuminated manuscripts,
paintings, carvings, drama, poetry, descriptive and devotional
prose: certainly the dramatic magnificence of the entry into the
city, and the final mighty climacteric of Calvary, have imposed a
demanding attraction on artists and writers at least as great as that

of Jesus' birth, the Christmas story. Even if one restricts one's gaze to the works concerning the historic actuality of Jesus, his life within the Holy Land, an immensity of material remains. In fact, such works stretch from long *before* his actual birth up to the present day. They begin before his time because the Middle Ages were certain that at least one classical writer had had a premonition of the Christian world. It was believed that the Fourth Eclogue of Virgil—mysteriously referring to the birth of a child who was to introduce a new epoch in history—was in fact a prophecy of the coming of Christ. Consequently, Virgil was afforded a respect and ranking second only to Old Testament prophets, and was grouped in the so-called *Ordo Prophetarum*, early religious plays from about the 12th century. Virgil also appears to have provided the model for the first poetic renderings in Latin of the Gospels—such as that of the Spanish priest Juvencus, in the third century, whose Virgilian hexameters surprisingly went through numerous editions until the beginning of the 18th century. We also know that Caedmon (considered by the Venerable Bede to be the father of English vernacular poetry) turned all the main events of sacred history into verse. About two centuries later, Cynewulf composed a highly interesting poem on Christ, and at roughly the same time the most important extant Old Saxon poem was written on the continent: the *Heliand*, the Saviour.

The theme of Jesus in Jerusalem has fascinated writers in every land and language. As is well known, his life plays a central role in the evolution of the drama from the cautious 'acting' of parts of the Easter liturgy to more extensive church plays, finally to the fully developed lay mystery plays in the vernacular, associated with Corpus Christi and staged as open-air pageants. Then with the Reformation there came a tremendous desire to personalize the Christian story, and with it came a new emphasis on the Hebrew elements in Christianity. By the 17th century mysticism had become a dominant element in Baroque poetry, providing many magnificent lyrics on the separate incidents of Christ's life, the parables, teachings, miracles, as well as on their relation to his life as a whole.

Perhaps with Milton some of the intense personal vision of these earlier poets lost its force and colour; instead, the towering epic of *Paradise Regained* gave a strength to the personal side of the Gospel that is still unsurpassed. The 18th century offers some charming verses on the theme of the warning of the Scribes and

Pharisees by Christ. There is a perfect sense of human observation in these poems which has the best qualities of the Age of Elegance. Such poems embrace, as might be expected, every grade of poetic skill and religious faith, whereas the Hymnals of all tongues are imbued with the simplicity of thought and expression that were likely to supply the masses with as many versions as possible of the perennial theme.

*

With the 19th century comes the rationalism that seemed at first to be wholly antipathetic to Christianity, but it gradually accepted and even hailed Jesus as a prophet. Notable amongst contemporary writers is the new Jewish approach to the human personality of Jesus. In a modern Jewish novel *Bamishol Hazan* (*The Narrow Path*), 1938, by the Israeli writer Abraham Aba Kabak, who died at Jerusalem in 1944, Jesus is the leading character. Kabak made full use of Jesus's authentic Jewish presence on Judean soil; in the key chapter, Jesus despairs because his followers are trying to exalt him as Messiah, and confesses to Judas his fears that the Messianic idea will mean his doom. Yet he decides not to retreat, and asks Judas to help him—and together they set off for Jerusalem. Sholem Asch portrayed a similar character in *The Nazarene*.

Other novelists in this century have claimed Christ as their own, and as a human figure—occasionally as a secular genius. Ernest Renan's immensely successful fiction set the fashion, followed by Giovanni Papini's *Storia di Cristo* (1921), Felix Timmerman's *Het Kindeken Jezus in Vlaanderen* (1917), Emil Ludwig's *Der Menschensohn* (1928), Edzard Schaper's *Das Leben Jesu* (1936). None of these equalled the violently controversial work of Renan's, who raised Jesus to the level of an incomparable but entirely human individual. Yet even Renan does not seem to have created quite the scandal that greeted *The Last Temptation of Christ* by Nikos Kazantzakis, who was promptly put in the *Index Librorum*, the chief accusation being that the Greek novelist has presented Christ 'as a beatnik'.

Clearly the personal actuality of Jesus, like that of David and other giant figures who stand out against the backdrop of Jerusalem, has not always been well served by modern writing. But perhaps there is an opportunity for new life in the treatment of Christ, growing out of recent discoveries that relate closely to him as a historical figure. The world has learned much from the Dead Sea Scrolls, found at Qumran, about that strange sect called the

Essenes—with their early idea of communistic living, their peaceful and devotional ethic, all of which cannot readily be separated from the Christian ideal. Here, obviously, is new light on the historicity of Jesus of Nazareth, and on the nature of his early life that drew him inevitably towards the culmination at Jerusalem. It may provide immeasurable food for thought both for modern creative artists as for theological scholars of all creeds and denominations.

Virgil (70–19 B.C.)

FOURTH ECLOGUE

A golden progeny from heav'n descends.
O chaste Lucina, speed the mother's pains,
And haste the glorious birth! thy own Apollo reigns!
The lovely boy, with his auspicious face,
Shall Polio's consulship and triumph grace;
Majestic months set out with him to their appointed race.
The son shall lead the life of gods, and be
By gods and heroes seen, and gods and heroes see.
The jarring nations he in peace shall bind,
And with paternal virtue rule mankind.
Unbidden earth shall wreathing ivy bring,
And fragrant herbs (the promises of spring),
As her first off'rings to her infant king.
His cradle shall with rising flow'rs be crown'd:
The serpent's brood shall die; the sacred ground
Shall weeds and pois'nous plants refuse to bear;
Each common bush shall Syrian roses wear.
But when heroic verse his youth shall raise,
And form it to hereditary praise,
Unlabour'd harvests shall the fields adorn,
And cluster'd grapes shall blush on every thorn;
Great cities shall with walls be compass'd round,
And sharpen'd shares shall vex the fruitful ground.

Translated by John Dryden, 1697

Anonymous

JESUS AND THE HOLY NAME

When King David had dug the foundation for the Temple, he found a stone resting on the mouth of the Abyss, with the Holy Name on it. He took up this stone and put it into the Holy of Holies in the Temple. The Sages of Israel began to fear lest some young men might learn the Holy Name and thus destroy the world—God forbid! They looked for means to prevent this. So they made two brazen lions, which they placed on iron pillars by the door of the Holy of Holies, one on the right and the other on the left. If anyone entered and learned the Holy Name, the lions would roar at him as soon as he came out, so that through terror and fright the Name would be utterly driven out of his mind and forgotten.

But Jesus of Nazareth came to Jerusalem in secret and, penetrating into the Temple, learned the holy letters of the Holy Name. These he wrote on parchment, and uttering the Name to prevent pain, he cut his flesh and hid the parchment therein. Then, again, pronouncing the Name, he caused the flesh to grow together . . . As he left the door, the lions roared and the Name was erased from his mind. When Jesus went outside the city he cut his flesh once more and drew out the parchment, and when he had studied the letters, Jesus learned the Holy Name again . . .

This is how Jesus was able to perform all his miracles and wonders. It is also said that after Jesus learned the Holy Name he went to Elijah's cave to hide himself. When he entered, Jesus uttered the Holy Name and the entrance of the cave shut itself. Then Rabbi Judah Gannana came to this cave and said: Cave, cave, open—becuase I am the messenger of the living God! When the cave heard this, it opened and Jesus escaped and stayed on Mount Carmel.

Legends of Palestine

William Langland (1332–1400)

THE GLORIOUS ENTRY

Ooon semblable to the Samaritan,
And som deel to Piers the Plowman,
Bare-foot on an asse bak
Boot-les cam prikye,
Withouten spores other spere,
Spakliche be lokede,
As in the kynde of a knyght
That cometh to be dubbed,
To geten hym gilte spores,
Or galoches y-couped.
Thanne was Feith in a fenestre,
And cryde a *fili David*,
As dooth an herand of armes,

94

Whan aventrous cometh to justes
Old Jewes of Jerusalem
For joye thei songem
Benedictus qui venit in nomine Domini.
Thanne I frayned at Feith
What al that fare by-mente,
And who sholde juste in Jerusalem.

The Vision of Piers Plowman, Passus Decimus Octavus, v. 818

John Donne (1573–1631)

IN THE TEMPLE

With his kind mother, who partakes thy woe,
Joseph, turn back; see where your child doth sit
Blowing, yea, blowing out those sparks of wit,
Which himself on the doctors did bestow.
The Word but lately could not speak, and lo,
It suddenly speaks wonders. Whence comes it,
That all which was, and all which should be writ,
A shallow-seeming child should deeply know?
His Godhead was not soul to his manhood,
Nor had time mellowed him to this ripeness:
But as for one which hath a long task, 'tis good
With the sun to begin his business,
    He in age's morning thus began,
    By miracles exceeding power of man.

Divine Poems, 1633

HOW HE WEPT FOR JERUSALEM

XCVII.f. (358) When Jesus went forth from the Temple, and saw how it was adorned with goodly stones and gifts, he wept, and said unto his disciples:

'See ye not these great buildings? O Jerusalem, Jerusalem, when the nations are gathered together to destroy thee, there shall scarce be left one stone upon another that shall not be thrown down!

95

'For thou has not known the time of thy visitation, neither hearkened to the voice that cried unto thee to repent.

'If thou couldst but know, in this thy last day, the things which belong to thy peace! But even now are they hid from thine eyes.

'As Isaiah prophesied in the name of the Lord: "I will camp against thee round about and will lay siege against thee, and raise forts against thee, and thou shalt be brought low."

'And again: "The heaven is My throne and the earth is My footstool. Where is the house that ye build unto Me, and where is the place of My rest?

'"For he that offereth an oblation there, it is as if he offered swine's blood; he that burneth incense, as if he blessed an idol. Yea, they have chosen their own ways, and their soul delighteth in abomination.

'"Behold, the Lord will come with fire and with His chariots like a whirlwind, to rebuke with flames of fire."

'And Micah likewise prophesied: "Zion shall be plowed as a field, for the sake of the princes of Israel that abhor judgement, and Jerusalem shall become heaps."

'Now is it again as in the days the Lord spake unto Jeremiah, saying: "Stand in the court of the Temple, and say unto all men that come up to worship:

'"'If ye will not walk in the Law that I have set before you, to hearken unto the words of My servants the prophets, which I sent you, to which ye have not hearkened, then will I make this house like unto that of Shiloh, and this city shall be desolate without an inhabitant!'"

'Then would the priests have stoned Jeremiah until he died, yet they could not. But in his stead they slew the prophet Urijah; whose innocent blood was on their heads until the prophecy of Jeremiah was fulfilled.

'Verily, I say unto you: so it shall be again!'

XXXIII.c (359) Jesus said also:

'Malachi proposed against the priest of Israel, saying: "Ye that offer polluted bread upon Mine altar, will I regard your persons?

'"For from the east unto the west shall My name be great among the Gentiles; yet have ye said of the table of the Lord: 'Behold what a weariness it is, and ye have sniffed at it.'"

'Therefore I say unto you, that though strangers came from the east and west and accept the Law with joy, and sit down to eat bread with Abraham, Isaac, and Jacob in the Kingdom of Heaven, yet of these sons of Levi, the children of the Kingdom, many shall be cast into outer darkness where shall be weeping and gnashing of teeth!'

XIII.z (360) 'Woe unto these faithless priests, unbelievers! For on their head shall fall all the righteous blood shed upon the earth; from the blood of righteous Abel until that of which Zacharias the son of Barachias prophesied, which is yet to be shed.'

XCVII.f (361) 'Yet shall the Lord raise up the righteous man and the prophet, before three days are fulfilled; as Hosea prophesied: "In the third day He will raise up and we shall live in His sight."

'In the third day also He shall restore the Temple which He Himself hath destroyed. As Enoch prophesied, saying: "I saw till the Lord of the sheep brought a new house, greater and loftier than that first, and set it up in the place of the first."'

LIX.c (362) 'Woe unto thee, Zion! As it is prophesied in the Book of Lamentations:

'"How hath the Lord cast down from heaven unto earth the beauty of Israel, and in the day of His anger remembered not His footstool!

'"He hath cast off His altar, He hath abhorred His sanctuary, He hath given up into the hand of the enemy the walls of her palaces."'

XCVII.g (363) 'Yet fear ye not, little ones, for David spake in a psalm, saying: "The Lord shall cover the earth with His feathers, and under His wings shalt thou trust.

'"A thousand shall fall at thy side and ten thousand at thy right hand; but it shall not come nigh thee!"'

XCIX.b (364) 'Isaiah prophesied of these days, saying: "Then shall the glory of Jacob be made thin, and his flesh shall wax lean, and it shall be as when the harvestman gathereth the corn and leaveth the gleanings.

'"Yet, gleaning grapes shall be left on his vine, two or three berries at the top of the uttermost bough.

'"In that day shall a man look to his Maker, and his eyes shall have respect for the Holy One in Israel."'

XCVIII.e (365) 'Behold, these are the days whereof Daniel prophesied, saying: "Know therefore that from the going forth of the commandment to restore and build Jerusalem, unto the Anointed One, shall be seven weeks, and three score and two weeks: the street shall be built again, and the wall as in troublous times. And after three score and two weeks shall the Anointed One be cut off and have nothing, and the people of the prince that shall come shall destroy both the city and the Sanctuary. And the end thereof shall be with a flood."'

XCVIII.f (366) The disciples ask Jesus: 'Lord, which shall this prince be?'

He answered: 'It is written in the Book of Job: "The eyes of the eagle behold afar off. Her young ones also suck up blood and where the slain lie, there shall she be also."

'Verily, I say unto you: wheresoever the carcass is, there shall the eagles be gathered together.'

XCVIII.g (367) 'Therefore, when ye shall hear of wars and rumours of wars, see that ye be not troubled. All these things must be, before the end cometh. And there shall be signs in the heavens, and upon the earth distress and perplexity; the sea and the waves roaring;

'Men's hearts failing them for fear, and for looking after those things which are coming on the earth. And because of iniquity the love of many shall wax cold.

'These are the beginnings of sorrows, but when they come to pass, lift up your heads: for your redemption draweth nigh.'

The Nazarene Gospel Restored, Chapter XXXVIII,
translated and edited by Robert Graves and Joshua Podro, 1953

Henry Vaughan (1621–1695)

MOUNT OF OLIVES

Sweet sacred hill! on whose fair brow
My Saviour sate, shall I allow
    Language to love
And idolize some shade, or grove,
Neglecting thee? Such ill-plac'd wit,
Conceit, or call it what you please
    Is the braines fit
    And meere disease;

Cotswold and Cooperes both have met
With learned swaines, and echo yet
    Their pipes, and wit;
But thou sleep'st in a deepe neglect
untouch'd by any; and what neede
The sheepe bleate thee a silly lay
    That heard'st both reede
    And sheepward play?

Yet, if poets mind thee well
They shall find thou art their hill,
    And fountaine too,
Their Lord with thee had most to doe;
He wept once, walkt whole nights on thee,
And from thence (his sufferings ended,)
        Unto gloorie
        Was attended;

Being there, this spacious ball
Is but his narrow footstoole all,
    And what we thinke
Unsearchable, now with one winke
He doth comprise; but in this aire
When he did stay to beare our ill
        And sinne, this Hill
        Was then his chaire.

Silex Scintillans, 1650

John Keble (1792–1866)

GETHSEMANE

There is a spot within this sacred dale
    That felt Thee kneeling,—touched thy prostrate brow:
One Angel knows it. O, might prayer avail
    To win that knowledge; sure each holy vow
Less quickly from the unstable soul would fade,
Offered where Christ in agony was laid.

Might tear of ours once mingle with the blood
    That from his aching brow by moonlight fell,
Over the mournful joy our thoughts would brood,
    Till they had framed within a guardian spell
To chase repining fancies, as they rise,
Like birds of evil wing, to mar our sacrifice.

So dreams the heart self-flattering, fondly dreams;
  Else wherefore, when the bitter waves o'erflow,
Miss we the light, Gethsemane, that streams
  From thy dear name, where in his page of woe
It shines, a pale kind star in winter's sky?
Who vainly reads it there, in vain had seen him die.

The Christian Year, 1827

Joseph Addison (1672-1719)

HIS PUBLIC ENTRY

The great change of things began to draw near, when the Lord of nature thought fit, as a Saviour and Deliverer, to make his public entry into Jerusalem with more than the power and joy, but none of the ostentation and pomp, of a triumph. He came humble, meek, and lowly; with an unfelt, new ecstasy multitudes strewed his way with garments and olive branches, crying with loud gladness and acclamation, *Hosanna to the Son of David! Blessed is he that cometh in the name of the Lord!* At this great king's accession to his throne, men were not ennobled, but saved; crimes were not remitted, but sins forgiven; he did not bestow medals, honours, favours, but health, joy, sight, speech. The first object the blind ever saw was the Author of sight, while the lame ran before, and the dumb repeated the hosanna. Thus attended, he entered into his own house, the sacred temple, and by his divine authority expelled traders and worldlings, that profaned it; and thus did he for a time use a great and despotic power, to let unbelievers understand that it was not want of, but superiority to, all worldly dominion, that made him not exert it.

The Spectator, 1711

Sholem Asch (1880-1957)

THE RABBI

And the way of our Rabbi is on this wise: he is not like other learned men who stay within the four ells of their commandments and preach the law in the study houses to their disciples who sit at their feet; but he is like a brimming well which standeth at the wayside so that all who pass may come and draw of its living waters. My Rabbi goeth about among the common people and guideth them into the right path. In the weekdays he goeth out to the port, where the fishers bring in the nets with the fish and the porters carry their burdens to the ships. Many folk are assembled there, for they come hither to sell the merchants the labour of their hands. And our Rabbi standeth there among the folk and teacheth them of the kingdom of heaven through beautiful parables, and this one he comforteth with a word and the other he healeth of a sickness. On the Sabbath he cometh to the synagogue and sometimes he preacheth on a text from the Torah, and sometimes he doth not so. But the Rabbi spreadeth his doctrine not only in the city of K'far Nahum, but he leadeth us through the towns and villages round about, and he showeth us how the modest people live and biddeth us take their example. Ofttimes it chanceth that as we come to a city the eventide encountereth us and the sky encloseth the earth in faith, and from the houses goeth up smoke where the bread is a-baking which labour hath earned. Then the man cometh home from the field or from his work to the house, and the goodwife waiteth at the door with the lamp in her hand, on the threshold of the house. And when the Rabbi cometh to the city, he goeth not to the house of study to the learned, but he turneth aside to the houses of the poor, and he stationeth himself at a door till that they bid him enter. He bringeth peace with him, he blesseth the house and sitteth with the folk to eat the bread of the poor, and saith a benediction thereon and praiseth the goodwife to the husband. And when they have eaten he calleth the children to him and inquireth of them concerning their lessons, and every child telleth him his text. Then he blesseth the children and saith, 'May your like multiply in Israel,' and the mothers sit on the thresholds of the doors, and when they hear that the Rabbi praiseth the fruit of their womb and maketh them beloved of their husbands, so they say to each other, It cannot be but that this is a man of God, for he bringeth peace with him into the house . . .

And when we come a second time unto this place, then the folk come of themselves to welcome us, and the women stand on the thresholds of their houses and they call unto the Rabbi, 'Let the Rabbi stay with me, let him lay his head under my roof and let my house be blessed for his sake.' And the children likewise run forth to greet him, and they make a circle about him and they seize his robe and they tell him the texts which they have learned that day in the school. And when we the disciples do sometimes speak angrily to the children and bid them begone from molesting the Rabbi, he will not have it so, but saith unto us: 'Suffer the little ones to come unto me, for theirs is the kingdom of heaven.' And thus

he goeth into the town with the children all about him, and the men come
forth to greet him and they call unto him:

'Come, thou blessed of God.'

And when eventide cometh he calleth them together in the house or
the yard of one of them, and they come bearing their lamps. And the
Rabbi sitteth with them, and breaketh bread, and telleth them of the
kingdom of heaven, and the people turn back to God. And the name of
the Rabbi spreadeth like an ointment through the land.

> *The Nazarene*, translated from the
> Yiddish by Maurice Samuel, 1939

Ernest Renan (1823–1892)

THE LAST JOURNEY TO JERUSALEM

His disciples, and the pious women who followed him, met him again in
Judea. But how greatly was all changed for him here! In Jerusalem Jesus
was a stranger. Here he felt a wall of resistance he could not penetrate.
Hemmed in by snares and difficulties, he was unceasingly dogged by the
enmity of the Pharisees. Instead of that illimitable faculty of belief, the
happy gift of youthful natures, which he found in Galilee—instead of
those good and gentle folk, amongst whom objections (which are always
in part the fruit of evil thinking and indocility) had no existence, here at
every step he met with an obstinate scepticism, upon which the means of
action that had succeeded in the north so well had little effect. His
disciples were despised as being Galileans. Nicodemus, who, on one of
the former visits of Jesus, had had a nocturnal interview, almost com-
promised himself with the Sanhedrim by his desire to defend him. 'Art
thou also of Galilee?' they said to him. 'Search and see that out of
Galilee ariseth no prophet.'

The city, as we have already remarked, displeased Jesus. Until now he
had always avoided great centres, preferring rural districts and towns of
small importance for his field of action. Many of the precepts which he
gave to his apostles were absolutely inapplicable except in a simple
community of humble folk. Since he had no conception of the world, and
was accustomed only to the kindly communism of Galilee, remarks
constantly escaped him, the simplicity of which might well appear odd at
Jerusalem. His imagination and his love of nature felt constraint within

its walls. It is not the destiny of true religion to emerge from the tumult of towns, but from the tranquil quietude of the fields.

The arrogance of the priests made the courts of the Temple disagreeable to him. One day some of his disciples, who knew Jerusalem better than he, wished him to notice the beauty of the Temple buildings, the admirable choice of materials, and the richness of the votive offerings which covered the walls. 'See ye not all these things' said he; 'verily I say unto you there shall not be left here one stone upon another.' He refused to admire anything, unless it was a poor widow who passed at that moment and threw a small coin into the box. 'This poor widow cast in more than they all,' said he; 'for all these did of their superfluity cast it unto their gifts: but she of her want did cast in all the living that she had.'

After having passed the day disputing in the Temple, Jesus used to descend at evening into the valley of Kedron, and rest awhile in the orchard of a kind of farm (probably a place where oil was made) called Gethsemane, which served as a pleasure garden to the inhabitants. Thence he would proceed to pass the night upon the Mount of Olives, which shuts in the horizon of the city on the east. This district is the only one, in the neighbourhood of Jerusalem, presenting an aspect that is in any way pleasing and verdant. Groves of olives, figs, and palms were numerous there, and gave their names to the villages, farms or enclosures of Bethphage, Gethsemane, and Bethany. Upon the Mount of Olives were two great cedars, the memory of which was long cherished amongst the dispersed Jews; their branches served as refuge for bevies of doves, and under their shade were established small bazaars.

From *Vie de Jésus*, 1863, translated by William Hutchison

Joseph Klausner (1874–1958)

THE LAST SUPPER

Since the disciples were, most of them, Galileans, they bestirred themselves and on the morning of Thursday asked Jesus where they were to eat the Passover and prepare the 'Seder'. This might not be done in Bethany since the rule was that in Jerusalem alone were the ceremonies to be performed. Furthermore the Passover 'could be consumed only in the night' and 'only by them for whom it had been prepared'.

For privacy's sake, Jesus had already made the necessary arrangements with a simple Jerusalem water carrier in whose upper chamber everything was made ready for Jesus and the disciples. All, apparently, was done in secret for the same reason which compelled Jesus to lodge outside the city during that week—fear of his persecutors; and but for Judas Iscariot, Jesus and the Twelve would not have been discovered.

In the evening Jesus 'and the Twelve' (including Judas Iscariot) came to the upper chamber, 'and they sat down and did eat' according to the Jewish Passover rule. From this state post-Pauline Christianity begins to elaborate the various episodes. After betraying Jesus, Judas Iscariot sat with him at table. Was it conceivable that Jesus the wonder worker, Jesus the Messiah, Jesus the Son of God, was unaware of the treachery? Such is the problem raised by the uncritical belief in Jesus the Messiah.

The only possible answer was that Jesus knew of the treachery from the beginning, indicated Judas as the traitor and actually referred to him as such by name. Yet again, since the rest of the Twelve, and even Peter their leader, were terrified at the time of the arrest and escaped in every direction, was it possible that Jesus the wonder worker, Jesus the Messiah, Jesus the Son of God, did not foresee this also? Again uncritical belief makes a like answer: Jesus prophesied to Peter that the same night before the cock should crow twice, he, Peter, should deny him thrice; and so, of course, did it happen exactly.

Jesus broke the bread ('Mazzoth,' the unleavened bread, 'the bread of affliction'), gave it to the disciples and said to them that they would take and eat it, for 'this is my body'; he also gave them to drink from his cup, saying, 'this is my blood, the blood of the new covenant, which is shed for many'; and he may have added, 'for the forgiveness of sins,' and also 'Do this in remembrance of me,' though this last occurs in neither Mark nor Matthew.

This was the origin of the rite of the 'Lord's Supper' and the mystical theory of 'Transubstantiation' (the conversion of the bread into the body of the Messiah, and the conversion of the wine into his blood), which induced the heathen of those days to believe that the Christians used blood for their Passover. And when, in their turn, the heathen became Christians they accused the Jews, on the basis of this Christian belief, of kneading their unleavened bread in Christian blood. But the rite arose much later than the time of Jesus.

He, as an observant Jew, celebrated the Passover 'Seder' on the night before the 14th of Nisan, since the 14th fell on the eve of the Sabbath and it was therefore not possible to kill the victim and roast it at the moment of sunset. Hillel's ruling, that the Passover was a public sacrifice abrogating the Sabbath laws, did not yet hold good among the priests who had charge over the sacrifices.

Scripture says of the Passover, 'With unleavened bread and bitter herbs shall they eat it'; therefore Jesus also ate unleavened bread with the Passover, and this is the 'bread' which the Gospels refer to. He said over it the prescribed liturgical blessings ('Blessed art thou, O Lord our God! King of the Universe; who bringest forth bread from the earth.' 'Blessed art thou, O Lord our God! King of the Universe, who has sanctified us with thy commandments, and commanded us to eat unleavened bread'); he 'brake it' (the usual Jewish way with the bread and 'Mazzoth', which then, as with the Arabs today, was not cut with a knife . . . and gave it to his disciples, and they all ate it as they sat. Jesus and the Twelve 'dipped' into the dish, and drank the first of the four cups, which he had blessed and given them all to drink (as is also the custom of the Jews today).

According to the Law they would eat bitter herbs, and these brought to Jesus' mind the 'panges of the Messiah'; they may also have drunk the four cups, following the usage laid down in the *Mishna*, which would seem to be fairly old. Finally they sang the *Hallel*, likewise an ancient use and one which gave rise to an early proverb: 'The Passover is like an olive, and the *Hallel* splits the roofs' (the point being, to make much ado about nothing). All was in line with the religious practices of the Jews.

Jesus may have urged the disciples to remember this solemn meal (the most ceremonious of all meals among the Jews), the first 'Seder' which he had celebrated in Jerusalem in their company. He may have said, 'Verily I say unto you, I shall in no wise drink of the fruit of the vine till that day when I shall drink it new in the kingdom of God,' since he considered the kingdom of heaven as very near, and the disciples, still less the authors of the Gospels, would not have attributed such a material sentiment to Jesus at a later stage.

But it is quite impossible to admit that Jesus would have said to his disciples that they would eat of his body and drink of his blood, 'the blood of the new covenant which was shed for many'. The drinking of blood, even if it was meant symbolically, could only have aroused horror in the minds of such simple Galilean Jews; and had he expected to die within a short space of time he would not have been so disturbed when death proved imminent.

Jesus of Nazareth, translated from the Hebrew
by the Rev. Herbert Danby, 1925

Phineas Fletcher (1582–1650)

DROP, DROP, SLOW TEARS

Drop, drop, slow tears,
   And bathe those beauteous feet,
Which brought from heaven
   The news and Prince of peace:
Cease not, wet eyes,
His mercy to intreat;
To cry for vengeance
   Sin doth never cease:
In your deep floods
   Drown all my faults and fears;
Nor let his eye
   See sin, but through my tears.

The Purple Island, 1633

Goethe (1749–1816)

JESUS AND AHASUERUS

As everything which I once warmly embraced immediately put on a poetic form, I now took up the strange idea of treating epically the history of the Wandering Jew, which popular books had long since impressed upon my mind. . . . I will now explain the way in which I treated this fable, and what meaning I gave to it.

   In Jerusalem, according to the legend, there was a shoemaker, of the name of Ahasuerus. For this character my Dresden shoemaker was to supply the main features. I had furnished him with the spirit and humour of a craftsman of the school of Hans Sachs, and ennobled him by an inclination to Christ. Accordingly as, in his open workshop, he liked to talk with the passers-by, jested with them, and, after the Socratic fashion, touched up everyone in his own way, the neighbours and others of the

people took pleasure in lingering at his booth; even Pharisees and Sad-
ducees spoke to him, and the Saviour himself and his disciples would
often stop at his door. The shoemaker, whose thoughts were directed
solely towards the world, I painted as feeling, nevertheless, a special
affection for our Lord, which, for the most part, evinced itself by a desire
to bring this lofty being, whose mind he did not comprehend, over to his
own way of thinking and acting. Accordingly, in a modest manner, he
recommends Christ to abandon his contemplative life, and to leave off
going about the country with such idlers, and drawing the people away
from their labour into the wilderness. A multitude, he said, was always
ready for excitement, and nothing good could come of it.

On the other hand, the Lord endeavoured, by parables, to instruct him
in his higher views and aims, but these were all thrown away on his mere
matter-of-fact intellect. Thus, as Christ becomes more and more an
important character, and finally a public person, the friendly workman
pronounces his opinion still more sharply and vehemently, maintaining
that nothing but disorder and tumult could follow from such proceedings,
and that Christ would be at last compelled to put himself at the head of
a party, though that could not possibly be his design. Finally, when
things had taken the course which history narrates, and Christ had been
seized and condemned, Ahasuerus gives full vent to his indignation when
Judas who undesignedly had betrayed his Lord, in his despair enters the
workshop, and with lamentations relates how his plans had been crossed.
He had been, he said, as well as the shrewdest of the other disciples,
firmly convinced that Christ would declare himself regent and head of the
nation. His purpose was only, by this violence, to compel the Lord, whose
hesitation had hitherto been invincible, to hasten the declaration.
Accordingly, he had incited the priesthood to an act which previously they
had not courage to do. The disciples, on their side, were not without
arms, and probably all would have turned out well, if the Lord had not
given himself up, and left them all in the most forlorn state. Ahasuerus,
whom this narrative in no ways tends to propitiate, only exasperates the
agony of the poor ex-apostle, who rushes out and goes and hangs
himself.

As Jesus is led past the workshop of the shoemaker, on his way to
execution, the well-known scene of the legend occurs. The sufferer faints
under the burden of the cross, and Simon of Cyrene is compelled to
carry it. Upon this, Ahasuerus comes forward, and sustains the part of
those harsh commonsense people, who, when they see a man involved in
misfortune through his own fault, feel no pity, but, struck by an untimely
sense of justice, make the matter worse by their reproaches. As he comes

out, he repeats all his former warnings, changing them into vehement accusations, which his attachment to the sufferer seems to justify. The Saviour does not answer, but at the instant the loving Veronica covers his face with the napkin, on which, as she removes it and raises it aloft, Ahasuerus sees depicted the features of the Lord, not indeed as those of the sufferer of the moment, but as of one transfigured and radiant with celestial life. Amazed by this phenomenon, he turns away his eyes and hears the words: 'Over the earth shalt thou wander till thou shalt once more see me in this form.' Overwhelmed at the sentence, it is not till after some time that the artisan comes to himself; he then finds that everyone has gone to the place of execution and that the streets of Jerusalem are empty. Disquiet and curiosity drive him forth, and he begins his wandering.

Dichtung und Wahrheit, translated by the
Rev. A. J. W. Morrison, London, 1849

Leonid Andreyev (1871-1919)

IN THE GARDEN OF GETHSEMANE

The Moon had already risen when Jesus prepared to go to the Mount of Olives, where of late he had been spending His nights. But He lingered strangely, and the disciples, ready to set out, hastened Him; and suddenly He said: 'He that hath a purse let him take it, and likewise his scrip: and he that hath no sword, let him sell his garment, and buy one. For I say unto you, that this that is written must yet be accomplished in Me: and He was reckoned among the transgressors.'

The disciples were amazed and looked at one another in dismay. And Peter replied: 'Lord! See we have two swords.'

He looked searchingly into their kindly faces, bent His head and said in a low voice: 'It is enough.'

Sonorously re-echoed in the narrow lanes the footsteps of those that walked—and the disciples were startled by the noise of their own footsteps; their black shadows stood out on a white wall lit by the moon—and of their shadows too they were afraid. So, in silence they passed through a sleeping Jerusalem, and now they were beyond the gates of the town, and in a deep ravine full of mysteriously unmoving shadows the brook of Kedron lay before them. Now everything frightened them. The quiet babbling and splashing of the water on the stones seemed to them the voices of men lying in wait; the monstrous shadows of the crags and trees that lay across the path disturbed them with their mingled colours; the immobility of night seemed to them like movement. But the higher they climbed the hill and the nearer they drew to the garden of Gethsemane, where in safety and quiet they had passed so many nights, the bolder they grew. Looking back every now and then, at the Jerusalem they had left behind them, white in the moon, they spoke amongst themselves of their vanished fears; and those who were walking behind heard snatches of the quiet words of Jesus. He was saying that all would abandon Him.

In the garden, just by the entrance, they halted. Most of them stayed there, preparing themselves with quiet words for slumber, spreading their cloaks in the transparent lacework of shadows and moonlight. And Jesus, worn by disquiet, together with four of his closest disciples went on into the depth of the garden. There they sat down on the ground from which the heat of the day had not yet departed, and while Jesus was silent Peter and John exchanged lazy words almost void of sense. Yawning with weariness, they said how cold the night was and how high the price of meat in Jerusalem, and how fish could simply not be bought anywhere. They endeavoured to assign an exact figure of the number of pilgrims who had gathered in Jerusalem for the feast, and Peter, drawing out his words in a noisy yawn, said there were twenty thousand of them, and John and his brother James asserted equally lazily that they were not more than ten thousand. Suddenly Jesus rose.

Judas Iscariot, 1907, translated from
the Russian by Walter Morison

Geoffrey Chaucer (1340–1400)

IF THOU WILT BE PERFECT . . .

But Christ, that of perfection is well,
Bad not every wight he should go sell
All that he had, and give it to the poor,
And in such wise follow him and his fore.
He spake to them that would live perfectly;
And lordings, by your leave, that am not I.

Robert Herrick (1591–1674)

GOING TO THE CROSS

Have, have ye no regard, all ye
Who pass this way, to pity me,
Who am a man of misery?

A man both bruised, and broke, and one
Who suffers not here for mine own,
But for my friends' transgression!

Ah! Sion's daughters, do not fear
The cross, the cords, the nails, the spear,
The myrrh, the gall, the vinegar:

For Christ, your loving Saviour, hath
Drunk up the wine of God's fierce wrath;
Only, there's left a little froth.

Less for to taste, than for to show,
What bitter cups had been your due,
Had he not drunk them up for you.

Robert Browning (1812–1889)

THE ALL-LOVING

So, the All-Great, were the All-loving too—
So, through the thunder comes a human voice
Saying, 'heart I made, a heart beats here!
Face, my hands fashioned, set it in myself.

Thou hast no power nor may'st conceive of mine,
But love I gave thee, with myself to love,
And thou must love me who have died for thee!'

H. G. Wells (1866–1945)

THE KINGDOM OF HEAVEN

When he first appeared as a teacher he was a man of about thirty. He went about the country for three years spreading his doctrine, and then he came to Jerusalem and was accused of trying to set up a strange kingdom in Judea; he was tried upon this charge, and crucified together with two thieves.

This doctrine of the Kingdom of Heaven, which was the main teaching of Jesus . . . is certainly one of the most revolutionary doctrines that ever stirred and changed human thought. It is small wonder if the world of that time failed to grasp its full significance, and recoiled in dismay from even a half apprehension of its tremendous challenges to the established habits and institutions of mankind. It is small wonder if the hesitating convert and disciple presently went back to the old familiar ideas of temple and altar, of fierce deity and propitiatory observance, of consecrated priest and magic blessing, and—these things being attended to—reverted then to the dear old habitual life of hates and profits and competition and pride. For the doctrine of the Kingdom of Heaven, as Jesus seems to have preached it, was no less than a bold and uncompromising demand for a complete change and cleansing of the life of our struggling race, an utter cleansing, without and within.

It was not merely a moral and social revolution that Jesus proclaimed; it is clear from a score of indications that his teaching had a political bent of the plainest sort. It is true that he said his kingdom was not of this world, that it was in the hearts of men and not upon a throne; but it is equally clear that wherever and in what measure his kingdom was set up in the hearts of men, the outer world would be in that measure revolutionized and made new.

Whatever else the deafness and blindness of his hearers may have missed in his utterances, it is plain that they did not miss his resolve to revolutionize the world. But even his disciples did not grasp the profound and comprehensive significance of that proposal. They were ridden by the old Jewish dream of a king, a Messiah to overthrow the Hellenized Herods and the Roman overlord, and restore the fabled glories of David. They disregarded the substance of his teaching, plain and direct though it was; evidently they thought it was merely his mysterious and singular way of setting about the adventure that would at last put him on the throne of Jerusalem.

He was too great for his disciples. Perhaps the priests and the rulers and the rich men understood him better than his followers. He was dragging out all the little private reservations they had made from social service into the light of a universal religious life. He was like some terrible moral huntsman digging mankind out of the snug burrows in which they had lived hitherto. In the white blaze of this kingdom of his there was to be no property, no privilege, no pride and precedence; no motive indeed and no reward but love. Is it any wonder that men were dazzled and blinded and cried out against him? Is it any wonder that to this day this Galilean is too much for our small hearts?

From *The Outline of History*, 1920

PONTIUS PILATE WRITES TO THE ROMAN EMPEROR

Pontius Pilate to Tiberius Caesar the Emperor—Greeting:

Upon Jesus Christ, whom I fully made known to thee in my last, a bitter punishment hath at length been inflicted by the will of the people, although I was unwilling and apprehensive. In good truth, no age ever had or will have a man so good and strict. But the people made a wonderful effort, and all their scribes, chiefs and elders agreed to crucify this ambassador of truth, their own prophets, like the Sibyls with us, advising the contrary; and when he was hanged supernatural signs appeared, and in the judgment of philosophers menaced the whole world with ruin. His disciples flourish, not belying their master by their behaviour and continence of life; nay, in his name they are most beneficent. Had I not feared a sedition might arise among the people, who were almost furious, perhaps this man would have yet been living with us. Although, being rather compelled by fidelity to thy dignity, than led by my own inclination, I did not strive with all my might to prevent the sale and suffering of righteous blood, guiltless of every accusation, unjustly, indeed through the maliciousness of men, and yet, as the Scriptures interpret, to their own destruction.

Farewell. The 5th of the Calends of April.

The Legend of Christ, a collection of medieval stories
printed from a MS. in the British Museum

Abraham Aba Kabak (1880–1944)

JESUS' FIRST VISIT TO JERUSALEM

The noise of the pilgrims came nearer and nearer. At the head came the instrumentalists: they clashed their cymbals, beat their drums, tinkled their bells and blew shrilly on their recorders. After the musicians came the elders of Nazareth eking out with their remaining strength their shaking steps. After them the heavy-footed camels, mules and asses adorned with coloured carpets, wreaths of vine and flowers and heavily laden with bags and baskets full of the fruits of the land. Farmers, towns-folk and villagers of Galilee accompanied them, some of them driving their animals with difficulty, some with ease. All were merry and joyful, striding along and dancing to the sound of the music. When the onlookers in the streets caught sight of them they began to clap their hands and shouted: 'Come in peace, our brothers, dwellers of the hills, come in peace!'

The guests went to rest in the city square which was beside the spring, and after them streamed the inhabitants of Nazareth.

*

The outskirts of Jerusalem, her streets and market places were filled with the bustle of pilgrims. The courtyard of the Temple was alive with a great multitude. Jews from all over the country and from abroad, from every part of the earth and the farthermost sea shores were here. Each was dressed differently from the other, each spoke a different language and had a different behaviour. They were all gathered here to appear before the Lord their God. And all were crowding, pushing and pressing on each other.

One of the people going up to celebrate the Festivals in Jerusalem was Jesus. His first pilgrimage was associated with an unpleasant memory. He was at that time a child, always pondering deeply and dreaming dreams. The new sights, the movement and noise of the great city, the big crowds in their differing and strange attire which streamed down the streets into the big market-places and the small, all these confused him. Lost completely he wandered away from his mother and father and became caught up with a crowd of strangers. From place to place they went until he found himself in a great hall. He saw there old men sitting in rows in a semi-circle and stood there awed at the impressive sight of them robed in

H

their splendid tallitot. They sat there unmoving and their speech was calm. One of the elders noticed the child with the golden curls and immediately a few of them entered into conversation with him requesting him to repeat the portion of the Torah which he had been learning. The people from Galilee who knew the child rejoiced to hear the sentences from the Torah, the Psalms and the prophet Isaiah which Jesus recited with the assurance of one who is familiar with them; they just fell from his lips.

The elders pointed long, bony fingers at Jesus and their hands stroked his cheeks lovingly. The faces withered by age and burdened by the yoke of this sudden and divine wisdom lightened; their wrinkles were cast away like a garment on seeing this young and bright-eyed child from Galilee. Eventually father and mother saw that their son was missing. They began to seek him everywhere, asking in every street and alleyway, and after much toil they found him in the Hall of the Sanhedrin. The child Jesus received a few blows from his parents; those blows were not forgotten many many days afterwards.

The Narrow Path, translated from
the Hebrew by Ronnie Greenberg

David Gascoyne (b. 1916)

ECCE HOMO (Fragment)

He who wept for Jerusalem
Now sees His Prophecy extend
Across the greatest cities of the world,
A guilty panic reason cannot stem
Rising to raze them all as He foretold;
And He must watch this drama to the end.

Though often named, He is unknown
To the dark kingdoms at His feet
Where everything disparages His words,
And each man bears the common guilt alone
And goes blindfolded to his fate,
And fear and greed are sovereign lords.

The turning point of history
Must come. Yet the complacent and the proud
And who exploit and kill, may be denied—
Christ of Revolution and of Poetry—
The resurrection and the life
Wrought by your spirit's blood.

Involved in their own sophistry
The black priest and the upright man
Faced by subversive truth shall be struck dumb,
Christ of Revolution and of Poetry,
While the rejected and condemned become
Agents of the divine.

Not from a monstrance silver-wrought
But from the tree of human pain
Redeem our sterile misery,
Christ of Revolution and of Poetry,
That man's long journey through the night
May not have been in vain.

Collected Poems, 1965

Hölderlin (1770–1843)

PATMOS (Fragment of a later version)
. . .
John. Christ. Of him would
I sing, like to Hercules or
That island, saved and held fast, refreshing
Its neighbour with cool sea-water from the vast
Desert of ocean, that expanse, Peleus. But this proves
Impossible. A destiny is different. More wonderful.
More rich for the singing. Measureless
The tale since then. And now
I would sing the journey of the nobles towards
Jerusalem, and anguish wandering in Canossa,
And Henri himself. May it be
That my courage does not overreach itself. We must
First grasp this. For like the morning air are the names
Since Christ. Become as dreams . . .

Translated from the German by Jean Eccles

V Pilgrimages

There's no discouragement
Shall make him once relent
His first avow'd intent
  To be a pilgrim
                    John Bunyan

And smale fowles maken melodye,
That slepen al the night with open ye,
(So priketh hem nature in hir corages):
Than longen folk to goon on pilgrimages
                    Geoffrey Chaucer

The most part (of pilgrims) that cometh,
cometh for no devotion at all, but only
for good company to babble thitherward,
and drinke dronke there, and then dance
and reel homeward.
          Sir Thomas More: *Dialogue on*
                the Adoracion of Images

Give me my scallop—shell of quiet,
  My staff of faith to walk upon,
My scrip of joy, immortal diet.
    My bottle of salvation,
My gown of glory, hope's true gage,
And thus I'll take my pilgrimage
          Sir Walter Raleigh: *His Pilgrimage*

The traditions of pilgrimage are known to most religions. Jerusalem, unique and immortal on her bare, tragic hills, has laid many fascinations on the hearts of men—but never more strongly than as the focal point of the secret dreams of countless pilgrims. Judaism, Christianity, and Islam have seen in Jerusalem the threshold to heaven, and the very air of the city seems charged with the long, slow accumulation of human hopes. From earliest times one glimpses those small, barefoot bands wending their way towards the city walls.

The Holy City holds a different significance for each of the three great religions of which it is the centre. Jew, Christian and Moslem have emphasized different sites (though some sites are, for all three, sacred for different reasons). While Christians and Moslems came to have other shrines—Rome, Canterbury, Walsingham, Compostella, Mecca—it was for Jerusalem that they *fought*. Only for the Jews did the city remain the unique sacred place, and the only goal of all their hopes. God dwelt in Zion and therefore going to Jerusalem on *Shalosh regalim* (the pilgrimage festivals) meant going to *see* God as well as be *seen* by God. *Alyyah*, the 'going up', was both a physical and a spiritual ascent, a supreme emotional experience. The earliest pilgrimages had a pan-Hebraic effect by bringing the scattered tribes of Israel to Jerusalem; after the destruction of the Temple and during the two thousand years of Diaspora, the Holy City became a symbol of the spiritual rejuvenation and resurrection of the dispersed Jewish people.

Christian pilgrimages to the city began in Apostolic times, although the earliest visit of which certain record survives was that of Bishop Alexander of Cappadocia in A.D. 217. But it was only after the conversion of Constantine in the fourth century that Christian pilgrims began to travel in large numbers, drawn by the report that Constantine's mother, the Empress Helena, had discovered the True Cross and the site of the Holy Sepulchre. Within a few years, Jerusalem had become the richest and most celebrated city in the Orient, with three great basilicas and many new churches. It became, too, a place of refuge for the proscribed and persecuted. But there was a darker side to the picture: not all pilgrims were moved to make the journey by the thought of spiritual gain, and as early as the fourth century, Gregory of Nyassa was denouncing the abuses which attended the practice of pilgrimage. 'Extreme licentiousness prevails in many hostelries and cities of the East which corrupt the ears, the eyes and the heart,' he wrote in a letter; and he urged the faithful to remember 'that believers in this land shall partake of the gifts of grace according to the measure of faith, not by a visit to Jerusalem.' St Jerome uttered a similar warning, and indeed it was to be reiterated throughout the Middle Ages, perhaps inspiring the unknown author of the proverb—

> He that on pilgrimage goeth ever
> Becometh holy late or never.

Nevertheless, pilgrimages became ever larger and more numerous. In the eighth century, to go on pilgrimages was a recognized way of gaining remission of sins. So important were they that civil and ecclesiastical laws were drawn up for their conduct. To facilitate the journey, routes were mapped, cities of call determined, and great hospices built. Gradually, however, Rome exerted its counter-attraction as a place of Christian pilgrimage, and after the Reformation the flow of Christian travellers further diminished. Yet still they came, even as late as the beginning of this century, from the farthest north of Russia and from the New World. One of the first acts of General Allenby, after he had taken the city in 1917, was to enter it on foot, together with detachments from the British and Allied forces, as a pilgrim.

For Moslems, Jerusalem became invested with a double significance—both as the city of Abraham, David, Solomon and Jesus (all prophets in the religion of Islam), and as the final goal of Mohammed's night journey, the flight in which he was carried on the winged steed al-Borak from Mecca to Sinai, then on to Bethlehem and finally to Jerusalem. There, he is said to have prayed before the Sacred Rock which once stood in the centre of Solomon's Temple, and then to have ascended from it by a ladder of light into heaven, where he received Allah's injunctions on the prayers his followers were to perform. It was over this rock that the Caliph Abd al Malik built the Dome of the Rock in A.D. 691 and south of it, at about the same time, the Aksa Mosque—both of which remain the chief places of Moslem pilgrimage to the present day.

The instinct of pilgrimage remains as deep and mysterious as any that sway the human heart. Jerusalem, at one and the same time an earthly site and a heavenly image, the old grey battle-scarred fortress of the Jebusites and the stirring modern city of glass and concrete, has seen the pilgrims come through twenty-five centuries and more, and still seems to hold the answer of their deepest aspirations.

Willibald (A.D. 721–727)

TRAVELS AS TOLD BY A NUN OF HEIDENHEIM

After the ceremonies of Easter were ended, the active champion (of Christ) prepared for his voyage with his two companions, and left Rome.

On their arrival at Jerusalem they first visited the spot where the holy cross was found, where there is now a church which is called the Place of Calvary, and which was formerly outside Jerusalem; but when St. Helena found the cross the place was taken into the circuit of the city. Three wooden crosses stand in this place on the outside of the wall of the church, in memory of our Lord's cross and of those of the other persons crucified at the same time. Before the door of the sepulchre lies a great square stone, in the likeness of the former stone which the angel rolled from the mouth of the monument. Our bishop arrived here on the feast of St. Martin and was suddenly seized with sickness. And then, being a little recovered, he rose and went to the church called St. Sion, which is in the middle of Jerusalem, and, after performing his devotions, he went to the porch of Solomon, where is the pool where the infirm wait for the motion of the water, when the angel comes to move it; and then he who first enters it is healed.

When at Jerusalem, Willibald bought balsam, and filled a gourd with it; and he took a gourd that was hollow, and had flax, and filled it with rock oil;[1] and poured some in the other gourd, and cut a small stalk, so that it fitted exactly and closed up the mouth of the gourd. So, when they came to Tyre, the citizens stopped them, and examined their burthens to see if they had anything concealed; for if they had found anything, they would immediately have put them to death. But they found nothing but Willibald's gourd, which they opened, and, smelling the rock oil in the stalk, they did not discover the balsam that was within.

Itinerarium S. Willibaldi, A.D. 750

Bernard the Wise (9th century)

THE VOYAGE OF BERNARDUS MONACHUS, THE WISE (867)

From the castle of Emmaus we went to the holy city of Jerusalem, and we were received in the hostel founded there by the glorious emperor Charles (Charlemagne), in which are received all the pilgrims who speak

---

[1] *Petrae Oleum.* No doubt the writer means naphtha, bitumen, or asphaltum.

the Roman tongue; to which adjoins a church in honour of St. Mary, with a most noble library, founded by the same emperor, with twelve mansions, fields, vineyards, and a garden in the Valley of Jehosaphat. In front of the hospital is the market, for which every one trading there pays yearly to him who provides it two *aurei*.

Within this city, besides others, there are four principal churches, connected with each other by walls. In the middle of the one to the west is the sepulchre of our Lord, having nine columns in its circuit, between which are walls made of the most excellent stones; of which nine columns, four are in front of the monument itself; which, with their walls, include the stone placed before the sepulchre, which the angel rolled away, and on which he sat after our Lord's resurrection. It is not necessary to say more of this sepulchre, since Bede has given a full description of it in his history.

I must not, however, omit to state, that on Holy Saturday, which is the eve of Easter, the office is begun in the morning in this church, and after it is ended the *Kyrie Eleison* is chanted, until an angel comes and lights the lamps which hang over the aforesaid sepulchre;[1] of which light the patriarch gives their shares to the bishops and to the rest of the people, that each may with it light up his own home.

Between the aforesaid four churches there is an unroofed court, the walls of which blaze with gold, and the pavement is laid with very precious stone; and in the middle four chains, coming from each of the four churches, join in a point which is said to be the middle of the world. To the north is the Temple of Solomon, having a synagogue for the Saracens.

The Itinerary of Bernard the Wise, 1893

Abu Mu'in Nāsir-i-Khusrow (1003–1060)

O LORD OF BOTH WORLDS!

It was the 5th of Ramadan, of the year 438 (5th March, 1047 A.D.), that I thus came to the Holy City; and the full space of a solar year had elapsed since I set out from home, having all that time never ceased to travel onward, for in no place had I yet sojourned to enjoy repose. Now, the

[1] This miracle was apparently instituted after the time of Charlemagne, as it is not mentioned prior to Bernard. It caused the persecution of the Christians and the destruction of the Church of the Holy Sepulchre by Khalif Hakim in A.D. 1008 or 1010. Abulfaragius, an Eastern Christian writer, wrote that Hakim was told by an enemy of the Christians that this was performed by greasing the chains of the lamp and lighting it from the roof. The impression to the worshippers inside was that the fire descended from heaven, and they burst into tears and cried out '*Kyrie eleison*'.

men of Syria, and of the neighbouring parts, call the Holy City (Bait al Mukaddas) by the name of Kuds (the Holy); and the people of these provinces, if they are unable to make the pilgrimage (to Mekkah), will go up at the appointed season to Jerusalem, and there perform their rites, and upon the feast day slay the sacrifice, as is customary to do (at Mekkah on the same day). There are years when as many as twenty thousand people will be present at Jerusalem during the first days of the (pilgrimage) month of Dhu-l Hijjah; for they bring their children also with them in order to celebrate their circumcision.

From all the countries of the Greeks, too, and from other lands, the Christians and the Jews come up to Jerusalem in great numbers in order to make their visitation of the Church (of the Resurrection) and the Synagogue that is there.

The country and villages round the Holy City are situated upon the hillsides; the land is well cultivated, and they grow corn, olives, and figs; there are also many kinds of trees here. In all the country round there is no (spring) water for irrigation, and yet the produce is very abundant, and the prices are moderate. Many of the chief men harvest as much as 50,000 Manns weight (or about 16,800 gallons) of olive-oil. It is kept in tanks and in pits, and they export thereof to other countries. It is said that drought never visits the soil of Syria. I heard from a certain person, on whose word I can rely, that the Prophet—peace be upon him, and the benediction of Allah!—was seen in a dream by a saintly man, who addressed him, saying, 'O Prophet of God, give me assurance for ever of my daily bread;' and the Prophet—peace be upon him!—replied: 'Verily it shall be warranted unto thee, even by the bread and oil of Syria.'

I now purpose to make a description of the Holy City. Jerusalem is a city set on a hill, and there is no water therein, except what falls in rain. The villages round have springs of water, but the Holy City has no springs. The city is enclosed by strong walls of stone, mortared, and there are iron gates. Round about the city there are no trees, for it is all built on the rock. Jerusalem is a very great city, and, at the time of my visit, there were in it twenty thousand men. It has high, well-built, and clean bazaars. All the streets are paved with slabs of stone; and wheresoever there was a hill or a height, they have cut it down and made it level, so that as soon as the rain falls the whole place is washed clean. There are in the city numerous artificers, and each craft has a separate bazaar. The mosque lies at the (south) east quarter of the city, whereby the eastern city wall forms also the wall of the mosque (court). When you have passed out of the mosque, there lies before you a great level plain, called the Sahirah, which, it is said, will be the place of the Resurrection, where all mankind shall be gathered together. For this reason men from all parts of the world come hither to make their sojourn in the Holy City till death overtakes them, in order that when the day fixed by God—be He praised and exalted!—shall arrive, they may thus be ready and present at the appointed place.

O God! in that day do Thou vouchsafe to Thy servants both Thy pardon and Thy protection! Amen. O Lord of both worlds!

At the border of this plain (of the Sahirah) there is a great cemetery, where are many places of pious renown, whither men come to pray and offer up petitions in their need. May God—be He praised and glorified! —vouchsafe unto them their desires. Grant unto us also, O God, our needs, and forgive our sins and our trespasses, and have mercy upon us, O most Merciful of the merciful!

Diary of a journey through Syria and Palestine, translated from the Persian by Georges Le Strange, 1888

Usamah Ibn Munqidh (1095–1188)

THE FRANKS IN THE CITY

A proof of the harshness of the Franks (the scourge of Allah upon them) is to be seen in what happened to me, when I visited Jerusalem. I went into the mosque Al-Aksâ. By the side of this was a little mosque which the Franks had converted into a church. When I went into the mosque Al-Aksâ which was occupied by the Templars, who were my friends, they assigned me this little mosque in which to say my prayers. One day I went into it and glorified Allah. I was engrossed in my praying when one of the Franks rushed at me, seized me and turned my face to the East, saying, 'That is how to pray'. A party of Templars made for him, seized his person and ejected him. I returned to my prayers. The same man, escaping their attention, made for me again and turned my face round to the East, repeating, 'That is how to pray'. The Templars again made for him and ejected him, then they apologised to me and said to me, 'He is a stranger who was only recently arrived from Frankish lands. He has never seen anyone praying without turning to the East.' I answered, 'I have prayed sufficiently for to-day'. I went out and was astounded to see how put out this demon was, how he trembled and how deeply he had been affected by seeing anyone pray in the direction of Kibla!

I saw one of the Templars go up to the emir Mou'în ad-Dîn (may Allah have mercy upon him), when he was in the cathedral of the Rock (As-Sakhra). 'Would you like,' he asked him, 'to see God as a child?' 'Yes, certainly,' answered Mou'în ad-Dîn. The Templar went before us and until he showed us an image of Mary with the Messiah as a child (may he be saved) on her lap. 'Here,' said the Templar, 'is God as a child'. May Allah raise himself high above those who speak such impious things.

The Franks understand neither the feeling of honours nor the nature of jealousy. If one of them is walking with his wife and he meets another man, the latter takes the woman's hand and goes and talks to her while the husband stands aside waiting for the end of the interview. If the woman prolongs it unreasonably, the husband leaves her alone with her companion and goes back.

Translated from the Arabic by George Richard Potter, 1929

Fetellus (*circa* A.D. 1130)

3102 YEARS FROM ADAM

According to the tradition of the Hebrews, it is said that the first-born of Noah, Shem, whom they call Melchisedech, first founded Salem after the flood, where he reigned as king and priest; afterwards the Jebusites were in possession of it, calling it Jebus after the name of their ancestor Jebus, the third son of Canaan. Joining these, it is called Jebus Salem. It was afterwards called by Solomon *Jerosolyma*, as if it were *Jebus Salomonia*. By poets it is called *Solyma*; by Elius Adrian, who restored it, *Elia*. This is Sion, which in Hebrew means *observation*, Jerusalem meaning *Vision of Peace*.

Jerusalem is the metropolis of Judaea—as it were, the navel of the earth, situated in the middle of the world. Whence David says: 'He wrought salvation in the midst of the earth'. Jerusalem excels all cities in the world in prayer and alms. In Jerusalem David reigned thirty-three years, after Saul was rejected. Of Jerusalem was Ysaias the Prophet, who was sawn with a wooden saw by King Manasseh. In Jerusalem is Mount Moria, *i.e.*, the threshing floor of Hornam the Jebusite, above which David saw the smiting angel, where also the Temple was afterwards built by Solomon.

3,102 years from Adam, 1,400 from the Flood, 1,200 from the departure of Abraham from Mesopotamia, 502 from the departure of Israel from Egypt, 240 from the foundation of Tyre, the Temple of the Lord began to be built. King Solomon built the Temple, *i.e.*, Bethel, and the altar, which he devoutly and solemnly dedicated at incomparable expense. The present temple is called the fourth. In the one before it the boy Jesus was circumcised. In Jerusalem is a Xenodochium, or Muscomion, a reception-house for strangers and the poor. Outside the city is a station for lepers. Hyrcanus, the prince of the Jews, is said to have been the first to institute Xenodochia with money which he abstracted from the Sepulchre of David. In the suburbs of Jerusalem, in the Valley of the Sons of Ennon, is Thopheth, the place in which the people of Israel were not ashamed to worship the idols of the Gentiles.

Translated from the Latin and annotated by
Rev. James Rose Macpherson

Jacques de Vitry (1180–1240)

THE CITY OF CITIES

Jerusalem is the city of cities, the holy of holies, great among the nations, and princess among the provinces, by especial prerogative called the City of the Great King. She standeth in the midst of the earth, in the centre of the world, and all nations shall flow unto her. She was the possession of the Patriarchs, the nursing mother of the Prophets, the teacher of the Apostles, the cradle of our Faith, the native country of the Lord, the mother of the Faith, even as Rome is the mother of the faithful; she hath been chosen and sanctified by God, trodden by His feet, honoured by the angels, and frequented by every nation under heaven.

The holy city of Jerusalem, as it exceeds all other places and cities in holiness and excellent grandeur, has drawn unto itself many religious persons, who visited the many venerable places at divers fitting times and seasons with fervour of spirit, were roused to devotion by one of them after another, and suffered not their souls to slumber through weariness, but kept them awake by the ardour of their love. This often-mentioned and often to be mentioned city is enclosed on all sides by a strong wall, and is neither straitened by excess of smallness nor is it likely to offend by over-greatness. It measures four bow-shots across from wall to wall, and has also on the west side a fortress of squared stone cemented together unbreakably with mortar and molten lead, which on one side serves as a wall to the city, and is called the Tower of David. The Lord's holy Temple is second to none of the holy and venerable places; for albeit it has been destroyed first by the Babylonians and afterwards by the Romans, yet it has been again rebuilt on the same spot by faithful and religious men in a round building, of wondrous and cunning workmanship, exceeding fair and stately. At this place, upon the rock which is still in the Temple, the Destroying Angel is said to have stood and appeared to David. Because of this, the Saracens to this day call the Lord's Temple the Rock, and hold it in such reverence that none of them dare to defile it with any filth, as they do at the other holy places; but from the time of Solomon even until now they come from distant countries to worship there. Whenever they possess the Holy City, they set up the image of Mahomet in the Temple, and suffer no Christian to enter it. Some believe that the Ark of the Lord is hidden in the aforesaid rock even to this day.

They who from the beginning of the recovery and redemption of the Holy Land have thoroughly known its condition and its divers alternations of fortune do affirm of a truth that no race of men and no plague has had greater power to hurt it than criminal and pestilent men, parricides, perjurers, adulterers, and traitors, corsairs—that is, pirates—whoremongers, drunkards, minstrels, dice-players, mimes and actors, apostate monks, nuns that are common harlots, and women who have left their husbands to live in brothels, or men who have run away from their true wives and taken others in their stead. Wicked people such as these in the West crossed the Mediterranean Sea, and took refuge in the Holy Land, where, as they had only changed their climate and not their character, they defiled it by numberless crimes and shameful deeds. They would claim sanctuary in the houses of regular clergy, and so they got off scot-free. Some men of blood and children of death when caught in their own country in their wickedness, and condemned to lose a limb or to be hanged, by entreaty or bribery could generally succeed in getting a sentence to perpetual exile in the Holy Land without hope of return. These men, who became denizens of the Holy Land, not by penitence but by force, used to let lodgings to pilgrims at immoderate rents, and cheated innocent strangers in every way that they could, worming money out of them for debts which they never incurred, and so made a wretched living by plundering their guests.

Historia Hierosolomyta, translated
by A. Stewart, 1896

Eusebius Hieronymus, Bishop of Caesarea (264–340)

NEW JERUSALEM, A.D. 333

Book III. Chapter 25. It seemed to the emperor Constantine beloved of God to be a duty to make conspicuous, and an object of veneration to all, the most blessed place of the Saviour's resurrection in Jerusalem. And so forthwith he gave orders for the building of a house of prayer, not having hit upon this project without the aid of God, but having been impelled to it in his spirit by the Saviour Himself.

Chapter 27. Nor did his zeal stop here. The emperor further gave directions that the material of that which was destroyed should be removed and thrown as far from the spot as possible. He also issued orders that, having dug up the soil to a considerable depth, they should transport to a far-distant spot the actual ground, earth and all, inasmuch as it had been polluted by the defilements of demon-worship.

Chapter 28. And as one layer after another was laid bare, the place which was beneath the earth appeared; then forthwith, contrary to all expectation, did the venerable and hallowed monument of our Saviour's resurrection become visible, and the most holy cave received what was an exact emblem of His coming to life. To the bishop Macarius who at that time presided over the Church in Jerusalem he sent the following letter, writing thus:

Chapter 30. 'This is always my first and only object, that as the faithfulness of the truth displays itself daily by fresh wonders, so the souls of us all may become more zealous for the holy law in all sobriety and earnestness with concord. Of all things it is most my care how we may adorn with splendour of buildings that sacred spot which, under Divine direction, I relieved as it were from an incumbent load and which has been made to appear still more holy since it brought to light the assurance of the Saviour's passion.

Chapter 31. It is therefore fitting that your sagacity make provision for everything necessary, that not only shall this basilica be the finest in the world, but that the details also shall be such that all the fairest structures in every city may be surpassed by it. Concerning the columns and marbles, whatever you shall judge after the plan has been inspected to be most precious and most serviceable, be careful to inform us in writing; that those things of whatever sort, and in whatever quantity, which we learn from your letter to be needful, may be procured from every quarter. For it is just that the place which is more wonderful than the whole world should be worthily decorated. As to the roof the basilica, I wish to know from you whether you think it should have a panelled ceiling or be finished in any other fashion. If it be panelled, it may also be ornamented with gold. It remains for your holiness to make it known with all speed how many workmen and artificers, and what expenditure of money, is needful.

God guard you, beloved brother!'

Chapter 33. These things did the emperor write, and his instructions were at once carried into effect. So on the monument of salvation itself was the new Jerusalem built, over against the one so famous of old, which, after the pollution caused by the murder of the Lord, experienced the last extremity of desolation. Opposite this the emperor reared, with rich and lavish expenditure, the trophy of the Saviour's victory over death. Perhaps this was that strange and new Jerusalem, proclaimed in the oracles of the prophets, to which long passages prophesying by the aid of the Divine spirit make countless allusions in song.

Vita Constantini, translated from the Latin by
Rev. John Bernard, London, 1891

Benjamin of Tudela (12th century)

JERUSALEM AND ITS SURROUNDINGS

. . . From there it is three parasangs to Jerusalem, which is a small city, fortified by three walls. There are many people in it, and the Ishmaelites call them Jacobites, Arameans, Greeks, Georgians, Franks, and peoples of all other tongues. There is a dyeing-house there, which the Jews rent annually from the king on condition that nobody besides the Jews should be engaged in dyeing in Jerusalem. There are about two hundred Jews dwelling under the tower of David, in one corner of the city. The first structure of the foundation of the wall of the tower of David, to the extent of ten cubits, is part of the ancient structure which our ancestors set up, but the remaining portion was built by the Ishmaelites. There is no structure in the whole city stronger than the tower of David.

The city contains also two buildings, one being a hospital, from which four hundred knights issue forth, and where all the sick that come hither are lodged and receive all their needs in life and in death. The second building is called the Temple of Solomon; it is the palace which was built by Solomon king of Israel, peace be upon him. Knights are quartered there, three hundred of whom issue forth every day for military exercises, besides the knights that come from the land of the Franks and from the land of Edom, having taken a vow upon themselves to serve there a year or two until their vow is fulfilled. In that city is the great place of worship called the Sepulchre; there is the burial-place of that man to which all the misguided repair.

There are four gates in Jerusalem; the gate of Abram, the gate of David, the gate of Zion, and the gate of Goshafat, which is the gate of Jehoshaphat, in front of the sanctuary which stood there in ancient times. There is also the Templum Domini, which is on the site of the temple upon which 'Omar the son of al-Khattab erected a very large and magnificent cupola. The Gentiles are not allowed to introduce there any image or effigy; they only come there to pray. In front of that place is the Western Wall which is one of the walls of the holy of holies. This is called the Gate of Mercy, and thither all the Jews repair to pray in front of the wall of the temple court.

In front of Jerusalem is Mount Zion; but there is no building on Mount Zion, except a place of worship belonging to the uncircumcised.

About three miles before Jerusalem are the sepulchres of the Israelites, for they used to bury their dead in caves in those days. Each sepulchre bears a date; but the children of Edom demolished the sepulchres, and of the stones thereof built their houses. These sepulchres reach as far as the border of Benjamin at Zelzah.

The Itinerary of Rabbi Benjamin of Tudela (1160–1173),
translated from the Hebrew by M. N. Adler, London, 1907

Abbot Daniel (12th century)

JOURNEYING IN HUMILITY

First Russian pilgrimage to the Holy Land (*circa* 1106–1107)
I, Daniel, an unworthy Abbot of Russia, the least among the monks, ill at ease by reason of my many sins and the insufficiency of my good works, was seized first with the idea, and then with an impatient yearning to behold the sacred city of Jerusalem and the Promised Land. By the grace of God I reached the holy city of Jerusalem, and saw the holy places: I visited the whole of Galilee and all the sacred places around the holy city

I

of Jerusalem, which Christ our God pressed with His feet, and where He manifested Himself by marvellous miracles.

I have seen all these places with my sinful eyes; and God in His mercy has deigned to show me all that I have for so many years longed to see.

Others, of whom I am the chief, after having visited the holy city of Jerusalem and the holy places, pride themselves as if they had done something meritorious, and thus lose the fruit of their labour. And again, others who have made the pilgrimage, return without having seen many valuable things, so eager were they to return home; for this journey cannot be made quickly, nor can all the holy places in Jerusalem and other localities be hurried through.

I then, unworthy Abbot Daniel, on arriving at Jerusalem, stayed for sixteen months in the Metochia of the Laura of St. Sabbas, and was thus able to visit and explore all the holy places. Now it is impossible to visit and explore all the sacred places without a good guide and an interpreter; I therefore gave all that I could out of my small means as a reward to those who were thoroughly acquainted with, and able to show me, the holy places of the city and other localities, so that I might see every detail; in this, accordingly, I was successful.

Jerusalem is a large city, protected by very solid walls, and built in the form of a square, whose four sides are of equal length: it is surrounded by many arid valleys and rocky mountains. It is a place absolutely destitute of water; one finds neither river, nor wells, nor springs near Jerusalem, with the exception of the Pool of Siloam. The inhabitants of the town, and cattle, have therefore nothing but rain-water for their use. In spite of that corn thrives well in that rocky land which lacks rain; but thanks to the pleasure and mercy of God the crop of wheat and barley is excellent. By sowing one measure, ninety and a hundred fold is reaped. Does not God's blessing rest upon this hallowed land? In the neighbourhood of Jerusalem there are plenty of vineyards and fruit-trees; fig-trees, syca-mores, olive-trees, carob-trees, and an infinite number of other trees.

Upon the Mount of Olives, on the southern side, near the place of the Ascension, there is a deep cavern, containing the tomb of Saint Pelagia, the courtesan. A stylite, a very austere man, lives there.

The Pilgrimage of the Russian Abbot Daniel in the Holy Land, adapted from a Russian manuscript (1496) by Colonel Sir C. W. Wilson, 1888

Henry Timberlake (?-1626)

A true and ſtrange diſcourſe of the Trauailles of two Engliſh Pilgrimes, what admirable Accidents befel them in their Journey to Jerusalem.[1]

Early next morning we aroſe and having ſaluted the Pater Guardian, he appointed us ſeven friars and an interpreter to ſhew us all the holy places in the city of Jeruſalem, except thoſe in Sepulchra Sancta, for that requir'd a whole day.

Now for the more eaſy comprehending how the country about Jeruſalem lies, I will compare the diſtance of places from thence with ſome of our Engliſh towns and villages from London, according as I have computed the ſame, the city of Bethlem—is as far from Jeruſalem, as Wanſworth from London. Joppa is from Jeruſalem as Ailſbury from London. The lake of Sodom and Gomorrah is from J. as Graveſend is from L.—The brook Kedron as Hounſditch, Mount Sion adjoins to J. as Southwark to L.

In the morning we mounted to take our journey for Jeruſalem (from Ramah)—and about four in the afternoon arrived at Jeruſalem at Joppa Gate where we tarried till the druggerman of the convent went to the laddy to procure a license for us to enter the city.

Edward Webbe (1554-1590)

HIS TRAUAILES

The Rare and moſt wonderful thinges which Edward Webbe an Engliſhman borne, hath ſeene and paſſed in his trauailes in the Citties of Jeruſalem, Bethlehem, Galely, and in the Landes of Iewrie, Egipt, Ruſſia, and in the Land of Preſter John. Born in 1554, ſon of Richard Webbe, Maſter Gunner of England, Edward was a Maſter Gunner, ſometime Chief Maſter Gunner of France. In 1566 in the ſervice of Captain Jenkenſon, and went to Ruſſia. He experienced 18 years of ſlavery. 'A ſimple man devoid of learning.'

The old Cittie of Ieruſalem is a very delicat place, and nothing there to be ſeene but a little of the old walles which is yet remayning. and all the reſt is Graſſe, Moſſe, and weedes much like to a peece of Rank or moiſt grounde. They have no Tillage at all in that partes. The Citty of Ieruſalem where the Temple now ſtandeth is almoſt a mile from the olde walls of Ieruſalem. it is a marvellous olde building, and there ſtandeth the old Relicks preſerved and kept as Monuments of great treaſure.

[1] Written in 1603, by 1629 this work had run through six editions. Five more issues followed between 1629-1759. The edition used here was printed in London in 1759.

The great Turk hath some profit comming by ye keeping thereof, and hath therefore builded at his owne charges an Hofpital within Ierufalem, —which is to receive all Pilgrims and trauellers to lodge in whenfoever they come. and all that come to fee the Sepulchre doe pay ten Crovmesapeece.—Such as come thither for Pilgrims have no beds at all, but lie vpon the ground on Turkey Carpets.

Printed by Ralph Blower for Thomas Power, London, 1590. 4°

Sir Richard Guylforde (1455?–1506)

PILGRIMAGE OF
SIR RICHARD GUYLFORDE KNYGHT

'A controuler unto our late soueraygne lorde Kynge Henry the VII. And howe he went with his seruants and company towards Ierusalem.' The pilgrimage was made to Palestine in 1506 at a time when such expeditions were generally in decline. The account was written by a priest, one of the company, whose name is unknown. Sir Richard died in Palestine, and was buried on Mt. Zion. The pilgrims were absent from England just under a year. (Written in original script.)

This Cytie of Jherufale is in a fayre Empynent place for it stondeth upon fuche a grounde that from whens foever a ma comyth thed he must ned alcede.—I sawe never cytie nor other place have fo fayre profpects. It sondeth fayre amoges hylles, there is nother Ryver Comynge thereto nor well in it, but the water comyth all by Condyte in grete plenty from Ebron which Condytts serve all the Cytie in euery place, fyll of piftynes which are in grete nombre and moche valer runneth nowe to waste.

This londe of Jherufalem hath been in the hands of many fondry Nacyons, as of Jewes, Cananeis, Parrcynens, Macedoynes, Medoyns, Grekes, Roma Cristen mon, Serrafyns, Barbaryns, Turkes, and many other Nacyons. Jherusale is in lande of Inde, it marcheth Estwards to the Kyndome of Araby, Southward to the Lande of Egipte, Westwards to the grete see, and Northwardes to the kyngdome of Surrey and to the see of Cypres in Some parte.

Printed by R. Pinson, London, 1511

Gerhard Tersteegen (1697-1797)

PILGRIM SONG

'Here we have no continuing city, but we seek one to come.' Hebrews xiii. 14

The Pilgrim's path of trial
   We do not fear to view;
We know His voice who calls us,
   We know Him to be true.
Then, let who will condemn
   But, stong in His almighty grace,
Come, every one, with steadfast face,
   On To Jerusalem!

If we would walk as pilgrims,
   We must not riches heap;
Much treasure to have gathered
   But makes the way more steep.
We march with haggard speed,
   Till every weight is cast aside,
Till with the little satisfied
   That pilgrimage can need.

Hymns from the Land of Luther, Edinburgh, 1853

Meshullam Ben Menahem of Volterra (15th century)

ADVICE TO THE TRAVELLER

And in order, my friends, that you may know the things we had to do and everyone has to do who takes this route, I will briefly relate them. From the balsam garden (Egypt) to Gaza and also close up to Jerusalem it is all desert, and every man must carry on his beast two sacks, one of biscuits and the other of straw•and fodder, also water skins, for there you cannot find sweet water, but only salt. You must also take with you lemons because of the insects which I wrote about above, and you must go in a big caravan because of the robbers who frequent the desert, and you must go slowly for two reasons; the one because in the desert there is much dust and sand and the horses sink in it up to their knees and go with difficulty, and secondly because the dust rises and gets into a man's mouth and makes his throat dry and kills him with thirst, and if he drinks of the hot brackish water he is troubled worse than before. Moreover, a man who does not know Arabic must dress like a Turk in order that he may not be taken for a Jew or Frank. When you come to the custom houses if you do a single thing not according to their usage they will at once understand that you are not a Turk or an Ishmaelite, and they are always on the watch, and if you ask me what their manner is and what to do, it is necessary that when you reach those places you must immediately take your shoes off and sit on the ground and bend your legs under you and never let your legs appear or stand upon them at all, but you must eat on the ground, and if crumbs fall from the bread pick them up, but do not eat the bread until you have put it on your head, and you must give to the people around you a little of all you eat, even if they are not eating with you; and you must never take any of your clothes off, but you must sleep in them at night, and if they pass you anything to eat you must stretch forth your hand to take it with a bow, and when you go to relieve yourself, take care not to lift up any of your clothes and keep close to the ground. You must never go to the house of anybody with shoes and never speak to anybody except seated with your legs bent beneath you, and even if you have only one loaf of bread and one cup of wine and a man comes and takes it and eats and drinks you must let him do so. Some people clean their hands in fine white dust somewhat scented, which in Arabic they call 'raihan'. It is also their custom to give no fodder to donkeys and nothing to drink, only all the caravan together, for it is by their law a great sin that the other horses or small donkeys should see one of them eat, because that would hurt those that are not eating, and that is cruelty to animals; and, therefore, every man must be careful not to transgress their customs lest, God forbid, they find out that he is a Jew or Frank, and unlucky is he that falls into this trap . . .

Translated from the Hebrew by Maurice Samuel

Obadiah Yareh di Bertinoro (*circa* 1450–d. Jerusalem 1510?)

MY JOURNEY FROM BEGINNING TO END

From Bethlehem to Jerusalem is a journey of about three miles. The whole way is full of vineyards and orchards. The vineyards are like those in Romagna, the vines being low but thick. About three-quarters of a mile from Jerusalem, at a place where the mountain is ascended by steps, we beheld the famous city of our delight, and here we rent our garments, as was our duty. A little farther on, the sanctuary, the desolate house of our splendour, became visible, and at the sight of it we again made rents in our garments. We came as far as the gates of Jerusalem, and on the 14th of Nisan, 5248, at noon, our feet stood within the gates of the city. Here we were met by an Ashkenazi who had been educated in Italy, Rabbi Jacob Calmann; he took me into his house, the most part desolate and in ruins. The inhabitants, I am told, number about four thousand families. As for Jews, about seventy families of the poorest class have remained; there is scarcely a family that is not in want of the commonest necessities; one who has bread for a year is called rich. Among the Jewish population there are many aged, forsaken widows from Germany, Spain, Portugal and other countries, so that there are seven women to one man. The land is now quieter and happier than before; for the Elders have repented the evil they have done, when they saw that only the poorer portion of the inhabitants remained; they are therefore very friendly to every newcomer. They excuse themselves for what has happened, and assert that they never injured anyone who did not try to obtain the mastery over them. As for me, so far I have no complaint to make against them; on the contrary, they have shown me great kindness and have dealt honourably with me, for which I give daily thanks to God.

The Jews are not persecuted by the Arabs in these parts. I have travelled through the country in its length and breadth, and none of them has put an obstacle in my way. They are very kind to strangers, particularly to anyone who does not know the language; and if they see many Jews together they are not annoyed by it. In my opinion, an intelligent man versed in political science might easily raise himself to be chief of the Jews as well as of the Arabs; for among all the inhabitants there is not a wise and sensible man who knows how to deal affably with his fellow-men; all are ignorant misanthropes intent only on gain . . .

Jerusalem, notwithstanding its destruction, still contains four very beautiful, long bazaars, such as I have never before seen, at the foot of Zion. They have all dome-shaped roofs, and contain wares of every kind.

All the necessities of life, such as meat, wine, olives, and sesame oil can be had very cheap. The soil is excellent, but it is not possible to gain a living by any branch of industry, unless it be that of a shoemaker, weaver, or goldsmith; even such artisans as these gain their livelihood with great difficulty. Persons of various nationalities are always to be found in Jerusalem from Christian countries, and from Babylonia and Abyssinia. The Arabs come frequently to offer up prayers at the temple, for they hold it in great veneration.

It is universally known here that the Arabs who make pilgrimages from Egypt to Mecca journey through a large and fearful desert, forming caravans of at least ten thousand camels. Sometimes they are overtaken in the wilderness by a people of gigantic stature, one of whom can chase a thousand Arabs. They call this people El-Arabes, that is, children of the Almighty, because in their battles they always invoke the name of Almighty God.

No Jew may enter the enclosure of the Temple. I do not know whether the Arabs enter the Holy of Holies or not.

Everyone is obliged to pay fifty ducats annually to the Niepo (the Governor of Jerusalem) for permission to make wine, a beverage which is an abomination to the Arabs. This is the whole amount of annual taxation to which the Jews are liable.

As for me, so far God has helped me, they have demanded nothing from me as yet; how it may fare with me in the future I cannot tell.

I have taken a house here close to the synagogue. I must thank God, who has hitherto vouchsafed me His blessing, that I have not been sick, like the others who came at the same time with me. Most of those who come to Jerusalem from foreign countries fall ill, owing to climatic changes and sudden variations of the wind, now cold, now warm. All possible winds blow in Jerusalem to prostrate itself before the Lord. Blessed be He that knoweth the truth.

Finished in haste in Jerusalem, the Holy City. May it soon be rebuilt in our days.

From your son, OBADIAH YAREH

The Miscellany of Hebrew Literature, London, 1872

Gedaliah of Siemiatycze (18th century)

SEEK YE THE PEACE OF JERUSALEM

Gedaliah of Siemiatycze, one of the company of the Rabbi Judah the Pious, records in 'Shaaru Shelom Yerushalaim' (Seek Ye the Peace of Jerusalem) how a company of some thirteen hundred Jewish pilgrims, hundreds of whom died on the way, set out for Jerusalem from Poland. Rabbi Judah himself was spared the difficulties of life in the Holy City, for he died almost as soon as he arrived.

Our master, Rabbi Judah the Pious, arrived together with his followers in Jerusalem on the New Year's Day of Marheshvan 5461 (1700). He at once acquired a house in the Synagogue Court of the Ashkenazim, rented dwellings for his faithful ones and distributed money for them to live on. Most of them were sick after the great exertions of the journey. Conditions on the ship had been bad, and the space allowed for all of us together was far too small.

*

In the late summer of the year, shortly before our arrival, a beginning was made at the building of the new synagogue, and of forty dwellings for the poor. The Turks in Jerusalem had to be heavily bribed before they permitted the building.

Now there is a law in Jerusalem that while building is going on the pasha has to be paid five hundred lion thalers a year for three years. But as the synagogue had been built higher than the old one without the permission of the Sultan, another pasha came and wished to stop the building. So he also received five hundred lion thalers. Finally, a new pasha came from Constantinople to whom five hundred lion thalers had to be given. Thus the Jews were compelled to borrow money from the Turks at a high rate of interest.

There are also many Christians dwelling in Jerusalem, almost more than Turks and Arabs. They also suffer greatly and must also pay taxes. Only the poor, the blind and the lame are exempt. Nevertheless the Turks demand it from them as well, and nothing much can be done about it, for it is a harsh *galut*. However, on Sabbaths and Festivals the tax collector may not press us. So on those days we walk the street without fear. But on weekdays it is different. The Official may not enter a house to demand money, or make his way into the synagogue. Sometimes the officials bribe the chief pasha of the Holy City, and in return receive permission to conduct their searches even in houses for two or three days.

But let us return to our great worries, which the synagogue building brought about. Our debts press like a heavy yoke on our necks. We are continually taken into custody and before one debtor can be redeemed, another has already been detained. One scarcely dares to go out in the street, where to cap it all, the tax collectors lie in wait like wolves and lions to devour us.

It is hard for us Ashkenazim to begin to trade here, for we lack knowledge of the languages. The Sephardic Jews talk Ladino, the Arabs talk Aramaic [*sic*] and the Turks Turkish. None of them understand German. And what should we deal with? There is indeed much wine in the Land of Israel, but Turks and Arabs drink neither wine nor brandy. If a Jew sells an Arab even a little wine or brandy and the Arab is seen drunk, then the Jew is imprisoned and beaten and has to pay a money fine.

A few Jews have grocery shops here. Some of them take a Turk as a partner in order to protect themselves against unfair treatment. There are also a couple of Jewish spice dealers in the non-Jewish markets. There are Jews here who are called Moghrabians (Moroccans), or 'Moriscos' in their own tongue. They have a language of their own, but also understand Aramaic [i.e. Arabic]. They go dressed like the Arabs and it is scarcely possible to distinguish them as the Arabs likewise follow the practice of leaving the beard uncut. These Moghrabians travel on their asses from place to place with spices and other things, and in return bring wheat and barley to Jerusalem. From this they make a meagre living. If they, who know the languages of the country, live in poverty, what shall we poor Ashkenazim do here when we have to pass to and fro among the non-Jews as though we were dumb? If we buy something from the Arab, he shows us the price on his fingers and we have to answer on our fingers; so we become a laughing stock in their sight and cannot make a living.

Jerusalem has two Jewish cemeteries, one from ancient times lying at a distance south of the town, and a new one to the east, on the slopes of the Mount of Olives. No gravestone can be recognized any more in the old cemetery, and there are many caves to be found there. There are no caves in the new graveyard and the graves are dug out after our European fashion. Burial may not take place without the written authorization of the Turkish Kadi (Moslem religious judge) who is paid for this according to the wealth of the dead person. He gives permission for the burial of a poor man immediately and free of charge.

The garments of the Turks are long like those of the Poles, but are multi-coloured. Round the turban they wrap a cloth of cotton or silk. The Sephardim wear a white under garment, and wear over it a black or coloured coat even on the Sabbath. The Ashkenazim go in gleaming white on the Sabbath, but the Sephardim wear white only on the Sabbath before the Ninth Day of Av. The Christians dress as in the kingdom of Poland. For the Turkish law prescribes that each nation should go in its own costume, in order to make the differences clear to see. There are also differences in footwear. The Jews wear blue and dark blue shoes, the Christians red, and yellow is reserved for the Turks.

The Arabs often wrong the Jew publicly. But if the Arab is a respectable man he will cause no injury to the Jew whom he meets in the street.

We have seen something very evil. There are some new-fangled fools who came to the Land only a short time ago, and who wish to revive the old disease of the year 5426[1] (1661). For these fools declare that the Divine

---

[1] Referring to the messianic movement of Sabbatai Zevi which reached its climax in 1666.

Presence is no longer in exile since then, and that there is therefore no reason to mourn its homelessness any longer.

For who does not know that we also shall return home with the return of the Divine Presence? Yet the Arabs will walk about our Holy Place and we are called the strangers to whom entry is forbidden. Even if it were true that the Divine Presence has forsaken our Exile, that fact does not help us and our wounds are not yet healed.

Yet it is a rare delight to dwell in the Land of Israel, and 'he who walks only four ells in the Land of Irsael has a share in the everlasting life'.

Translated from the Hebrew by I. M. Lask

Martin Buber (1878-1965)

BAALSHEM AT JERUSALEM

At times Baalshem heard voices calling to him in the night, and his hearing was keen and awake, though sleep lay heavy upon his senses. He could then clearly distinguish the sound, which came to him as though from an immeasurable distance; it reached him from the mouth of many primeval things in their pilgrimage, and a single note of immense woe surrounded his couch. The sound reached his heart and woke it up; but it came to him from past ages, and his heart could not understand the meaning of its language, he was only overwhelmed by a sense of the distress, far away in the distance, which was causing it. But the sound shattered him day and night from this time forward. One night, however, the voices came quite near to the Master's ear, trembling from the weariness of their long pilgrimage. He recognized them and whence they came, and he was aware of one that till now had been foreign to him, and which now spoke to him out of the shame of its ruin. It was the ancient vineyard, now an arid waste, which the flocks of alien, wandering tribes trampled on year by year with their hated hoofs. Its walls were buried, its ore was scattered beneath the weight of countless rocks, and in the place of its gleaming forests there was but a stony slope, and its spring of water was dried up.

And the voice spoke to Baalshem: 'Come, come, and tarry not. You are the one whom we await, whose breath shall lift the stones from our graves, as the wind of spring lifts the down that falls from a bird's nest. The stream will flow, the forest will grow, the vine will bear fruit, and the rock will be clothed. Come and lay your hand upon us.'

From this night onward Baalshem was sure in his soul that he ought to arise and go to the Land. He got up and cried to God: 'Give me leave, O Lord, and time. Release me from that to which Thou hast here kept me bound, so that I may go to Thy Land, which calls to me.'

But God spoke to him at night, and answered: 'Israel, my sentence on thee is that thou shouldst stay in thine own place, and that thou shouldst not arise and go to my Land.'

Then Baalshem lay many nights in misery. The voices were in his ear, but the words of the Lord were in his heart. The lamentations of the voices rose as a storm in the air, and there was a commotion as of a great death, as on the day when Jerusalem the splendid fell. Then the longing of the dying earth prevailed over the word of Heaven, and the master prepared to journey to Jerusalem. It was the first night that Baalshem and his scribe and scholar, Zwi, lay down to rest under a strange roof. In that night the voices of affliction turned back to the place whence they had come. And when they returned home a great whisper flew to meet them, the old earth trembled with greeting, and everything that lay buried, benumbed, and deserted, lifted itself up and listened. And the voices cried: 'Stand up, ye sleepers and ye who are dumb, prepare, for your deliverer is at hand.' Then the body of the earth trembled, and with a monstrous breath it shook off the sleep of ages. In heartfelt tones everything shouted the call of life, a mighty murmur of joy was in the air, there was light, and a great, mysterious upheaval from the ravines up to the mountain-tops. The buried land blossomed, the dried-up waters flowed, and the sap rose again into the corn and the vine, and the stars rose over the old world in this night of expectation.

Baalshem stepped forward unfalteringly, but he had lost his brightness and joy. He was quiet and full of thought, and when Rabbi Zwi spoke of the wonderful end of the journey the Master hardly answered at all, save with a stifled sigh. Something weighed upon his heart and grew heavier as he went on his way. This was the voice of God, which his longing had silenced and which was now dumb, but it lingered all the while in his heart and did not fade away. At times it seemed to the Master as though a tender child were within his breast, and at nights there was a sound of lamentation without words, so deep and passionate that he heard it when he awoke, and was forced to listen to it. And each morning, when he journeyed onward, he carried with him this ever-growing burden.

And so he left town and country behind him, the familiar and the strange. The moon had changed over him many times when, one evening, he came in his wanderings to the coast of that sea that separated him from his goal. But there was neither house nor town to be seen as far as the eye could reach; no sail was on the water; there was only the beach, shimmering and distant, the water breaking on the sand, and a long, silent night, lit only by the stars. Then they both threw themselves down on the earth, which still breathed forth the warmth of the past day; here they could rest and await the morrow. In the middle of the night, the Master found himself on the waves in a rudderless ship, with only a sail of flaming red and yellow over him. The little ship was tossed hither and thither by a fearful storm, and round about it neither heaven nor earth could be seen, nothing but the storm-tossed waters on all sides, and the wind howling above. Baalshem gazed around him, but there was nothing but the deadly solitude of the waters. Then he searched within himself; but all had faded from him, all wisdom and mastery. Then he felt a desolation greater than the depth of the ocean, and his soul felt as empty as the cast-off rind of a fruit. He was overcome by great weeping. He threw himself beside his companion till it should all pass away. But while he lay for long, a miserable, deaf thing, a voice came to him, first quite softly, gently, and mysteriously; but gradually the voice rose, and the raging of the sea was swallowed up in its sound as a mere whisper. And the Master drank in the voice of God.

In the morning twilight Baalshem and Rabbi Zwi rose from the sand. Hair, face, and raiment were wet, as with those whom the sea throws up on its shores. They did not speak, each avoided the other's eye, and they turned, and without a word walked back along the path by which they had come the night before. When they had travelled several hours, and the sun had risen high and had dried their garments, by chance the Rabbi looked at his Master, and was aware of the old holy light on his countenance.

In the night in which Baalshem had fought with the loneliness of the waters and with the loneliness of his own soul, the land which had called to him lay awaiting him. The voices of those awoken from the grave spoke from out of the earth, and asked of the voices of the air: 'What do you hear?' Then the sisters of the air answered and said: 'A storm is raging, and he who would deliver us struggles on the angry waters.'

Some time passed, and again the voices of the earth asked: 'Does he draw near to the land?' And the answer came: 'The word is upon him.' Again time passed, and once more came the question: 'What do you hear?' Like the sound of wings tired to death came the answer: 'We hear in the distance the sound of his steps, and he is turning back again.' On that the old world opened its mouth and answered: 'Then I will lay me down and die.' It hid its face and shut its eyes, and everything turned back to the place of its rest and prepared for death. A silence spread over the land, and in the silence was grief and in the grief was death.

But the silence was broken by a living cry which shattered it. The cry encircled the land, and said to it: 'You will not die, my friend. Earth of the Lord, you will grow and will live, and find no quarrel with him whom you have called. For he is born as one who shall live again and shall return, and the Lord's hand is upon his roots, that He may bring him back in His own time.'

The Legends of Baalshem, translated from
the German by Lucy Cohen, 1956

VI The Crusades

Jerusalem, grant damage me fais,
Qui m'as tolu ce que je plus amoie
Anon. 12th or 13th century

Dieus, quant crieront 'Outree',
Sire, aidiez au pelerin
Pour qui sui espoentee,
Car felon sont Sarrazin.
Guiot de Dijon: Chanson d'outree,
13th century

It was not in the spirit of peace and repentance that the knights and their companions left the Western shores for the Holy Land. They came in armour against the infidel, and they came with the sword. Jerusalem acted as a burning glass upon the tinder of men's conflicting aspirations.

The subject of the Crusades has been a powerful and constant inspiration to the historian; and the legends which enshrine the exploits of the Crusaders derive from actual historical events. Both religious ardour and warlike enthusiasm have stimulated the imagination and inventiveness of the storytellers. The Crusades have provoked differing reactions: Gibbon, taking the point of view of the 18th-century enlightened rationalist, denounced their 'enthusiasm'. Before him Calvin's campaign against these exploits was inspired by religious objections to the claim that relics brought back from Jerusalem possessed the power of self-reproduction. But the Crusades should perhaps here be regarded in their widest possible aspect, as part of the age-old contest between East and West; and, moreover, as an inevitable clash between two world religions, Christianity and Islam, and between two contrasting types of civilization. The period of the Crusades may therefore be considered both as one of horrible confusion between the earthly Jerusalem and the heavenly, and also as one in which a noble effort was made to bring the two together.

It is not within the scope of this section to trace the history of the Crusades; indeed, only three out of the eight were both directed towards Jerusalem and managed to achieve their objective. We can merely name some of the main heroes in the kaleidoscopic story of the Holy City: Peter the Hermit, Godfrey of

Bouillon, Tancred, Richard Coeur de Lion, Frederick Barbarossa, Saladin. Few other historical events have been more productive of good literature. The vision of the Holy City in general and of the Holy Sepulchre in particular can be considered as one of the basic themes in the literature of chivalry and romance to which the Crusades gave tremendous impetus if not actual birth. The *Gesta Francorum et aliorum Hierosolymitanorum,* probably completed in A.D. 1101, was written by an anonymous South Italian knight who took an active part in the First Crusade. Many medieval historical and poetical works stem from the *Gesta Tancredi* of Ralph of Caën, the *Hierosolomyta* of Ekkehardus Uragiensis (1095–1151), the anonymous *Libellus de expugnatione Terrae Sanctae,* Benedict of Peterborough's *Gesta Henrici II et Richardi Angliae,* and especially from William of Tyre's monumental *Historia rerum in partibus transmarinis gestarum* (History of the Deeds done Beyond the Seas), a history of the Crusades in twenty-three books which are an inexhaustible treasury of tales well told. We are fortunate in being able to read the first English translation of Ambroise's *Estoire de la guerre sainte,* an account of the Third Crusade written in octosyllabic couplets by a Norman knight who was minstrel to Richard I and probably an eyewitness of the spectacular events he relates. There are also many other literary works still hidden in the *Recueil des historiens des Croisades,* the *Collection des poètes français du Moyen Age,* and the *Collection des Chroniques belges*—true sagas in their vivid description of desperate battles, in their richness of colour, and most of all in their fabulous and fascinating inconsistencies . . .

Today one is very much aware of the equivocal and less holy character of the Crusades; of the combination of religious zeal and commercial gain by which they were inspired; of the spirit of conquest and colonialism that lay behind them. Moreover, recent interpretations of the historical documents show how Western Europe had in fact cruelly provoked the comparatively tolerant Moslems.

However, whatever historical or political assessments may be made about this turbulent era, the greatness of such works as Tasso's *Gerusalemme Liberata* and Lope de Vega's *Jerusalén Conquistada* is indisputable; nor are English and French literatures lacking in works which exalt the Crusades as the central expression of Christian revival. Surely, Lessing was not yielding to the spirit engendered by the Crusades when he wrote *Nathan der Weise;*

but it is symbolic that he should stage the fable which teaches religious toleration in the capital of the Latin kingdom of Jerusalem . . .

However unholy they may have been (though to ordinary people of the time they were 'holy wars'), in perspective the Crusades are seen to have played an important part in the shaping of Western civilization as we know it. Though the knights who went on Crusades against both Jews and Moslems to avenge the death of Jesus may have slain hundreds during the day, at night they would kneel at the altar, and if truly penitent receive remission of their sins.

Jerusalem provided the Church with an ideal channel into which to direct the often cruel instincts of the Middle Ages and gave feudal society an impulse towards action, which in turn tended towards the re-instatement of Christianity in the very place from which it has sprung. Knights who went on crusade took a solemn vow to deliver the Holy Places from Mohammedan oppression; and as the sacred places stirred the imagination of many heedless and impetuous warriors, they also led some of the sinful pilgrims to the Christ of the Gospels.

PLANGITE, CORDIS DOLORE

(The Templars' Lament from 'The Liturgy of the Templars')
'Let Jerusalem come into your mind, remember, Lord.'

Weep today the bitterest tears,
Pour thy heart, grief, tell thy fears,
'Tis the day of wrath and shame:
    Jerusalem! Jersualem!

Where are now thy Fathers old?
Where thy Temple—warriors bold?
Wail their loss, thy tarnished fame,
    Jerusalem! Jersualem!

Kings and Princes, all are ta'en;
They who fought for thee are slain;
What is left thee but thy name?
    Jerusalem! Jersualem!

See! the foes thy walls have gained,
Zion's Temple is Profaned,
Fort and tower are wrapped in flame!
    Jerusalem! Jerusalem!

Fly! ye ne'er can stay her fall,
And if memory recall
Aught of beauty, aught of fame,
    Cry, then, to your God, her name.
        Jerusalem! Jerusalem!

Translated from the Latin by Robert Maude Moorsom

Thomas Warton (1728–1790)

THE CRUSADE

Bound for holy Palestine,
Nimbly we brushed the level brine,
All in azure steel arrayed;
O'er the wave our weapons played,
And made the dancing billows glow;
Many a warrior-minstrel swung
His sounding harp, and boldly sung:
    'Syrian virgins, wail and weep,
English Richard ploughs the deep!

146

From Sion's turrets, as afar
Ye ken the march of Europe's war!
Saladin, thou paynim king,
From Albion's isle revenge we bring!
In vain to break our firm array,
Thy brazen drums hoarse discord bray:
Those sounds our rising fury fan:
English Richard in the van,
On to victory we go,—
A vaunting infidel the foe!'
    Soon we kissed the sacred earth
That gave a murdered Saviour birth!
Ye trampled tombs, ye fanes forlorn,
Ye stones, by tears of pilgrims worn;
Your ravished honours to restore,
Fearless we climb this hostile shore!
For thee, from Britain's distant coast,
Lo, Richard leads his faithful host!
Proud Saracen, pollute no more
The shrines by martyrs built of yore!
    'Salem, in ancient majesty
Arise, and lift thee to the sky!
Soon on the battlements divine
Shall wave the badge of Constantine.
Ye barons to the sun unfold
Our cross, with crimson wove and gold!'

Collected Works, 1791

Richard Knolles (1550–1610)

PETER THE HERMIT

He diligently noted by the way, as he travelled, the manners and fashions
of these barbarous nations, their government, their cities, their power and
strength; but, above all, the grievous miseries of the poor oppressed
Christians, that they lived in most miserable thraldom among them,
without hope of release; all which he in the habit of a poor pilgrim at
liberty safely viewed in the midst of these miscreants, being withal a
little low, hard-favoured fellow, and therefore in show more to be

condemned than feared; yet under such simple and homely feature lay unregarded a most subtle sharp and piercing wit, fraught with discretion and sound judgment, still applying to some good use what he had in his long and painful travel most curiously observed. He cometh to Jerusalem, and performing his devotions there, saw the grievous misery of the poor devout Christians, so great and heavy, as that greater or more intolerable could none be: wherewith not a little grieved, he entered into a deep discourse thereof with Simon the Patriarch and with the Master of the Hospitaliers. After much grave conference, it was at length agreed upon that the Patriarch and the Grand Master should write their letters unto the Pope and the other Christian Princes concerning their miseries, and to crave their aid for the recovery of those places out of the hands of those cruel Infidels: of which letters the devout Hermit promised himself to be the trusty carrier and of their petitions the most careful solicitor.

The Generall Historie of the Turks, 1603

Edward Gibbon (1737–1794)

A.D. 1099

... (A.D. 1099). Jerusalem has derived some reputation from the number and importance of her memorable sieges. It was not till after a long and obstinate contest that Babylon and Rome could prevail against the obstinacy of the people, the craggy ground that might supersede the necessity of fortifications, and the walls and towers that would have fortified the most accessible plain. The obstacles were diminished in the age of the crusades. The bulwarks had been completely destroyed, and imperfectly restored; the Jews, their nation and worship, were forever banished; but nature is less changeable than man, and the site of Jerusalem, though somewhat softened and somewhat removed, was still strong against the assaults of the enemy. By the experience of a recent siege, and a three years' possession, the Saracens of Egypt had been taught to discern and in some degree to remedy, the defects of a place which religion as well as honour forbade them resign. Aladin, or Iftikhar, the caliph's lieutenant, was intrusted with the defence: his policy strove to restrain the native Christians by the dread of their own ruin and that of the holy sepulchre; to animate the Moslems by the assurance of temporal and eternal rewards. His garrison is said to have consisted of forty thousand Turks and Arabians; and if he could muster twenty thousand of the inhabitants, it must be confessed that the besieged were more numerous than the besieging army. Had the diminished strength and number of the Latins allowed them to grasp the whole circumference of four thousand yards (about two English miles and a half) to what useful purpose should they have descended into the valley of Ben Hinnom and torrent of Cedron, or approached the precipices of the south and east, from whence they had nothing to fear or hope? Their siege was more reasonably directed against the northern and western sides of the city. Godfrey de Bouillon erected his standard on the first swell of the Mount Calvary: to the left, as far as St. Stephen's gate, the line of attack was continued by Tancred and the two Roberts; and Count Raymond established his quarters from the citadel to the foot of Mount Sion, which was no longer included within the precincts of the city. On the fifth day the crusaders made a general assault in the fanatic hope of battening down the walls without engines, and of scaling them without ladders. By the dint of brutal force, they burst the first barrier; but they were driven back with shame and slaughter, to the camp: the influence of vision and prophecy was deadened by the too frequent abuse of these pious strategems; and the time and labour were found to be the only means of victory. The time of siege was indeed fulfilled in forty days, but they were forty days of calamity and anguish. A repetition of the old complaint of famine may be imputed to some degree to the voracious and disorderly appetite of the Franks; but the stony soil of Jerusalem is almost destitute of water; the scanty springs and hasty torrents were dry in the summer season; nor was the thirst of the besiegers relieved, as in the city, by the artificial supply of the cisterns and aqueducts. The circumjacent country is equally destitute of trees for the use of shade or building; but some large beams were discovered in a cave by the crusaders: a wood near Sichem, the enchanted grove of Tasso, was cut down; the necessary timber was transported to the camp by the vigour and dexterity of Tancred; and the engines were framed by some Genoese artists, who had fortunately landed in the harbour of Jaffa. Two movable turrets were constructed at the expense, and in the stations, of the duke of Lorraine and the count of Tholouse, and rolled forward with devout labour, not to the most accessible, but to the most neglected, parts of the fortifications. Raymond's tower was reduced to ashes by the fire of the besieged, but his colleague was more vigilant and successful; the enemies were driven by his archers from the rampart; the drawbridge was let down; and on a Friday, at three in the afternoon, the day and hour of the Passion, Godfrey of Bouillon stood victorious on the walls of Jerusalem. His example was followed on every side by the emulation of valour; and about four hundred and sixty years after the conquest of Omar, the holy city was rescued from Mahometan yoke. In the pillage of public and private wealth, the adventurers had agreed to respect the exclusive property of the first occupant; and the spoils of the great mosque, seventy lamps and massy vases of gold and silver, rewarded the diligence and displayed the generosity of Tancred. A bloody sacrifice was offered by his mistaken votaries to the God of the Christians: resistance might provoke, but neither age nor sex could mollify, their implacable rage: they indulged themselves three days in a promiscuous massacre, and the infection of the dead bodies produced an epidemical disease. After seventy thousand Moslems had been put to the sword, and the harmless Jews had been put to death in their synagogue, they could still reserve a multitude of captives, whom interest or lassitude persuaded them to spare. Of these savage heroes of the cross, Tancred alone betrayed some sentiments of compassion; yet we may praise the more selfish lenity of Raymond, who granted a capitulation and safe-conduct of the garrison of the citadel. The holy sepulchre was now free; and the bloody victors prepared to accomplish their vow. Bareheaded and barefoot, with contrite hearts, and in humble posture, they ascended the hill of Calvary, amidst the loud anthems of the clergy; kissed the stone which had covered the Saviour of the world; and bedewed with tears of joy and penitence the monument of their redemption. This union of the fiercest and most tender passions had been variously considered by two philosophers: by the one, as easy and natural; by the other, as absurd and incredible. Perhaps it is too rigorously applied to the same persons and the same hour: the example of the virtuous Godfrey awakened the piety of his companions; while they cleansed their bodies, they purified their minds; nor shall I believe that the most ardent in slaughter and rapine were the foremost in the procession to the holy sepulchre.

Decline and Fall of the Roman Empire, 1788

Joseph Ha-Cohen (16th century)

IN THE YEAR 4856

In the reign of Philip, son of Henry, King of France, Peter the Hermit went to Jerusalem, saw the sufferings of the Christians who lived there and, on his return, related it to his brothers; this was in the year 4856, which is the year 1096. The Christian Kings then offered to go and conquer Judah and Jerusalem; from all countries there gathered an enormous concourse of men and women who would go with them, and with this year began a time of pitiless desolation for the Israelites in Christian countries, wherever they were scattered; and the times were such that they became sick of life; terrible and numberless were the afflictions which they bore, for there rose against them the multitude of France and of Germany which had gathered for the Crusade, an evil-faced multitude, which neither spared the aged nor took pity on children. Their cry was: 'Let us avenge our Saviour on the Jews, let us wipe them out from among the peoples, unless they accept another god and become Christians like ourselves: and only when this is accomplished will we set out.' When the Jews of Germany heard this, their hearts melted in them and became like water, and pain and trembling seized them as with a woman in labour; they lifted their eyes to heaven, set aside fast days and cried to the Eternal in their misery, but the Eternal had hidden himself behind clouds which no prayer could pierce. On the twenty-third day of the month the Crusaders descended like night wolves against the holy community of Worms, and many of the members took refuge in the house of the Bishop for fear of disaster. The attackers rushed into the houses and put to the sword whomsoever they found, sparing neither man nor woman; they sacked the houses, broke down the towers, and stretched out their hands to the plunder, and there was none to save from them in that day of divine wrath. They threw down the scrolls of the law, tore them to pieces and trampled them underfoot, and they shouted in the house of God as on a day of celebration, devouring Israel, and leaving alive but a small remnant, whom they forced to deny their God, the God of Israel, but who, when the fury was once passed, returned again to the God of their fathers. As to the slaughtered, they sanctified the Holy One of Israel in the open light, and chose death rather than life that they might not become faithless to God. Many immolated themselves, and this one slew his brother, or his friend, his beloved wife, his sons and daughters: tender mothers slaughtered with firm hand and heart their little children, and the little ones pronounced the Unity of God as they gave up their souls on the bosoms of their mothers.

Emek ha-Bacha (The Vale of Tears), A.D. 1575

Torquato Tasso (1544–1595)

THE CRUSADERS ARRIVE AT THE GATES

The purple morning left her crimson bed,
And donned her robes of pure vermilion hue,
Her amber locks she crowned with roses red,
In Eden's flowery gardens gathered new,
When through the camp a murmur shrill was spread,
Arm, arm, they cried; arm, arm, the trumpets blew,
   Their merry noise prevents the joyful blast,
    So hum small bees, before their swarms they cast . . .

Feathered their thoughts, their feet in wings were dight,
Swiftly they marched, yet were not tired thereby,
For willing minds make heaviest burdens light.
But when the gliding sun was mounted high,
Jerusalem, behold, appeared in sight,
Jerusalem they view, they see, they spy,
   Jerusalem with merry noise they greet,
    With joyful shouts, and acclamations sweet.

As when a troop of jolly sailors row
Some new found land and country to descry,
Through dangerous seas and under stars unknowe,
Thrall to the faithless waves, and trothless sky,
If once the wishèd shore begin to show,
They all salute it with a joyful cry,
   And each to other show the land in haste,
    Forgetting quite their pains and perils past.

To that delight which their first sight did breed,
That pleasèd so the secret of their thought
A deep repentance forthwith did succeed
That reverend fear and trembling with it brought,
Scantly they durst their feeble eyes dispreed
Upon that town, where Christ was sold and bought,
   Where for our sins he faultless suffered pain,
    There where he died and where he lived again . . .

Their naked feet trod on the dusty way,
Following the ensample of their zealous guide,
Their scarfs, their crests, their plumes and feathers gay,
They quickly doffed, and willing laid aside,
Their molten hearts their wonted pride allay,
Along their watery cheeks warm tears down slide,
    And then such secret speech as this, they used,
    While to himself each one himself accused.

'Flower of goodness, root of lasting bliss,
Thou well of life, whose streams were purple blood
That flowèd here, to cleanse the soul amiss
Of sinful man, behold this brinish flood,
That from my melting heart distilled is,
Receive in gree these tears, O Lord, so good,
    For never wretch with sin so overgone
    Had fitter time or greater cause to moan.'

Godfrey of Bulloigne or The Recoverie of Ierusalem. Book III,
translated by Edward Fairfax, 1600

Lope de Vega (1562–1635)

THE ORIENT'S CRADLE

She lies in Asia between the two mounts Carmel,
The Holy Land, upon Jordan reclining . . .

The Orient's cradle, bathed in light
Of that first dawn in snowy Bethlehem
And that setting of the sun,
The mortal bed of suffering Christ.

Will Jerusalem then be like the cloak
Of the divinest Captain, and the soldiers
Those Christian Kings of Europe
Casting lots over the seamless cloth?

Jerusalén Conquistada, Book I, translated from
the Spanish by Amalia Leguera

Imam Jalal-Addin Al Saycuti[1] (15th century)

THE DELIVERANCE FROM THE INFIDELS

The Temple of Jerusalem, from the time of the great victory, hath remained in the hands of the Musulmans, to be sought by pilgrims, and to be magnified in all successive ages; and still to remain in the power of Islam, with glory, perpetuated (if it please God Almighty) until the day of judgment shall arrive. May, then, the lover of symmetry enjoy much good in this clear collection of accounts respecting this victory!

To proceed—When God Almighty had transferred the consecrated Temple (to the Moslems) from the hands of the Christians, and had purified it from their dirt and their filth; when the victory was consummated, and affairs reduced to order;—the Sultan Salah-Uddin (upon whom may the mercy of God remain!) began to consider the means of perfecting that which God Almighty had established; namely to exalt the rallying word of the Faith. Therefore, for the rest of the year 593, he occupied himself in arranging large collections of money. He wrote to the people of the open country and to the dwellers in the chief cities, begging them to collect armies for the sacred war, and to send troops for the purpose of accomplishing those designs which his breast entertained respecting cutting off all places of strength or of value from the people of error, and deviators from the right road, and adversaries of the truth. To this they agreed, and came to join him from all quarters. And in the year 580 the Sultan Salah-Uddin set off from the Holy Land, and left Jerusalem, and all those coasts near to it. And his army laid waste the lands of the Franks far and wide, and cut down their trees, and all the constructions of these wanderers from truth, that were to be found.

And in the year 585 the Franks began to bestir themselves, and to burn with rage, and to be full of boiling fury; and all the priests and monks assembled, and they put on black garments, publicly to denote their indignation and sorrow. So the Franks rose in the morning, looking with an evil eye for slaughter; and they sallied forth, resembling a wide stream of locusts, and filled the land with their length and breadth. Then they began to attack single men. Then the Moslems hastened, and some of them stood their ground, and firmly closed their ranks. And the Sultan made with them a charge in right earnest, and made a tremendous slaughter of the Franks, and took the whole of them prisoners: and the

---

[1]Al Saycuti was an Arab historian believed to have been born in the year of the Hejira 848 (A.D. 1443). This is an extract from his *History of the Temple of Jerusalem*, translated by Rev. James Reynolds, London, 1836.

number of those slain on that day was ten thousand. So the Sultan commanded them, and they cast them into the river, of which the Franks drank. Battles continued between the Moslems and the Franks for eight days, being incessantly renewed by each party.

And there set out the King of Alman (Germany), who was the most eminent for insolence and haughtiness, and had expressed the most confident opinion that he would recapture the Consecrated Temple. Their number was about 160,000; but, one day, their king went down to bathe himself in a river near Antioch, and was drowned in a place where the water did not reach the middle of a man; and his son took the command after him. Nevertheless, the force of the divine destiny of the Lord caused them to perish on the road. Glory and power be ascribed to God! For he determines in equity.

Now there still continued much fighting with the Franks. The great Patriarch forbade them, under pain of God's curse, to enjoy any pleasure, and shut the gates of the churches. And they clothed themselves in mourning garments, and were straightly prohibited from approaching their wives. Nor were they to cease these observances until they should obtain an entrance into the Holy City. The siege of Akka lasted two years, and more than one hundred thousand Franks were killed in it. And in the year 588 peace took place between the Sultan Salah-Uddin and the infidels.

I will omit the enumeration of all that happened between the year 588 and 725, as also of the transactions with the Franks, and the Tartars and others—the expeditions, the numerous pitched battles, and the wars, the storms, and the sieges, and the migrations; because the minute explication would be long. (In order to expel) Nasir from Damascus Al Kamil called in the assistance of the Franks; upon which, Al Abruz, king of the Franks (Frederic Barbarossa), came forward with a great army; and Al Kamil gave him the Holy City, whose walls had been destroyed. This affair caused great grief to the Moslems; for the inhabitants of Jerusalem were left in the same town with the Franks; and the sound of the bells was plainly heard, whilst the *viva-voce* summons to prayer was mute. The Faith was struck dumb with surprise; for in every quarter where *those* were, *these* were also, even (associating) in their prayers; for the same place was used for their Infidelity, their Trinitarianism, and Temple of public concourse (for worship).

Now, the Prince Al-Nasir-Uddin, lord of Karak, earnestly desired to accomplish his blessed design, to rescue the Consecrated House from the hands of the Franks,—that wicked race who sit on one side in the saddle, hoping to receive a recompense both in this world and in the next. He assembled, then, a great array, and arranged them for the purpose of making a sudden attack upon the Franks, on the feast of the Temple, at a time when they would be negligent. Now the Christians were all occupied with their errors, their games, their infidelity, their Trinitarianism, and their drunkenness. Then the Musulmans kindled their lights, and raised up their standards, and cried out, Allah Akbar! and before the dawn of morning suddenly attacked the Christians in the very shrine of their infidelity and their Trinitarianism. Therefore they were astounded and stupefied when they heard the cry, Allah Akbar! from every quarter of Jerusalem. The Moslems then laid the sword on them, and continued to slay, to carry captive, and to plunder. The king then came to Al Nasir and his army, and began to call out loudly upon Al Nasir for an explanation of what had occurred. But he drew his sword, and cut off the head of the king of the Franks.[1] Upon this the Moslems shouted the Allah Akbar, and chanted the jubilate of praise. This massacre was terrific; nor did the dawn arise before the brilliant valour of the Moslems had prevailed. Thus God graciously prospered this sudden attack and illustrated his saying, 'The work incumbent on you shall not be a grief.'

There was an Ode, or Didactic Poem, by Ibn Nabat, the Egyptian, wherein Al Nasir was panegyrized. This poem was of the kind called 'The Long'. The following couplets were contained in it:—'Truly a regular recurring train of vicissitudes seems to be the lot of the Mosque Al Aksa. It undergoes one change, and again reiterates a similar course. First, its turn was to be an abiding-place for the Infidels; then God sent unto it Nasir (a protector). Thus Nasir purified it first, and Nasir purified it last.' Then did the tongues of men utter prayer and praise; and now, at this moment, may we praise the Giver of good success! He who hath assembled Victory, Power, and Conquest, in one abiding-place, which is the Baitu-l-Mukaddas[2]—that point of direction, and goal whereunto we must perform pilgrimage; which we must magnify, until the conclusion of the revolting course of years!

From *History of Jerusalem*, translated from the Arabic by the Rev. James Reynolds, London, 1836

---

[1] In fact, Barbarossa was drowned during the crusade in Syria in 1190.

[2] Another Arabic name for Jerusalem.

Hilaire Belloc (1870–1953)

IN SIGHT OF THE CITY

Jerusalem, with its large Egyptian Fatimite garrison, was close at hand; by the time the Crusaders got to Ramleh it was only one day's riding away—say twenty-five miles by the shorter of the two roads. They therefore broke the rule they had hitherto followed of keeping all together; they left a small garrison in Ramleh to guard against surprise and made for the uplands of the Holy City. For three days they stood at Ramleh, at the foot of the final ascent.

This halt at Ramleh was used for a last council of war. It is interesting that one of its members boldly proposed to neglect Jerusalem for the moment and march straight on Egypt, arguing that if they could hold Cairo they would hold all Palestine as well; for it was the heretic Mohammedans of Egypt who now held Jerusalem and the Holy Land.

On Monday, the sixth of June, the little column—we may call it little for the task it had undertaken and in comparison with the great body of which it was the last poor survivor—set out upon the rising road. On the morning of the next day, Tuesday the seventh, they at last saw their goal, dark against the morning sun—the flat domes, the few towers and the long line of the western wall, standing sharply against what was then bare, stony and empty land, a slight lift of which hides the Holy City from the sea.

As they came nearer to the object of all that terrible journey, the end of those two years of marching through enemy lands, of continual combat, famine, desertion and waste of every kind, this elect, this sacred band, which had endured to the end, was filled with glamour. They were illuminated, entranced, moved by one of those enthusiasms which breed triumph. Already outriders had visited Bethlehem, and in the rare words of those who witnessed the thing, you feel the vibration of their souls. Here are those words:

'In procession did they (that is, the Christians of Bethlehem) lead them (the hundred Christian knights led by Tancred, who had galloped all night to reach Bethlehem) to the Church built on the place where the Glorious Mother brought forth the Saviour of the world: there did they set eyes on that cradle where lay the Beloved Child Who was also the Maker of Heaven and of Earth; and the people of the town for joy and for proof that God and their leader would give our people victory, took Tancred's banner and set it high over the Church before the Mother of God.'

The encirclement of Jerusalem was accomplished within a week; to the Norman tents on the north side opposite the Damascus Gate were added in their order the men following Robert of Flanders, who pitched camp at the corner of the walls, where they turn down southwards towards the citadel at the Jaffa Gate. In front of that citadel and the Jaffa Gate itself Godfrey and Tancred stood guard.

On the Monday, the sixth day after the first sight of the city, all was thought ready for attack and an assault was made; but it just failed, for lack of leaders. And naturally, seeing the failure of the assault, that failure cost the besiegers dearly in lives. Further, it meant the necessity for a fully ordered formal siege, and the peril of this lay in the lack of water. Once more the test had come, as at Dorylaeum, as at Antioch, in the torrid heat of an Eastern summer. Skins had to be filled even as far off as the Jordan, and brought on camels from over twenty miles away and up more than three thousand feet. The few stagnant pools remaining were quite insufficient for the fifteen thousand armed men and as many pilgrims and followers. It was further necessary to build engines, catapults and high moving towers and all that was required for the attack on the walls.

The besieged within, under the Fatimite commander of the garrison, Iftikkar Al Dawla, had plenty of supply and plenty of material to construct their great machines for hurling stones. The besiegers, in that denuded country, wherein so many centuries of Mohammedan rule had already destroyed nearly all the trees, had to send far and wide for the scanty wood they needed. The council of war, two days after the first assault, decided on the immediate building of the movable towers, ladders and catapults. Whether there were sufficient local supplies of material is doubtful, but happily the day after the morrow two galleys from Genoa anchored before Jaffa, bringing not only cargoes of food, but timber as well.

A hundred knights of Provence rode down to make contact with the Genoese and the move was made only just in time; a body of Moslem ships from Ascalon attacked just after the cargoes had been landed, and the Genoese barely escaped; but they escaped with their task accomplished. The energy and rapidity of the Crusaders, even after such a march and in such a foreign burning air, amazes the reader of those chronicles today. Within twenty-four hours the whole mass of material had been transferred to the camps of the besiegers, north, west and south of the city. And still the enthusiasm rose, and still that exaltation, in which all things seem possible and the miracles of history are accomplished, continued. The passing of the days, the increasingly impossible heat, did not check this rising mood. Adhemar the Legate, long dead, he who had lent that unity of command to the host (which had since been so grievously lacking, but was now for a moment recovered) appeared in a dream to one who then preached the marvel throughout the ranks.

A general fast was ordered. When the completion of the engines approached, the army marched in procession round the walls (it was upon the eighth of July). They went in solemn train, chanting the holy chants, from the Mount of Olives, round by the north and west to Zion hill; and all the walls were crowded with the Negroes and the Saracens, jeering at them and their chanting—planting crosses in full sight of the Christians, which they spat upon and otherwise defiled, until the warriors singing in columns below cried out that they would soon avenge this dishonour done to Jesus Christ. It was the Friday, the day of the Passion of the Lord, that these things were done.

Under cover of the Saturday night, Godfrey and Robert of Flanders and the Duke of Normandy brought up the wooden wheeled castles against that part of the north wall which lies east of the Damascus Gate, standing on a traditional spot where St. Stephen was stoned. Further west they could not attack, for the defences were too strong. On the Sunday morning the garrison in the first dawn were astonished to see the high wooden stages topping the wall and threatening escalade.

The main assault was not delivered until the third night, the night of the Wednesday, the 13th–14th of July. On the fourteenth the hammering at the walls continued and the counter hurling of great stones from within, and the rain of Greek fire with which the garrison sought to destroy the wheeled towers in spite of their covering of horse-skins. So all that day the furious attempt blazed on; but they never got a foothold on the wall, thrown back perpetually by the flame-bearing arrows, the Greek fire and the hot oil poured upon every effort to scale. It was not till the morning of the Friday, the fifteenth, that the first of the besiegers forced his way in, bursting forward along the gangways from the towers to the summits of the wall.

Who was the first man into the city we shall never know; local legend is not to be despised, and I have always hoped that it was indeed that Lord of Sourdeval, the Norman from the Cotentin. But those who were with Godfrey and his brother, Eustace of Boulogne, on the high wooden tower will have it that when, about noon, two Flemings pushed a gangway forward, these were the first in Jerusalem, Godfrey and Eustace themselves immediately following. But no eye-witness can tell us to whom this honour should fall, for simultaneously by the north and south the eager armed groups were mounting the scaling ladders and holding the wall upon either side. The host poured in, the garrison fell back upon the height of the Temple enclosure—where a violent resistance ended in general massacre.

That massacre spread from the great Mosque throughout the city. Tancred had attempted to check it, but the madness of the successful attack, coming after the violent insults and provocations, was too strong for any orders to be heard. The wholesale killing went on all that Friday afternoon; it continued on the Saturday; at last before night it was ended. The garrison of the Fatimite Caliphs of Egypt, their black soldiers and their trained Arab bands had perished together. Such few as survived paid ransom, and it makes us understand what the temper of the moment was that when the Count of Toulouse accepted such ransom from one unhappy victim, hardly spared, the cry of avarice arose against him.

This carnage—a thing of uncalculated fury—was politically an error. It was claimed by some of those from whom we have the tale that the terror of that Friday broke down all resistance and made certain of victory throughout the land. It is the very plea of those who defend Cromwell and his massacres in Drogheda and Wexford. But there is another side to the question, and a more important one. Ever since the Crusaders had come down towards the sea from Ma'arret the policy of conciliation, of tolerance, which was politically a policy of alliance between the petty Moslem chiefs and the Crusaders, had been fruitful. The awful story of what had happened at Jerusalem would make the pursuit of such a policy for the future more difficult. It is true that those who had fallen in the Holy City (holy to the besieged as to the besiegers) were not the amenable and free chiefs of the Lebanon, but of a very different sort, mercenaries of the Egyptian Caliph who had turned from a proposed alliance and had become an enemy to the death. It is also true that when the shock of the news came to Baghdad it stunned and paralysed that capital of Islam, instead of provoking reaction and a holy war. Whether it were politically serviceable or not (and it was not serviceable) the massacre was an ill ending.

But the great march had been accomplished, the objective had been reached—just barely reached—by one fragment left from the half-million that had set their faces first from Nicaea towards the East. Of those who had cried 'Jerusalem! Jerusalem!' throughout two years and a thousand miles of way, not one in twenty came up at last to the town.

The World's Debate, 1937

Jehan de Neuville (12th century)

JHERUSALEM, GRANT DAMAGE ME FAIS

There is grief in Jerusalem and grief in the land
Where the Lord of His goodness, in suffering died,
That on this side the sea, few are the friends to God
And scarce the help they bring.

If each could but remember the judgment to come,
The holy place where God His agony hath borne,
And to Longius forgave the final wound of death,
Loath is he then to turn from his Crusade.

For whoso takes the Cross for God, pure though he be,
When he but forsakes the Cross; then his God denies.
So he, with Judas, be lost to Paradise.

> *Les Chansons des Croisades*, translated from the
> Old French by Rachel Melrose

Ambroise[1] (13th century)

THE PREACHING OF THE THIRD CRUSADE

Who has a lengthy tale to tell
Must needs watch carefully and well,
Lest he begin by taking on
A task that he cannot make done.
So let him to his task attend
That he may bring it to good end;
Thus, that my burden be not too
Heavy, I start without ado.
My care I fain would dedicate
To matter worthy to relate,
Which tells the troubles dolorous
That rightfully afflicted us
In Syria, but yesteryear,
Where our rank folly cost us dear,

---

[1]Ambroise was a minstrel in Richard Lionheart's service.

161

L

Which God could not do otherwise
Than make us sorely realise:
He made us feel it certainly
In France, likewise in Normandy,
As well as through all Christendom,
Where much or little it had come.
In little time he made us feel
It, by that cross at which all kneel
And which was then by pagan hand
Transported to another land
Than that where it was wont to lie,
Where God deigned to be born and die . . .
Then stilled was joy of word or tongue,
Stilled was the dancing, hushed the song
And hushed the joy and hushed the mirth
Of Christian folk throughout the earth,
Until the Pope of Rome, through whom
God has saved many men from doom
(He was the eighth called Gregory,
So it is told in history),
Proclaimed a grace of sovereign might
For God and in the devil's spite:
That he should have all sins forgiven
Who would attack those foes of heaven
Who had despoiled in very sooth
The great and noble King of Truth.

Estoire de la guerre sainte, translated from the Old
French by Merton Jerome Hubert, New York, 1941

Sir Walter Scott (1771–1832)

RICHARD AND SALADIN

The hermit followed the ladies from the pavilion of Richard, as shadow
follows a beam of sunshine when the clouds are driving over the face of
the sun. But he turned on the threshold, and held up his hand towards
the King in a warning, or almost a menacing posture, as he said: 'Woe
to him who rejects the counsel of the Church, and betaketh himself to the
foul divan of the infidel! King Richard, I do not yet shake the dust from

my feet and depart from thy encampment—the sword falls not—but it hangs but by a hair.—Haughty monarch, we shall meet again.'

'Be it so, haughty priest,' returned Richard, 'prouder in thy goatskins than princes in purple and fine linen.'

The hermit vanished from the tent and the King continued, addressing the Arabian—'Do the dervises of the East, wise Hakim, use such familiarity with their princes?'

'The dervise,' replied Abondec, 'should be either a sage or a madman; there is no middle course for him who wears the khirkhah, who watches by night, and fasts by day. Hence, hath he either wisdom enough to bear himself discreetly in the presence of princes, or else, having no reason bestowed on him, he is not responsible for his own actions.'

'Methinks our monks have adopted chiefly the latter character,' said Richard. 'But to the matter.—In what can I pleasure you, my learned physician?'

'Great King,' said El Hakim, making his profound Oriental obeisance, 'let thy servant speak onward, and yet live. I would remind thee that thou owest—not to me, their humble instrument—but to the Intelligences, whose benefits I dispense to mortals, a life—'

'And I warrant me thou wouldst have another in requital, ha?' interrupted the King.

'Such is my humble prayer,' said the Hakim, 'to the great Melech Ric—even the life of this good knight, who is doomed to die, and but for such fault as was committed by the Sultan Adam, surnamed Aboulbeschar, or the father of all men.'

'And thy wisdom might remind thee, Hakim, that Adam died for it,' said the King, somewhat sternly, and then began to pace the narrow space of his tent with some emotion, and to talk to himself. 'Why, God-a-mercy—I knew what he desired as soon as ever he entered the pavilion!—Here is one poor life justly condemned to extinction, and I, a king and a soldier, who have slain thousands by my command, and scores with my own hand, and to have no power over it, although the honour of my arms, of my house, of my very Queen, hath been attained by the culprit?—By Saint George, it makes me laugh! By St. Louis, it reminds me of Blondel's tale of an enchanted castle, where the destined knight was withstood successfully in his purpose of entrance by forms and figures the most dissimilar, but all hostile to his undertaking! No sooner one sunk than another appeared! Wife—Kinswoman—Hermit—Hakim—each appears in the list as soon as the other is defeated!—Why, this is a single knight fighting against the whole mêlée of the tournament—ha! ha! ha!

The Talisman, 1825

VII Messiah

Jesus was not considered as the Messiah by most of his Jewish contemporaries, and the high priest sternly refused to treat him as such in the Sanhedrin. The new Christian concept derived from the fact that Jesus, while accepting the Messianic mission, stripped it of all political and national significance. In Christian literature, the idea of the Messiah embraces the whole work of redemption, and also the spiritual regeneration performed by Jesus. It is the single instance in the history of the world when God and man are fused. It is by the same token a unique moment which must either be accepted or rejected.

With the dispersal of the Jews, Palestine ceased to be a Jewish national centre in the racial sense, and was not to be one again until the 20th century. Despairing of secular ambitions when confronted with the ruthless conquerors who were to affect their destinies in every country but their own, the dispersed people put their faith for the regeneration of their homeland in Messiah—the 'Anointed of the Lord'. Isaiah, Micah, Hosea had all referred to the king of the future, the deliverer of the nation; while post-exilic writings carried on in this strain with even greater confidence. There were Messianic expectations prior to the notion of a unique personal Deliverer. The chief elements in these early conceptions of the Messiah were: He will be a descendant of David; He will be the ideal king, whose mind and action shall be in full harmony with the will of God, in whose days and through whom God will make good all His promises, and who will lead all men to honour the God of Israel. With the Messiah's arrival the age-long covenant between the people and the Lord would be fulfilled.

The Diaspora and the long residence among strange peoples and strange gods gave the Jewish thinkers and prophets a new conception of the world. The faith in Messiah transcends races, languages and customs to become world-embracing. God will establish His rule through the 'coming of the Kingdom' ('one thousand years of blessedness'), but not in Israel alone and not for the sole benefit of His chosen people.

Jerusalem, spiritual head of the world, thus appeared in all literatures as the natural and only centre where Messiah's return can be celebrated and the 'divine kingdom of righteousness and peace on earth' be ushered in.

MESSIAH AMONG THE ARABS

David ha-Reubeni, who had proclaimed himself Messiah of Israel, came to Jerusalem from Haibar in Arabia. He was on his way to Rome to petition the Pope for help in his endeavour to restore the Jewish people to their land.

In the month of Adar in the year 1523, he entered the Mosque of Omar (Dome of the Rock), and he relates the following: 'When I entered the Temple all the Arab guards came to prostrate themselves before me and kissed my feet, and they said: 'Come, you blessed of the Lord, our Master, the son of our Master.' Then two of the chief guards led me to the cave which is beneath the Stone of Foundation, and they said to me, 'Here prayed Elijah the prophet, and here King David, and here prayed Mohammed!' I said to the guards, 'Now that I know all this, go your way, for I wish to pray here alone.' I remained in the Temple, and I fasted five weeks, no bread did I eat, and no water passed my lips, except on the eve of Sabbath.

Now on the top of the Dome of the Rock there is a crescent which faces westward. On the first day of the Feast of Pentecost (*Shabuot*), this crescent was seen to face the East, and when the Arabs saw this, they shouted in alarm. I asked them, 'Why do you shout?' and they answered, 'Because of our sins this crescent has turned towards the East, which is an evil omen to the Arabs.'

A workman climbed to the Dome and turned the crescent to its former position, but on the next day it was again facing the East. And the Arabs continued to shout and to weep as they vainly tried to turn the crescent.

Then I knew that it was time to leave Jerusalem, for the wise men had told me, 'When you behold this sign, it is time to proceed to Rome!'

Legends of Palestine,
collected by Zev Vilnay, 1932

Cynewulf (737–780)

THE KING OF GLORY

O holy Jerusalem,   Vision of peace,
Fairest of royal seats,   City of Christ,
Homeland of angels,   in thee for ever
Rest the souls   of the righteous alone
In glory exulting.   No sign of sin
In that city-dwelling   shall ever be seen,
But from thee all evil   shall flee afar,
All trouble and toil.   Thou art wondrously filled
With holy hope,   as thy name is named.
  Lift up thine eyes   on the wide creation,
The dome of heaven,   on every hand;
Behold His coming;   the King of Glory
Himself approaches   to seek thee out,
To abide in thee,   as the blessed prophets
In their books foretold   the birth of the Christ,
To they comfort spoke,   thou fairest of cities!
Now is the Babe come   born to transform
The works of the Hebrews.   He brings thee bliss,
Looses thy bondage,   draws nigh unto men,
For He only knows   their harrowing need,
How man in his wretchedness   waits upon mercy.

Christe, Boston edition, 1900

Alexander Pope (1688–1744)

MESSIAH

Ye Nymphs of Solyma! begin the song:
To heav'nly themes sublimer strains belong.
The mossy fountains, and the sylvan shades,
The dreams of Pindus and th'Aonian maids,
Delight no more—O thou my voice inspire
Who touched Isaiah's hallow'd lips with fire!
  Rapt into future times, the Bard begun:
A Virgin shall conceive, a Virgin bear a Son!
From Jesse's root behold a branch arise,
Whose sacred flow'r with fragrance fills the skies:

168

Th'Aethereal spirit o'er its leaves shall move,
And on its top descends the mystic Dove.

*

See by bright altars throng'd with prostrate Kings,
And heap'd with products of Sabaean springs!
For thee Idume's spicy forests blow,
And seeds of gold in Ophir's mountains glow.
See heav'n its sparkling portals wide display,
And break upon thee in a flood of day!
No more the rising Sun shall gild the morn,
Nor ev'ning Cynthia fill her silver horn;
But lost, dissolv'd in thy superior rays
One tide of glory, one unclouded blaze
O'erflow thy courts: the light himself shall shine
Reveal'd, and God's eternal day be thine!
The seas shall waste, the skies in smoke decay,
Rocks fall to dust, and mountains melt away;
But fix'd his word, his saving pow'r remains;—
Thy realm for ever lasts, thy own Messiah reigns!

From *Messiah*, a sacred eclogue in imitation of Virgil.
First published in *The Spectator*, 1712

Charles Wesley (1707-1788)

THE JUDGEMENT

Lo! He comes with clouds descending
   Once for favoured sinners slain;
Thousand thousand saints attending.
   Swell the triumph of his train;
   Hallelujah!
God appears on earth to reign.

Every eye shall now behold him
   Robed in dreadful majesty;
Those who set at nought and sold him,
   Pierced and nailed him to the tree,
   Deeply wailing
Shall the true Messiah see.

Maimonides (1135-1204)

THE MESSIAH

Let it not enter your mind that the Messiah will perform miracles, or create new things, or resurrect the dead, as the stupid relate; we must await nothing of this kind. Rabbi Akiba, one of our greatest scholars in the Mishna, was equerry to Bar Kozba; he, and the scholars of his time, took him to be the Messiah until the day he was killed (for his sins) and only then did they know that he was not the Messiah. These sages asked of him neither signs nor miracles. But an important principle is that our Torah, and its precepts and commandments, are eternal; nothing can be added and nothing taken away; whosoever does this, or whosoever brings a different sense into the Torah, or interprets it so as to change it, should be treated as an impostor, a criminal and a despiser of the Law. If therefore there should arise a king of the race of David, who will turn his spirit toward the Torah, and, like his forefather, David, will practise both the written and the oral commandments of the Law, and if he shall cause all Israel to live according to the Law and to strengthen it; and if his labour prospers, and if he conquers the surrounding peoples, rebuilds the Temple and reassembles the scattered remnants of Israel, then there will be no doubt: it will be the true Messiah. But if fortune does not attend his labours, if he falls in combat, then it was not he whom the promises announced: he is only like the other pious kings of the House of David who have been defeated, and God will have sent him to be a trial to great numbers of men, as it is said: 'And some of them of understanding shall fall, to try them, and to purge, and to make them white, even to the time of the end.' (Daniel). As for the man who shall give himself out as the Anointed, and who, in consequence, shall suffer the just punishment of death—what greater error could there have been? All the prophets had proclaimed that the Messiah would redeem the children of Israel and would deliver them from their sufferings, that he would reassemble the dispersed and would strengthen them in the observance of the commandments, while this man brought it about that Israel, as a nation, should be destroyed by the sword, should be scattered and humiliated; he introduced changes into the Law, and brought the world to err in adoring something outside of the true God. Nevertheless, no human mind can apprehend the designs of the Creator, for His ways are not our ways; so that this man, like the founders of all other later religions, has served to make smooth the way for the true Messiah, who shall bring all the peoples of the world to the one service of God, as it is said: 'For then will I turn to the people a pure language, that they may all call upon the name of the Lord, to serve him with one consent.' (Zephaniah iii: 9). Thanks to these new religions, the world has been filled with the idea of a Messiah-Redeemer, and with the words of the Law and the commandments; these words have now been spread to the furthest islands, and to numerous peoples which are barbarous; all of them to-day study the words of the Torah and are exercised by the question of its validity; some assert that the Commandments of the Torah are true, but have now been abrogated; others give them a secret meaning, and say that their contents have already been realized; but when the true Messiah will come, all will be converted and will recognize their errors.

The Guide of the Perplexed, translated from the Hebrew by M. Friedlander, 1885

TO THE JEWS OF MOROCCO

Fez, about 1160

I have no patience with people who console themselves with the thought that the Messiah will soon appear and lead them to Jerusalem. They who remain in the country, expecting the Messiah, are causing others to transgress the Law. Besides there is no definite time for which the appearance of the Messiah is foretold. It is not known whether his coming will be in the near future or at some remote period. A sincere wish to observe the Jewish law has no relation to the appearance of the Messiah.

TO JACOB AL FAYUMI AND TO THE JEWS OF YEMEN

Cairo, 1172

Regarding the manner in which the Messiah will present himself, and the place where his operations will begin, let me offer some information. It would seem that the land of the patriarchs is destined to be first trodden by his steps . . . but touching his presentation to our notice, it will not happen until events shall prove him worthy of our confidence. I mean, that he will not commend himself to our allegiance by reason of his distinguished descent, but the marvellous deeds he shall perform will show him to be the expected Messiah. . . . And after having revealed himself in the Holy Land, having gathered the dispersed in Jerusalem and received recognition from countries nearer to Palestine, the fame of our nation through him will spread eastward and westward, reaching at length you of South Arabia, and those still further in India, who will acknowledge the mission of our leader. . . .

171

Cairo, last quarter of the 12th century

Thus says Moses the son of Rabbi Maimon, one of the exiles from Jerusalem, who lived in Spain:

I received the question of the master Obadiah, the wise and learned proselyte, may the Lord reward him for his work, may a perfect recompense be bestowed upon him by the Lord of Israel, under whose wings he has sought cover.

Maimonides Epistolae

Chasdai Ibn Shaprut (915–970 or 990)

KING JOSEPH ANSWERS THE KHAZARS

With reference to your question concerning the marvellous end,[1] our eyes are turned to the Lord our God, and to the wise men of Israel who dwell in Jerusalem and Babylon. Though we are far from Zion, we have heard that because of our iniquities the computations are erroneous; nor do we know aught concerning this. But if it please the Lord, He will do it for the sake of His great name; nor will the desolation of His house, the abolition of His service, and all the troubles which have come upon us, be lightly esteemed in His sight. He will fulfil His promise, and 'the Lord whom ye seek shall suddenly come to His temple, the messenger of the Covenant whom ye delight in: behold he shall come, saith the Lord of Hosts' (Mal. iii. 1). Besides this we only have the prophecy of Daniel. May God hasten the redemption of Israel, gather together the captives and dispersed, you and I, and all Israel that love His name, in the lifetime of us all.

Finally, you mention that you desire to see my face. I also long and desire to see your honoured face, to behold your wisdom and magnificence. Would that it were according to your word, and that it were granted me to be united with you, so that you might be my father and I your son. All my people would pay homage to you: according to your word and righteous counsel we should go out and come in. Farewell.

Miscellany of Hebrew Literature, translated from the Hebrew by A.I.K.D., 1893

[1] The restoration of the Jews to their former glory by the Messiah.

Benjamin Disraeli (1804–1881)

DAVID ALROY BEHOLDS JERUSALEM

And Alroy gazed upon the silent loneliness of earth, and a tear stole down his haughty cheek.

'This is singular! but when I am thus alone at this still hour, I ever fancy I gaze upon the Land of Promise. And often, in my dreams, some sunny spot, the bright memorial of a roving hour, will rise upon my sight, and, when I wake, I feel as if I had been in Canaan. Why am I not? The caravan that bears my uncle's goods across The Desert would bear me too. But I rest here, my miserable life running to seed in the dull misery of this wretched city, and do nothing. Why! the old captivity was empire to our inglorious bondage. We have no Esther now to share their thrones, no politic Mordechai, no purple-vested Daniel. O Jerusalem, Jerusalem! I do believe one sight of thee would nerve me to the sticking point. And yet to gaze upon thy fallen state, my uncle tells me that of the Temple not a stone remains. 'Tis horrible. Is there no hope?'

*

To his infinite astonishment he beheld Jerusalem. That strongly-marked locality could not be mistaken: at his feet were Jehoshaphat, Kedron, Siloam; he stood upon Olivet; before him was Sion. But in all other respects, how different was the landscape from the one that he had gazed upon a few days back, for the first time! The surrounding hills sparkled with vineyards, and glowed with summer palaces, and voluptuous pavilions, and glorious gardens of pleasure. The city, extending all over Mount Sion, was encompassed with a wall of white marble, with battlements of gold; a gorgeous mass of gates and pillars, and gardened terraces; lofty piles of rarest materials, cedar and ivory, and precious stones; and costly columns of the richest workmanship and the most fanciful orders, capitals of the lotus and the palm, and flowing friezes of the olive and the vine.

And in the front a mighty Temple rose, with inspiration in its very form; a Temple so vast, so sumptuous, that there needed no priest to tell us that no human hand planned that sublime magnificence!

'God of my fathers,' said Alroy.

The Wondrous Tale of Alroy, 1833

PART TWO The Image of Jerusalem

VIII Behold the City: sightseers and wayfarers

> *Walk about Zion, and go round about her:*
> *That ye may tell it to the generation following*
> Psalm xlviii. 12, 13.

> *Ten measures of beauty came down;*
> *nine were taken by Jerusalem and one by*
> *the rest of the world.*
> *Talmud: Kiddushim,* 49 B.C.

Equal in impressiveness to its extended and dramatic history through time is Jerusalem's visual reality in space. Emphatically not a city of ruins (few Biblical and pre-Christian sites can be described as having been truly identified), Jerusalem is perhaps nearer architecturally to the ancient part of Rome than to Athens. It lies at the end of a barren limestone plateau on which valleys converge, such as the steep-sided valley of Hinnom, enclosed on the south by the 'Hill of Evil Counsel' (that of Judas Iscariot). Jerusalem is actually built on four hills, though their outline is now hardly discernible through the centuries-old debris covering the intervening valleys. The vista embracing this lofty quartet is memorable. The sides of the hills are beautifully terraced, bright with flowers—cyclamens, geraniums, roses.

Within the old city walls, the thrice holy history of Jerusalem announces itself in a varied and poetic nomenclature: Herod's Gate is known to the Arabs as *bab es-jahireh* (Gate of Flowers), while St. Stephen's Gate (where the saint was reputedly stoned) is in Arabic both *bab es-asbat* (Gate of the Tribes) and *bab es-sitti maryam* (Gate of our Lady Mary). Damascus Gate, the most impressive and at present the main entrance to the old city, is for Jews *Shaan Shechem* while the Arabs call it *bab el-amud* (Gate of the Pillars). Zion Gate is also the 'Gate of the Prophet David'.

A detailed itinerary would here hardly be in place: we should rather touch on the more significant facets of the city's structure and essence to help the reader grasp their historical and spiritual impact. For instance, most authorities identify the site of the Holy Sepulchre with Golgotha (in Hebrew *gulgoleth*, meaning skull).

From earliest times the Church was composite, and was to become more so, at the cost of artistic integrity in its architecture. (But this is to some extent accounted for by the successive fury of destructive conquerors, Persian and Saracen.) Rebuilding of the Sepulchre occurred in the middle of the 11th century, but the crusaders did not find the new edifice worthy of so sublime a purpose and site. Later a French architect, Maître Jourdain, erected a Romanesque ensemble, more harmonious than any of the former or later structures. Barely surviving the great fire of 1808, the whole was remodelled, not in the best taste perhaps, with a group of Franco-Russian architects adding in 1869 an 'iron-fitted cupola'. Within, the pillar by the entrance is the 'Stone of Unction' where Christ's body is said to have been laid for anointing. In the Chapel of the Holy Sepulchre, forty-three lamps, unceasingly alight, illuminate the marble-cased tomb in which Joseph of Arimathea and Nicodemus are traditionally believed to have laid the crucified Christ. (Their own reputed tombs are in the Chapel of the Syrians.) The labyrinth of relics leads from the Column of the Flagellation to the controversial site of the resurrected Christ's meeting with Mary Magdalene; from the lance of the centurion Longinus the way leads to the Column of Derision and to an altar with two holes in which Christ's feet were allegedly placed before the Crucifixion.

Irrepressible rivalry between the many denominations saddens the history of the place. Each Christian sect continues to celebrate its own rite. To the Greek Orthodox belongs the curious Chapel of Adam, deep beneath the Golgotha Rock: legend has it that Adam, buried there, was revivified by drops of Christ's blood on the cross. A dramatic height is reached in front of a marble slab pierced with holes which are believed to be those for the bases of the Three Crosses. A few yards to the left, one can see the 'Cleft in the Rock', caused when 'the veil of the Temple was rent in twain from the top to the bottom, and the earth did quake, and the rocks rent'.

In Holy Week the Sepulchre area is alive with a whole variety of spectacles. On Good Friday, for instance, the Franciscans nail a figure to the Cross; but perhaps the most memorable rites of all are the Orthodox and Armenian, called the 'Miracle of the Holy Fire', where thousands of pilgrims rush with candles and tapers to kindle flames in the minute Chapel of the Angel, containing a marble stone which 'closed the door of the sepulchre'.

The whole vicinity is rich in religious institutions and monologues contradicting each other. Typical of Jerusalem is the controversy between the Greek Orthodox and the Abyssinians, as to which olive-tree (that in Abraham's Chapel or the one of the Abyssinian Monastery) is the genuine plant in which the first of the Patriarchs entangled the horns of the ram sacrificed by him in place of his son Isaac.

Beyond the Christian monuments, a single walk through the old city takes the visitor to the Jewish Wailing Wall and the Moslem *Haram-esh-Sharif* (The Venerable Sanctuary). Not that this positioning implies sympathy between the two Semitic faiths: indeed, in 1929, the mere rumour that the Jews intended to build an open-air synagogue in front of the Wailing Place was enough to occasion one of the most violent riots. For the Moslems, this is a most sacred site, for here Mohammed tied up his mare after his miraculous flight from Medina in a single night. The Wailing Wall (*Kotel Hama' aravi*) was ever since A.D. 70 one of the most tragic yet hopeful of the world's sites; a whole race has come here for centuries to mourn the destruction of the Second Temple. Surrounded by a mosque and by the Moslem Religious Courts, visitors to Jerusalem could see an island of inextinguishable Jewry. The bareness and almost primeval grandeur of the Wall itself, with its vast limestone blocks (part of which are believed by both Jews and Moslems to have belonged to Solomon's Temple), has added to the city a sense of pathos and persistent hope. In the 4th century St. Jerome referred movingly to the Jewish mourners who reached the Wailing Wall by bribing Roman soldiers. People still insert pieces of paper bearing prayers into the crevices between the stones. And in 1967 battle-hardened Israeli soldiers wept when they had made their way to the Wall.

In a truly lordly area, on Mount Moriah's summit, where the Hebrew Temple once stood, is now the 'Dome of the Rock', surrounded by raised places for prayer and exquisite fountains. The decorative genius of the Arabs is manifest in the pavements lined with mosaics. The same artistry appears in the Dome itself with its superb calligraphies (white on blue enamel). This remarkable monument has often changed hands between Moslems and Christians, but fortunately the artistic result was not spoilt. Few religious buildings excel this Dome in its wealth of legends, where Moslem and Talmudic imagery unite. The Sacred Rock 'hovers over the waters of the flood', is 'the centre of the earth', the place 'where Abraham offered his son Isaac', and the place 'from

M

which Mohammed was translated into heaven'. The Last Judgment, too, is to take place in the Valley of Jehosaphat nearby. Below the Dome, a tongue of the rock 'replied' to the Prophet's greetings; the places of prayer of David, Solomon and Elijah are still pointed out to pilgrims and travellers; while the souls of the dead meet for prayer in the cavity called the 'Well of the Spirits'. Not far away are Solomon's Stables, described already by John of Würzburg in the 12th century, and a small chamber called the 'Cradle of Christ', where the babe is said to have been circumcized.

Volumes both mystical and scientific have been written depicting still more buildings within the city's walls: the Church of St. Anne; the resplendent Armenian Patriarchate (capable of accommodating several thousand pilgrims); the Palace of Caiaphas (with 'the prison of Christ' and the altar-stone 'rolled away from Christ's tomb'); the Tomb of David, *nebi Daud*, which paradoxically, also contains the *Coenaculum*, or Chamber of Christ's Last Supper —a splendid symbol of the trinity of faiths.

Most vital of all for Christian visitors is the *Via Dolorosa*, a narrow street intense with religious associations. High and often picturesque, it is at least thirty feet above the road supposed to have been traversed by Christ. Tablets in the walls denote the Fourteen Stations, such as Pilate's Judgment Hall; the Binding of the Cross (on Christ's shoulder); the place where the Virgin fainted; the three Falls of Christ; the holes where the Cross was inserted; the *Stabat Mater* altar (the Descent from the Cross), while the fourteenth and last station is the Sepulchre itself. Today it is a discontinuous lane, so that sightseers and pilgrims must often enter side-streets to continue the route. On or near it stand churches, convents, the 'Ecce Homo' Arch and the Gate of Judgment (by which gate Christ left the city towards Calvary).

Outside the walls the same devotional interest continues. Above the Grotto of Jeremiah, we find the Skull Hill or 'Place of Stoning', a strange knoll believed by General Charles Gordon and other explorers to be the true site of the Crucifixion. Biblical references as well as Christian and Moslem traditions give interest to such places as the Tombs of Absalom, Jehosaphat and Zachariah, to the 'Virgin's Fount', the Pool of Siloam, Tophet (scene of the infant sacrifices said to be practised in honour of Moloch), the Apostles' Cavern (where they may have hid themselves after forsaking Jesus). Two thousand and seven hundred feet above sea-level rises a still more enduring site: the Mount of Olives. Here the

Garden of Gethsemane is reached by a road bearing the imposing building of the old Hebrew University inaugurated in 1925.

Hills, valleys, domes and vegetation allure the visitor as far as, or farther than, the Dead Sea. The impressive new part of Jerusalem, equally alive with religious and secular buildings of a score of nationalities, bears on the whole the seal of modernity, energy and optimism.

Pliny the Elder (23–79)

RACE WITHOUT WOMEN

To the east of Lacus Asphaltites (Dead Sea) lies Arabia of the nomads, towards the south Machaerus, which in former days was the most important stronghold in Judaea after Jerusalem. On its western side, beyond the unhealthy strip of shore, dwell the Esseni, a solitary people, the strangest among the inhabitants of the world, for there are no women among them, and they have abjured all sexual pleasure, and possess no money, but abide in the palm-groves. Day by day the number of these refugees is renewed, being largely swelled by the accession of those whom the vicissitudes of fortune drive, weary of life, to adopt their usages. In this way, marvellous though it seems, a race exists perpetually in which no one is born, for it is propagated by other men's dissatisfaction with life.

Historia Naturalis, v, 71–73, translated
from the Latin by H. T. Riley, 1857

Palladius, Bishop of Hellenopolis (364–431)

OF A CERTAIN VIRGIN IN THE HOLY CITY

And, moreover, I saw a certain virgin in Jerusalem who had been clothed in sackcloth for three years, and she had secluded herself in a solitary cell, and had never permitted herself to enjoy the desirable things wherein there is pleasure.

Now this woman, having been forsaken by the Divine Providence, because of her immeasurable pride and arrogance fell into the ditches of fornication, and she opened the window of the habitation in which she had secluded herself, and received (therein) the man who ministered unto her, and she had intercourse with him. And because she did not continue to persevere in faith and in the ascetic life with a perfect will, and with a mind which possessed Divine love, but (departed therefrom) for the sake of men, that is to say, for the sake of vain glory, doing so, more-over, with an evil intent and with a corrupt and lascivious mind—for her own thoughts having been cut off, since they had been robbed of the Divine understanding, she came to the condition of casting blame upon others—the guardian of chastity did not remain with her.

Stories of the Holy Fathers, Chapter XXVI, translated
from the Syriac by Sir Ernest Wallis Budge, 1934

Torquato Tasso (1544-1595)

HIERUSALEM

Hierusalem is seated on two hills
Of height unlike, and turned side to side,
The space between a gentle valley fills,
From mount to mount expansèd far and wide.
Three sides are sure imbarred with crags and hills,
The rest is easy, scant to rise espied:
  But mighty bulwarks fence that plainer part,
  So art helps nature, nature strengtheneth art.

The town is stored of troughs and cisterns, made
To keep fresh water, but the country seems
Devoid of grass, unfit for ploughman's trade,
Not fertile, moist with rivers, wells and streams;
There grow few trees to make the summer's shade,
To shield the parching land from scorching beams,
  Save that a wood stands six miles from the town,
  With aged cedars dark, and shadows brown.

By east, among the dusty valleys, glide
The silver streams of Jordan's crystal flood;
By west, the Midland Sea, with bounders tied
Of sandy shores, where Joppa whilom stood;
By north Samaria stands, and on that side
The golden calf was reared in Bethel wood;
  Bethlem by south, where Christ incarnate was,
  A pearl in steel, a diamond set in brass.

Godfrey of Bulloigne, Book III, translated from
the Italian by Edw. Fairfax, 1600

William Lithgow (1582–1645?)

A SCOTCHMAN IN THE HOLY LAND (1612)

William Lithgow was born at Lanark about 1582. His Total Discourse, *published in 1632, records travels covering nearly twenty years, and the writer claimed to have 'traced over thirty-six thousand and odd miles, which draweth near to twice the circumference of the whole earth.')*

Spring come, I pretended to visit Jerusalem in my backcoming; and for the furtherance of my determination I joined with a caravan of Armenians and Turks, that were well guarded with janissaries and soldiers . . . At last we beheld the prospect of the City, which was not only a contentment to my weary body but also being ravished with a kind of unwonted rejoicing, the tears gushed from my eyes for too much joy. In this time the Armenians began to sing in their own fashion psalms to praise the Lord; and I also sung the 103rd Psalm all the way till we arrived near the walls of the city, where we ceased from singing for fear of the Turks.

The sun being passed to his nightly repose before our arrival, we found the gates locked and the keys carried up to the Pasha in the castle; which bred a common sorrow in the company, being all both hungry and weary. Yet the Caravan entreated the Turks within to give us over the walls some victuals for our money, showing heavily the necessity we had thereof; but they would not, neither durst attempt such a thing. In this time the guardian of the monastery of Cordeliers, who remaineth there to receive travellers of Christendom, who having got news of our late arrival, came and demanded of the Caravan if any Franks of Europe were in his society. And he said only one. Then the guardian called me, and asked of what nation I was of; and when I told him he seemed to be exceeding glad, yet very sorrowful for our misfortune.

He having known my distress, returned, and sent two friars to me with bread, wine, and fishes, which they let over the wall (as they thought, in a secret place), but they were espied. And on the morrow the guardians paid to the sub-Pasha or Sanzack a great fine, being a hundred piastres, thirty pounds sterling; otherwise both he and I had been beheaded. which I confess was a dear-bought supper to the grey friar; and no less almost to me, being both in danger of my life for starving and then for receiving food, therefore suspected for traitor. For the Turks alleged he had taken in munition from me and the other Christians to betray the city. This they do oft for a lesser fault than that was only to get bribes and money from the grey friars, which daily stand in fear of their lives.

Anno 1612, upon Palm Sunday in the morning, we entered into Jerusalem.   *Rare Adventures and Painful Peregrinations,* 1632

Anonymous (19th century)

THE BREATH OF DEATH

Dawns leaden day: a grey
    Wind moaning low;
Through empty street no feet
    Echoing go.

Ways dank with breath of death,
    All day in gloom
Drift grim, white-draped, escaped
    Shapes from the tomb.

Men's doors fast-barred to guard
    Living from dead;
Cold-cramped, each heart apart
    Crazes with dread;

Ten thousand groan and own
    Terror their guest;
One lying lone in stone
    Only knows rest.

The Sacred Year, 1856

Chateaubriand (1768–1848)

AMONG THE RUINS

The houses of Jerusalem are heavy square masses, very low, without chimneys or windows; they have flat terraces or domes on the top, and look like prisons or sepulchres. The whole would appear to the eye one uninterrupted level, did not the steeples of the churches, the minarets of the mosques, the summits of a few cypresses, and the clumps of nopals, break the uniformity of the plan. On beholding these stone buildings, encompassed by a stony country, you are ready to inquire if they are not the confused monuments of a cemetery in the midst of a desert.

Enter the city, but nothing will you there find to make amends for the dullness of its exterior. You lose yourself among narrow, unpaved streets here going up hill, there down, from the inequality of the ground, and you walk among clouds of dust or loose stones. Canvas stretched from house to house increases the gloom of this labyrinth. Bazaars, roofed over, and fraught with infection, completely exclude the light from the desolate city. A few paltry shops expose nothing but wretchedness to view, and even these are frequently shut, from apprehension of the passage of a cadi. Not a creature is to be seen in the streets, not a creature at the gates, except now and then a peasant gliding through the gloom, concealing under his garments the fruits of his labour, lest he should be robbed of his hard earnings by the rapacious soldier. Aside, in a corner, the Arab butcher is slaughtering some animal, suspended by the legs from a wall in ruins: from his haggard and ferocious look, and his bloody hands, you would suppose that he had been cutting the throat of a fellow-creature, rather than killing a lamb. The only noise heard from time to time in the city, is the galloping of the steed of the desert: it is the janissary who brings the head of the Bedouin, or who returns from plundering the unhappy Fellah.

Amid this extraordinary desolation, you must pause a moment to contemplate two circumstances still more extraordinary. Among the ruins of Jerusalem, two classes of independent people find in their religion sufficient fortitude to enable them to surmount such complicated horrors and wretchedness. Here reside communities of Christian monks, whom nothing can compel to forsake the tomb of Christ; neither plunder nor personal ill-treatment, nor menaces of death itself. Night and day they chant their hymns around the Holy Sepulchre. Driven by the cudgel and the sabre, women, children, flocks, and herds, seek refuge in the cloisters of these recluses. What prevents the armed oppressor from pursuing his prey, and overthrowing such feeble ramparts? The charity of the monks: they deprive themselves of the last resources of life to ransom their suppliants.[1] Cast your eyes between the Temple and Mount Sion; behold another petty tribe, cut off from the rest of the inhabitants of this city. The particular objects of every species of degradation, these people bow

[1] Dr. Clarke, an English nineteenth-century traveller, draws a somewhat different picture of these holy friars: he describes them, in the first place, as the most corpulent he had ever seen issue from the warmest cloisters of Spain or Italy. 'Their comfortable convent, compared with the usual accommodations of the Holy Land, is,' he says, 'like a sumptuous and well-furnished hotel. By contrasting one of these jolly fellows with the *Propaganda* missionaries, the latter are as meagre and as pale as the former are corpulent and ruddy.' The Franciscans complain heavily of the exactions of the Turks, who make frequent and large demands for money. 'But,' remarks Dr. Clarke, 'the fact of their being able to answer these demands affords a proof of the wealth of their convent. According to Hasselquist the sum that yearly passed through the hands of the procurator of the convent to be at least half a million of *livres*. This considerable sum is devoured by Turks and by monks who are useless inhabitants in Europe, and unnecessary at Jerusalem, where they are of no sort of advantage to Christianity.'

their heads without murmuring; they endure every kind of insult without demanding justice; they sink beneath repeated blows without sighing; if their head be required, they present it to the scimitar. Enter the abodes of these people, you will find them, amid the most abject wretchedness, instructing their children to read a mysterious book, which they in their turn will teach their offspring to read. What they did five thousand years ago, these people still continue to do. Seventeen times have they witnessed the destruction of Jerusalem, yet nothing can discourage them, nothing can prevent them from turning their faces towards Sion. To see the Jews scattered over the whole world, according to the Word of God, must doubtless excite surprise. But, to be struck with supernatural astonishment, you must view them at Jerusalem; you must behold these rightful masters of Judea living as slaves and strangers in their own country; you must behold them expecting, under all oppressions, a king who is to deliver them. Crushed by the Cross that condemns them, skulking near the Temple, of which not one stone is left upon another, they continue in their deplorable infatuation. The Persians, the Greeks, the Romans, are swept from the earth; and a pretty tribe, whose origin preceded that of those great nations, still exists unmixed among the ruins of its native land.

Travels to Jerusalem and the Holy Land, translated from the French by Frederic Shoberl, London, 1835

Alexander William Kinglake (1809–1891)

TERRA SANTA

The contests waged by the priests and friars certainly do not originate with the lay-pilgrims, for the great body of these are quiet and inoffensive people. It is true, however, that their pious enterprise is believed by them to operate as a counterpoise for a multitude of sins, whether past or future, and perhaps they exert themselves in after-life to restore the balance of good and evil.

If you stay in the Holy City long enough to fall into anything like regular habits of amusement and occupation, and to become, in short, for the time 'a man about town' at Jerusalem, you will necessarily lose the enthusiasm which you may have felt when you trod the sacred soil for the first time, and it will then seem almost strange to you to find yourself so entirely surrounded in all your daily pursuits by the signs and sounds of religion.

Eöthen, 1844

Frederika Bremer (1801–1865)

LOOKING AROUND   *January 24th, 1859*
'I lift my hands rejoicing
To God's hill and house!'

Unspeakably thankful to have arrived safely in Jerusalem, to be able here
in a quiet dwelling to rest from weariness and danger, and with a gladness
free as a bird to look around me spiritually and physically.

I am in Jerusalem, I am living on the Hill of Zion on King David's
Hill, and from the windows and roof of my loftily situated dwelling—
the Hotel Rosenthal—I can look over the ancient memorable city; but
the whole glorious city, which the Seer of Patmos beheld descending
from heaven prepared as a bride for her husband, brilliant with noble
pearls and precious stones, with the pure river on the shores of which the
tree of life bears twelve different kinds of fruit, for the healing of the
nations; the city in which also the glory and honour of the nations are
introduced, in which all the pomp and beauty of the earth is assembled,
where there is no more night, neither any weeping nor death, neither
anything which can do evil, because the Lord God Almighty is Himself
the temple therein and the light therein, and the nations and all who are
saved so walk in His light,[1]—that Jerusalem is a long, long way from
earthly Jerusalem into which I will conduct you, if you will accompany
me on my journey from Jaffa, on the 21st and 22nd of this month.

'To horse!' Such was the terrible command which I obeyed with
beating heart, yet with determination, as I took my seat in men's fashion
on the Arabian saddle. But, oh! my astonishment and delight. I found
myself when seated, as comfortable and as much at my ease as if in an
armchair (and as I never before found myself on any English ladies-
saddle, mounted on an ass), and the stirrups—as large as a pair of shoe
soles—are very convenient as supports to my feet; in a word, I sit so
perfectly at ease on my Rosinante, that I myself can hardly comprehend
it. But the Arab saddle is very easy, and is provided, both back and front,
with an elevated support, which serves as a something to hold fast by as
one clambers into one's seat.

EASTER WEEK
'The quiet week' as the Passion Week is called with us, is in Jerusalem
a week of disquiet, of bustle and confusion. With each succeeding day
arrived some new procession of pious pilgrims and inquisitive travellers.

[1] Revelations of St. John xxi. 22.

The people flooding the streets in all colours and costumes, with their camels, horses and asses. Convents and hotels are full to overflowing. Every day has its festivals and processions to the Church of the Sepulchre, but the crushing and the rudeness of the people render it actually dangerous to life to venture thither without the protection of the Kavasses. At the same time the streets and courts on the way to the Church are occupied with Turkish soldiers whose business is to keep the Christians under control and they do it sometimes in the rudest manner, with blows and pushing them out of the way by force. Nevertheless it must be confessed that the Christian pilgrims are themselves rude and brutish, and cannot be managed by any other means. It is not without cause that the Jews and Mohammedans regard them with a certain contempt. The Jews have lately concluded the celebration of their Purim, in memory of the deliverance of their nation by Queen Esther, and they now are preparing themselves for their Passover at the same time with the Easter of the Christians. Every Jewish family consumes on this occasion a paschal lamb, which they eat standing, clothed in the manner and with the ceremonial prescribed by the Mosaic Law; but this is done in profound quietness within the family. The Mussulmans celebrate also the Easter week, which falls this year at the same time with their Feast of Bairam. A garland of lamps is lit every evening on their minarets, which produces a very awful effect from the Mosque of Omar, and they, too, eat a lamb, according to the ancient usage, in direct conformity with the Hebrew tradition. But this also takes place in quietness, and the orthodox Christians, as they of the Greek Church designate these, constitute the peculiarly fanatical and dangerous population of Jerusalem at this season. Nevertheless the Christian Church has here also its better representatives. The small Evangelical Community celebrate on Mount Zion a divine worship, in spirit and in truth, which is both an enjoyment and an edification of witness.

> *Travels in the Holy Land*, translated from
> the Swedish by Mary Howitt, London, 1862

Eça de Queiroz (1845-1900)

MODERN SION

And, not satisfied with this, he looked out again on Sion, the divine, through the bleary windows. Under the melancholy rain the white walls of the convent opposite could be seen, with green shutters let down in front of its windows and two enormous zinc drain-pipes one at each corner, one of which was emptying itself noisily into a deserted alley-way; the other fell softly into an allotment planted with cabbages where an ass was braying. On the other side there was an endless mass of terrassed roofs, lugubrious and mud-coloured, with a little brick cupola in the shape of a furnace and long rods to hang out rags on; the roofs were almost all decrepit, dismantled, very poverty-stricken; it looked as if they would fall to pieces under the water that was flooding them. Further off still, there was a hill clustered with sordid dwellings with kitchen-gardens, looking tumbled-down and in pieces beneath the damp mist. A scrambling, narrow alley with steps led among these; up and down it there were going monks in sandals with umbrellas, sombre Jews with long hair falling down their backs, or some slow Bedouin throwing back the sleeves of his burnous . . . The grey sky seemed like a weight above us. And that is what ancient Sion, the well-built city, bright with clarity, the joy of the earth, looked like to me.

A Reliquia (*The Relic*), translated from
the Portuguese by C. David Ley

William Henry Leighton (1826–1883)

A COOK'S TOUR TO THE HOLY LAND IN 1874

Camp. Jerusalem,
Tuesday, 17th November, 1874

The rest at the hotel on Sunday did us both a deal of good, and I am now pretty well recovered. On Saturday the camp was to have arrived. I went up the Mount of Olives and on my return came on a familiar group of horses and found the party had just gone into the so-called Garden of Gethsemane, where I joined them. The Garden of Gethsemane is a small enclosure between stone walls with lots of *cultivated* flowers, and I understand the rest of the party were shown the impressions which the Apostles left on the stone on which they slept. I am happy to say I did not see them. Touching Jerusalem as a whole it certainly looks rather striking from the Mount of Olives across the Valley of Jehoshaphat, but it is like all other Eastern cities, a dreary network of covered streets with stalls at each side; and the surrounding country is all the same colour as the houses. On Sunday we went to church at the

English church on Mount Zion, where a nigger read the prayers and the Bishop did part of the Communion Service, and a German Jew preached. In the evening there was an informal service at the schoolroom, where one of our party, Professor Lindsay, preached, the Bishop and the two other clergymen being present. Mount Moriah, where the Temple is believed to have stood, is occupied by a range of Mahommedan buildings of which the Mosque of Omar is the most celebrated. *Externally* the Mosque of Omar is by no means as striking a building as I had expected: the dome is no great size and does not form a particularly striking feature in a general view of the city. *Internally* it is the most gorgeous mosque I have seen. The interior of the dome is something like the Hall of the Abencerrages, but the work is very rude like everything Eastern and does not bear investigation. The dome is erected over an unhewn piece of Mount Moriah, which has a very singular appearance, looking like an enormous model of some mountainous country with the map washed off. Tradition makes this rock the site of the altar of *burnt offering*. It also made an attempt to follow Mahomet to Heaven, but was held down by an angel who has left the impression of his fingers in it. We have seen the Church of the Holy Sepulchre, where the Sepulchre, Calvary, the place where the rock was rent by the earthquake, the centre of the earth, and about thirty-five other things all conveniently brought together under one roof. I am sick of traditions. Even the approximate place of the Crucifixion is really very doubtful, and the greater part is pure and wilful invention. Murray says 'the whole writings and teachings of the Apostles tended to withdraw men from an attachment to times, places, and physical objects etc. etc.; and it is not in fact until the 4th century, or about three hundred years after the Crucifixion, that we find any reference in history to the site of the Holy Sepulchre.'

The Letters of William Henry Leighton to his brother Robert,
edited by Douglas Leighton, 1947

Lady Judith Moses Montefiore (1784–1862)

CAMPING IN JERUSALEM

Thursday, 6 June 1830. What the feelings of a traveller are, when among the mountains on which the awful power of the Almighty once visibly rested, and when approaching the city where he placed his name; where the beauty of holiness shone in its morning splendour; and to which, even in its sorrow and captivity, even in its desolation, the very Gentiles, the people of all nations of the earth, as well as its own children, look with profound awe and admiration. Oh! what the feelings of the traveller are on such a spot, and when listening to the enraptured tones of Israel's own inspired King, none can imagine but those who have had the privilege and the felicity to experience them!

As we drew nearer to Jerusalem the aspect of the surrounding country became more and more sterile and gloomy. But solemn as were the feelings excited by the melancholy desolateness of the rocky hills and valleys through which we were passing, they were suddenly lost in a sense of rapture and indescribable joy, for now the Holy City itself rose full into view, with all its cupolas and minarets reflecting the splendour of the heavens. Dismounting from our horses, we sat down and poured forth the sentiments which so strongly animated our hearts in devout praises to him whose mercy and providence alone had then brought us a second time, in health and safety, to the city of our fathers.

The pure air of the Mount of Olives breathed around us with the most refreshing fragrance.

Friday, 7 June. Thanks to Almighty God, we rested in peace and comfort beneath our tents. The governor, Moukhamed Djizdar, a good-tempered man, attended by his suite, and several of our brethren, came to visit us. The governor presented us with five sheep, the fattest of which was killed, and part given to the priest, a quarter to some poor families of our nation, and half to the mukkaries, to be dressed with rice for their supper.

We are strongly persuaded not to enter the city, cases of plague having occurred within the last few days. It is therefore our determination to remain in our present position on this beautiful mount, where the finest air, the most sublime views and associations of the noblest kind unite to comfort us and elevate our thoughts.

Wednesday, 12 June. We entered the city through the Gate of the Tribes. The streets were narrow, and almost filled up with loose stones, and the ruins of houses which had fallen to decay. Our guards on each side were busily engaged in keeping off the people, a precaution rendered necessary to lessen the danger of contagion. Having passed through the bazaar, we entered the Jewish quarter of the town, and which appeared the cleanest of any we had traversed.

The streets, every lattice, and all the tops of the houses were thronged with children and veiled females. Bands of musicians, and choirs of singers welcomed our arrival with melodies composed for the occasion.

Having reached the synagogue the governor entered with us, and then said addressing M. he would leave us to our devotions, and that his officers should attend us, when we pleased to return to our encampment.

On our return the streets presented the same thronged and festive appearance as before, and thousands of good wishes and prayers were presented to heaven for our peace and happiness. In our progress we called at Mr. Young, the British Consul, and his lady, and were received with great kindness, and treated with coffee, sherbet and cakes. We returned by the Tower of David, the valley of Jehosaphat, Mount Zion, and Mount Moriah. M. was as fatigued as myself, though both full of thankful and satisfactory reflections. He sent the governor a present of a hundred dollars, which in handsome terms he declined accepting.

It is a lovely evening: the new moon is up, and the heavens are full of stars, while a disposition to thought clears away the mists of time. Fresh and sweet sounds the song of David: 'The heavens declare the glory of God, and the firmament sheweth his handy work: day unto day uttereth speech, and night unto night sheweth knowledge!'

Oh! who could dwell upon such themes, and not glow with devotion and holy love! Oh! who could look upon such scenes, and not ask: 'When shall the days come when the voice of the Lord shall be heard, saying "Break forth into joy: sing together, ye waste places of Jerusalem, he hath redeemed Jerusalem".' (Isaiah).

Private Journal of a visit to Egypt and Palestine
by way of Italy and the Mediterranean.
Privately printed, London, 1885

Benjamin Disraeli (1804–1881)

SABBATH IN THE CITY

Morn came; the warriors assembled around the altar and the sacrifice. The High Priest and his attendant Levites proclaimed the unity and the omnipotence of the God of Israel, and the sympathetic responses of his conquering and chosen people re-echoed over the plain. They retired again to their tents, to listen to the expounding of the law; even the distance of a Sabbath walk was not to exceed that space which lies between Jerusalem and the Mount of Olives. This was the distance between the temple and the tabernacle, it had been nicely measured, and every Hebrew who ventured forth from the camp this day might be observed counting the steps of a Sabbath-day's journey. At length the sun again set, and on a sudden fires blazed, voices sounded, men stirred, in the same enchanted and instantaneous manner that had characterized the stillness of the preceding eve. Shouts of laughter, bursts of music, announced the festivity of the coming night; supplies poured in from all the neighbouring villages, and soon the pious conquerors commemorated their late triumph in a round of banqueting.

The Wondrous Tale of Alroy, 1833

G. K. Chesterton (1874–1936)

THE GATES OF THE CITY

I need not say I did not expect the real Jerusalem to be the new Jerusalem; a city of charity and peace, any more than a city of chrysolite and pearl. But neither did I find what I was much more inclined to expect; something at the other extreme. Many reports had led me to look for a truly conquered town. I looked for a place like Cairo, containing indeed old and interesting things, but open on every side to new and vulgar things. It does not, like Cairo, offer the exciting experience of twenty guides for one traveller. The town is quite inconvenient enough to make it a decent place for pilgrims.

The first part of the sensation is that the traveller, as he walks the stony streets between the walls, feels that he is inside a fortress. But it is the paradox of such a place that, while he feels in a sense that he is in a prison, he also feels that he is on a precipice. The sense of being uplifted, and set on a high place, comes to him through the smallest cranny, or most accidental crack in rock or stone; it comes to him especially through those long narrow windows in the walls of the old fortifications; those slits in the stone through which the medieval archers used their bows and the medieval artists used their eyes, with even greater success. Then I remembered that in the same strips of medieval landscape could be seen always, here and there, a steep hill crowned with a city of towers. And I knew I had the mystical and double pleasure of seeing such a hill and standing on it.

The greater part of the actual walls now standing were built by Moslems late in the Middle Ages; but they are almost exactly like the walls that were being built by the Christians at or before that time. The Crusaders and the Saracens constantly copied each other while they combated each other. The curse of war is that it does lead to more international imitation; while in peace and freedom men can afford to have national variety. The wall and gates which now stand, whatever stood before them and whatever comes after them, carry a memory of those men from the West who came here upon that wild adventure, who climbed this rock and clung to it so perilously from the victory of Godfrey to the victory of Saladin.

I do not forget, of course, that all these visible walls and towers are but the battlements and pinnacles of a buried city, or of many buried cities. Nor do I forget the long centuries that have passed over the place since these medieval walls were built, any more than the far more interesting centuries that passed before they were built.

Therefore my immediate impression of the walls and gates has not remained primarily a thing of walls and gates; a thing which the modern world does not perhaps understand so well as the medieval world. There is involved in it all that idea of definition which those who do not like it are fond of describing as dogma. A wall is like a rule; and the gates are like the exceptions that prove the rule. From this standpoint the Holy City was a happy city; it had no suburbs. That is to say, there are all sorts of buildings outside the wall; but they are outside the wall. The first sight of the sharp outline of Jerusalem is like a memory of the older types of limitation and liberty. Happy is the city that has a wall; and happier still if it is a precipice.

Again, Jerusalem might be called a city of staircases: this shape is symbolic; as symbolic as the pointed profile of the Holy City. For a creed is like a ladder, while an evolution is only like a slope. A spiritual and social evolution is generally a pretty slippery slope; a miry slope where it is very easy to slide down again. Such is something like the sharp and even abrupt impression produced by this mountain city.

When the walls of the Holy City were overthrown for the glory of the German Emperor, it was for the glory of a single day. It destroyed a monument to make a procession. There is the true barbaric touch in this oblivion of what Jerusalem would look like a century after, or a year after, or even a day after.

When the critic says that Jerusalem is disappointing he generally means that the popular worship there is weak and degraded, and especially that the religious art is gaudy and grotesque. What is wrong with the critic is that he does not criticise himself. He does not honestly compare what is weak, in this particular world of ideas, with what is weak in his own world of ideas. The lesson he ought to learn from it is one which the western and modern man needs most, and does not even know that he

N

needs. It is the lesson of constancy. No man living in the West can form the faintest conception of what it must have been like to live in the very heart of the East through the long and seemingly everlasting epoch of Moslem power. It must have seemed as if the whole earth belonged to Mahomet to those who in this rocky city renewed their hopeless witness to Christ. What we have to ask ourselves is not whether we happen in all respects to agree with them, but whether we in the same condition should even have the courage to agree with ourselves. It is not a question of how much of their religion is supersitition, but of how much of our religion is convention; how much is custom and how much a compromise even with custom. That is the real lesson that the enlightened traveller should learn; the lesson about himself.

I can understand a man who had only seen in the distance Jerusalem sitting on the hill going no further and keeping that vision for ever. If he has not come for a poetic mood he has come for nothing; if he has come for such a mood, he is not a fool to obey that mood. No great works will seem great, and no wonders of the world will seem wonderful, unless the angle from which they are seen is that of historical humility.

The New Jerusalem, 1920

Eric Gill (1882–1940)

LETTERS FROM THE CITY OF STONE

Couvent des Dominicains, Jerusalem   5-4-1934

Dear Carey: We arrived here a fortnight ago. The weather is not yet too hot. It is an astonishing place. Words fail me. I can't begin to describe it. There is a mad balance (preserved by Brit. Govt.) between ancient & utter loveliness & mod. bestial commercial enterprise—in fact they cancel out.[1] There is also a mad confusion of religions, all worshipping & scrapping at same shrines. I expect to be here till end of June.

> *S.S. 'Sagaing' Sailing i.e. steaming along coast of Spain, expecting to arrive at Gibraltar this evening*

'My dear Graham! This is simply to say that our Palestine interlude is now coming to a close (. . . .) It would be impossible to tell you everything about it. We have had a marvellous time in many ways. A.H. lives on the S. side of the city in a very beautiful house with fine arab vaults to all the

[1] i.e. between the two you may say there is no real Jerusalem at all.

194

rooms. (Item: I am much gone on the arab vaulting system—an alternative solution, to the medieval European one, of the problem of cross vaults. Instead of the pointed arch they use ellipses. They make *the diagonals first*, & always semicircular, but not necessarily crossing at right angles.

It is a jolly fine system giving very strong vaults & is as flexible as the Gothic—moreover it harmonizes with the round headed window . . . if that's a comfort to you! (I think it rather is to me.), and it's much more suave and restful to the eye & naturally never developed into a complication of groining.) Jerusalem was much the same as three years ago.

Jerusalem is a city of stone & as there are no streets wide enough for wheeled traffic (except a few hundred yards by the Jaffa gate & the Bab Siti Miriam) there is no noise save that of human voices & footsteps &, inside the walls, there is a complete absence (except in the cheap factory stuff & tinned foods which they sell in their little shops—or in some of them) of our filthy western life & none of its filthy apparatus. And, in the midst, the Holy Sepulchre (which, whatever one may say about the silly squabbles of the rival caretakers, Catholic, Greek & Copt etc., is a palpably holy place) and, occupying all one corner, the Haram el Sheraf (called by us 'the Temple Area'), than which nothing, nothing, nothing could be lovelier, holier, more dignified, more humane or more grand. Thank God I got a permit from the Grand Mufti to go in and out every day ('cept Fridays, when it is reserved for Moslems exclusively & jealously). I did a few drawings sitting on the roof of a house in the via Dolorosa. Which, whatever the valuelessness of the drawings, was a fine way of staying put & thus really soaking up the scene.

Well, well, this is all absurdly inadequate to convey to you (a) my overwhelming love for Jerusalem & for Palestine—oh my dear Graham you can't believe how lovely they are.

Letters of Eric Gill, 1947

Selma Lagerlöf (1858–1940)

THE CITY OF HATRED

In truth, everyone is not strong enough to live in Jerusalem. Even if they can stand the climate, and even if they escape infectious diseases, they sometimes succumb. The Holy City depresses and weighs upon them, or else they go out of their minds—ay, it can even kill them outright. One cannot live there for a week or two without hearing people say about this or that person who has suddenly died: 'Jerusalem has killed him.'

Those who hear this cannot help being greatly surprised. 'How can this be possible?' they ask. 'How can a city kill? These people cannot be in earnest.' And whilst wandering hither and thither in Jerusalem, one cannot help thinking: 'I should like to know what people mean when they say that Jerusalem kills. I should really like to know where that Jerusalem is which is so terrible that it kills men.' One remembers that the remains of walls which cover the ground are ruins of what were once the halls of Kings; that the hill opposite is the Rock of Offence where Solomon sinned; that the valley beneath, the deep Valley of Hinnom, was once filled to its very edge with the bodies of human beings who were killed in Jerusalem when the Romans destroyed the city.

A strange feeling comes over one as one walks there; one fancies one hears the noise of battle, one sees great armies advancing to attack the walls of the city, one sees Kings approaching in their war-chariots. This is the Jerusalem of war, of strife, of violation, one thinks, and one is terrified at the thought of all the misdeeds and horrors that open out before one's mind.

Then a moment can come when one wonders if it should be this Jerusalem that causes men to die. But the next moment one shrugs one's shoulders, and says: 'It is impossible. It is much too long ago since the mighty swords met and the red blood flowed.'

When walking there one thinks: 'Yes, this is the Jerusalem of death and judgment. Here both heaven and hell open their gates.' But one immediately says: 'No, it is not this Jerusalem, either, that kills. The trumpets of the Judgment Day are too far away, and the fire of Gehenna burns no more.

Again one continues one's way along the city wall, and comes to the northern side of the city. Here it is barren, lonely, and monotonous. One stops a moment, looking meditatively on the solemn and gloomy darkness. 'It is not this Jerusalem, either, that kills men,' one thinks, and wanders onwards.

But if one goes further towards the north-west and west, what a transformation! Here in the new part of the town, outside the city wall rise the splendid palaces of the missionaries and the big hotels. On this side expand the important Jewish and German agricultural colonies. Here are the large convents, the manifold charitable institutions; here crowd monks and nuns, sick-nurses and sisters of charity, missionaries and Russian popes, here reside men of science, who study Jerusalem's past, and old English ladies, who can't live anywhere else; here are the splendid missionary schools, that give their pupils free education, and board and lodging and clothes, in order to gain an opportunity of winning their souls; here are the mission hospitals, where one simply begs the sick to come and be nursed that one may have a chance of converting them; here are held religious services and prayer-meetings where they fight for souls. Here it is where the Roman Catholic speaks evil of the Protestant, the Methodist of the Quaker, the Lutheran of the Reformed Church, the Russian of the Armenian; here envy sneaks about; here the fanatic looks askance at the worker of miracles; here the orthodox disputes with the heretic; here no mercy is shown; here one hates one's fellow-men to the glory of God. And here one finds what one has been looking for. This is the Jerusalem of soul-hunting, this is the Jerusalem of evil-speaking, this is the Jerusalem of lies, of slander, of jeers. Here one persecutes untiringly; here one murders without weapons. It is this Jerusalem which kills men.

Jerusalem, translated from the Swedish by Jessie Bröchner, 1903

Keith Douglas (1920–1944)

SATURDAY EVENING IN JERUSALEM

In summer evenings the moonstruck city fills
with movement of people, tides of speech
and the whole evening moving where
the words stream down into the square;
the street is full of shoulders. Watch
moonlight leap out between the hotels.

Young men and girls linked in fours and twos
under the moon sitting so high so bright
are drawn uphill between the figures of trees
now softening hot walls appear to freeze
and silver children go in and out
stumping on the pavements with their shoes.

It is a collaboration between things
and people; the cat moonlight prowling about
rubs against friendly legs, leaps upon
the shoulders of a family. Family song,
incense of talk and laughter mounting the night;
in the dome of stars the moon sings.

But among these Jews I am the Jew
the outcast, wandering down the steep road
into the hostile dark square:
and standing in the unlit corner here
know I am alone and cursed by God
as if lost on my first morning at school.

Collected Poems, edited by G. S. Fraser
and John Waller, 1946

Kaj Munk (1898–1944)

A LUTHERAN'S VISIT

'And when he was come near, he beheld the city and wept over it.'

If the ministry of Jesus had had nothing else to show for it, one result
is at any rate traceable: hotel prices in the tourist city of Jerusalem are
half as high again as anywhere else. A man went down from Jericho to
Jerusalem, and near the end of his journey he fell among thieves. The inn
where the Good Samaritan found him board and lodging for two denarii
has been pulled down. One gets the impression that a famous text from
Holy Writ that has been put up on the original site is now taken to mean
that, if a man takes away your coat, then he is entitled to your waterproof
as well.

And what do we get for our money? Experiences to strengthen our
faith and further our sanctity? Ah, well, even though a sober individual
like myself has for years known perfectly well that in Palestine the popu-
lace no longer stands about in white robes with palm-branches in their
hands singing *Halleluja* all day long, nevertheless it is galling to find out
that one was right. It is not aesthetically exhilarating to meet in person the
shepherds in the field whom romantic poets and colour-drunk painters
have for centuries depicted for us with such delusive charm. It is heart-
rending to see all over the land of Jehovah the half-moon of Mahomet

swaggering cocksurely at the new, while his lazy lousy Arabs sprawl and lounge along the pavements, purple with the chill of spring. It is maddening at every sacred memorial to have to engage with chauffeurs and guides and seedy-looking Greek-Catholic priests in the usual vulgar dispute over a small gratuity. But worst of all is it to come across the various mendacious assumptions of the Christian churches, the cynical boldness with which they point out the unknown locus of every incident concerning Christ, and the tactlessness—the lack of respect and a decent reserve—that leads them, instead of removing their shoes and keeping quiet, to make a display with church houses and to tinkle bells and bleat out masses and put on airs and attitudes.

What does one look for in Jerusalem? David is not here, nor David's Son either. It is possible that statistics may show that as a result of immigration in recent years the Jews in the city are once more in a majority after an interval of one thousand eight hundred and sixty years, and that the Christians of all sorts come number two in the population, so that the Arabs have to be content with third place. But what difference can that make? Where is the Temple? Oh, I could shed tears, could line up among the old Jews down by the Wall of Weeping and stand like them knocking my head against the stones, for very grief that the Temple has gone—not a chip of it left; but on its broad noble site, that leads straight out to the precipitous rock and in that way dominates the whole surrounding country, are two gaudy mosques which they tell me are splendid specimens of Mahometan art. But I don't want to look at them—honestly, I don't.

As to-day is Sunday, let us force ourselves to be as devout as possible. Let us go to Golgotha—or where they say Golgotha was. Here the Catholics have put up Jesus' fourteen stations of the Cross on the houses. Here he is weeping over Jerusalem; and there—yes, of course—*there* stands a monstrosity of a church. Just where one imagined that mankind in tremulous piety might have set apart a plain simple plot of ground for silence and meditation to kneel down together, there are a number of chapels and stairways and hiding-places, hundreds of lamps in every colour of the rainbow, and shoals of priests whose appearance makes one as frightened as Peer Gynt in the madhouse—and you glance round to see if the way out is still open.

Those Greek-Catholic priests are pretty formidable fellows. Their matted jet-black hair falls like a horse's mane in plaits over their shoulders, and the swarthy sea pours down from cheek and chin over chest and stomach. And then they have voices like archangels. They stand and peer round about them in the chapels, while the congregation swarms singing outside. Suddenly the priests dart forward in the doorway and utter ferocious howls. Finally they assemble for a mass procession; there is a lightning of silks and purple and gold and flaming tapers, and a thunder of Greek anthems; then the procession sets off round the church. In front pace two scimitared cherubim whose weapons strike the church floor with a measured bump as they march, and after them follow the whole motley crowd of savages, ending up with a super-savage who, wading forward in his long beard and plastered all over with brocade, wears a massive gold crown on his head and makes minatory gestures right and left with a silver cross. Is it to be supposed that God in his heaven is really so stage-struck that a revue act like this can be acceptable to him on the very spot where his Son's blood once flowed? Doesn't one find oneself momentarily in perverse sympathy with those bloodthirsty gentlemen in Russia who have acquired the notion that these hundred per cent male persons might perhaps give God greater joy by making themselves useful in some other form of activity?

With nerves jarred and jangled we escape from this profanity, and our souls are refreshed at the sight of an evangelical church. We must go inside. Better to hear a clergyman in everyday clothes uttering a few quiet commonplaces, and a congregation after that being helped along with a modest hymn, than all this buffoonery of the fair-ground. So we devoutly compose ourselves. The church is light, without undue ornamentation, friendly, simple and chaste—bless you, it does one good. A good Christian is a good German. And then—but I have had enough. Away! Away! Dear Lord Jesus, Thou wast naive enough in this very place to say, 'It is finished!' Ah, what a lot there is still to be done!

No, there is no message for us here. The Golgotha that speaks to our hearts no longer exists geographically, but is a place in a book—the central point in our New Testament. There we can make a pilgrimage with some hope of profit—a pilgrimage, thank God, that is not reserved for those who can afford a ticket, but is available for all mankind. It begins to dawn upon us that there is now nothing left of our Jerusalem, but a name. Such was God's will. All the holy places have disappeared, so that man shall not by them be tempted to outward adoration instead of adoration in spirit and in truth. Only the garden of Gethsemane—with its memories of humiliation, of agony, of perplexity, of his cry that the cup might pass from him, of his disciples' pitiable desertion—still survives to admonish us . . .

Translated from the Danish by R. P. Keigwin

Sir Ronald Storrs (1881–1957)

LEAVING THE CITY

I had always dreaded the day when I should have to leave Jerusalem, but the reality was sharper than I have ever dreamed. I realised with a pang that I must wind up Pro-Jerusalem. Under Clifford Holliday who succeeded Ashbee in 1922, we had completed the restoration of the City Walls, Ramparts, and Citadel; repaired the Damascus Gate, Herod's Gate, and the Zion Gate; and removed the offence of the Turkish 'Jubilee' Clock Tower from the Jaffa Gate. Under the provisions of a Town Planning Ordinance, developing and legalising my first arbitrary Proclamations, we had maintained the architectural style of the Old City by preserving flat roofs, vaults, domes, street arches, abutments and buttresses, and by prohibiting asbestos sheets, Marseilles tiles and corrugated iron. We had placed the ceramic industry on a sound financial footing, organised six more art exhibitions, and published a portfolio of architectural photogravures (with letterpress in English, Arabic and Hebrew) and the first practical modern map of Jerusalem. We had made a Civic Survey of the City and surrounding district, and enacted a definitive town-planning scheme for the Old and New Cities; comprising the conservation of historic monuments, new roads, zones for industries with shops and housing, the establishment of a green belt round the City, and the natural reservation of the valleys of Hinnom and of Jehoshaphat and the Mount of Olives. And it is owing to Pro-Jerusalem that the only surviving gravestone of a Crusader, the English Philip d'Aubigny, signatory of Magna Charta, Governor of the Channel Islands and tutor to King Henry the Third, is preserved, safe at last under a wrought iron grille from the trampling of feet, before the Church of the Holy Sepulchre. Meanwhile the Departments concerned had grown in scope as well as efficiency; whilst subscriptions to Pro-Jerusalem steadily decreased. Holliday had obtained an official Municipal appointment, and by his private architectural practice was providing a corrective to the Central European proclivities of some of his colleagues. Pro-Jerusalem had always been a personal, perhaps a too personal, Society. In the absence of any clear perspective

> . . . *it were a greater grief*
> *To watch it withering, leaf by leaf*
> *Than see it pluck't today.*

There were three very drastic weeks of farewells, receptions, and addresses; tiredness and sadness mingled with speeches abroad and the continual hammering of packing cases at home. The Life Honorary Presidentships of Chamber of Commerce, Musical Society and the other bodies we had founded or helped to found, meant to us very much more than an empty compliment. On the eve of our going we climbed the Russian Tower of the Ascension and drank in for the last time that doubly magnificent view. A City set in the midst of mountains gaunt, austere, uncompromising but yet of a perfect distinction and in a supreme style: of an atmosphere at once thrilling and poignant, which from the first had taken my heart. At midnight I made my final inspection of the Police Posts, checked the registers and verified the attendances. Next morning we ran the kindly gauntlet at the station; and at noon of November 29th, accompanied by the boxes containing everything I had acquired in life since the age of twenty-two, we embarked at Jaffa upon His Majesty's Sloop *Cornflower* and sailed for Cyprus.

I cannot pretend to describe or analyse my love for Jerusalem. It is not wholly sentimental, aesthetic or religious—still less theological or archaeological; though I hope it contains something of all five. A little perhaps also that I had worked and enjoyed and suffered there from the beginning; that I knew the people so well and liked them so much; that after misunderstandings had always followed understanding; that I had shared the delight there of my father and mother; that I had begun there the happiness of my married life. Persons of wider experience and more facile emotions have often come there to pray and gone away to mock. For me Jerusalem stood and stands alone among the cities of the world. There are many positions of greater authority and renown within and without the British Empire, but in a sense that I cannot explain there is no promotion after Jerusalem.

Orientations, the definitive edition, 1943

Maria Kuncewicz (b. 1899)

ANNO DOMINI 1936

The streets with their steps and crevices and caves wound like dark canyons up and down the Holy City. Dusk and silence were closing in upon me as this, the ancient part of Jerusalem, emptied itself of its daytime life. On doorsteps cats stood, their backs arched, refusing admittance, while overhead huge vultures gazed down upon them as they beat the air noiselessly with their wings.

A marble slab, almost transparent with age, caught my eye. It jutted above the floor, candles flamed round it, and out of the darkness the brilliant Byzantine lampades came flowing down on silver chains, their milky glass etched with flowers and crosses. My heart stopped, and time with it. When the emotion subsided I somehow knew that the yellow slab was the bed on which Joseph of Arymathea had washed the body of Christ; that somewhere near was the hill of the Passion; and that in an awkward bulky chapel, as in a chest, was hidden the Tomb. I also knew that I was fulfilling the dream of many generations; I was kneeling as my ancestors had wished to kneel, the countless Byelo-Russians, Masovians, Lithuanians and Podolians, deeply immersed in sin and work, people long since dead who had called to Jesus in their hour of death. To live through that moment in a way that would not disappoint the dead—what a responsibility! The world was dropping away from me and the God of Judas, of the fishermen, the lepers and the whores was again walking the earth. It lasted seconds, or ages, and I had been deaf to the shouts of the Arab youth. He tugged at my sleeve, then with a great clatter he ran up the steps to a gallery. From there he yelled again:

Kommen hier! Golgotha, Golgotha ist hier!

He came back. Close to my face I saw a pair of those poetic eyes whose blackness is the colour, perhaps, of the innocent wickedness of animals and of the storm.

Heilig Grab sehen, he cried. *Alles für dreissig Piaster sehen.*

It was not my peace he was shattering, he was robbing the dead of their chance.

Lassen sie mich, I begged him.

But then his wrath poured out in a flood.

Dreissig Piaster nicht billig? Sie Jehüd! Hier verboten!!

A hand was reaching towards my neck.

Kreuz zeigen! Jehüd hier verboten.

I had no cross to show. I fled.

The City of Herod (Miasto Heroda),
translated from the Polish by the author

IX The Heavenly City

*So speaketh the Lord: This is Jerusalem. I
have set in the midst of the nations, and round
about it are countries.*
            Ezekiel

*New Jerusalem coming down from God out of
heaven, prepared as a bride adorned for her
husband.*
            Rev. of St. John xxi. 2

*Four great walls in the New Jerusalem
Meted on each side by the angel's reed,
For Leonard, Rafael, Agnolo and me
To cover.*
            Robert Browning: Andrea del Sarto

*Time is, time was, but time shall be no more.
At the last blast the souls of universal
humanity throng towards the valley of
Jehoshaphat, rich and poor, gentle and simple,
wise and foolish, good and wicked.*
            James Joyce: A portrait of
            the artist as a young man

*And saintly men, who walk with God on earth,
would fain be away, to walk with him on the
golden pavements of the New Jerusalem.*
            Nathaniel Hawthorne:
            The Scarlet Letter, *1850*

Ever since the time of the captivity in Babylon, there is much
fascinating evidence of the idea of Jerusalem as a heavenly city,
as distinct from the physical city for which the exiles longed. The
Jews believed that exactly on the top of the earthly Jerusalem, and
forming a part of it, there is a Jerusalem of the Upper World
(*Yerushalaim shel Ma'alah*), with its Temple, high priest and small
elite of prophets. It is a place of endearing symbols and of lofty
eternity, summing up in an imaginary whole the farthest boundaries of emotion, the quest for perfection. In the Messianic
prophecies of Deutero-Isaiah and Jeremiah, Jerusalem becomes
the city from which world redemption will flow—the spiritual
capital of the world.

Christianity found Jerusalem holy to the Jews of every land and
made it holier still by associating it with the life, passion, crucifixion and resurrection of Jesus. The new persecuted faith turned
indeed to its incarnate Saviour, while persecuted Jewry longed

nostalgically for its 'incarnate' city. Jerusalem became the focus of Christian mysticism, the image of Christ's completed work of redemption. Generations of visionaries have depicted in poems and hymns the city as the essence of goodness and beauty. Thus the confessed fantasy spoke the language of an accepted reality of the spirit. Whenever despair or the burden of human sin seemed intolerable, poets and theologians named the comfort they longed for, the 'happy home' that life on earth could never give them— Jerusalem.

In the Apocalyptic writings, there also appears the idea of a new Jerusalem, a heavenly city of God. Even without these Jerusalem would have been the world centre of three religions; but the spiritual significance of the city of God captivated men's minds as the physical city had never done. The ideal of a rebuilt Jerusalem is a characteristic of Old Testament prophecies and of some Apocalypses; this gives way to the idea of a New Jerusalem first mentioned by name in the *Testament of the Twelve Patriarchs* as to be set up by God; or a heavenly Jerusalem revealed by Him, or built by the Messiah (these ideas recur in Hebrews and Galatians, and are also a familiar theme in Rabbinic theology).

On the other hand St. Augustine's view regarding the duration of the church, literally interpreted, gave rise to the idea that the world would end in A.D. 1000, with all its far-reaching consequences. Medieval maps showed Jerusalem as the centre of the world, the *umbilicus vitae* (cf. Ezekiel). The chiliastic views of the Middle Ages included the passing away of heaven and earth, their destruction or transformation, and the appearance of a new heaven and a new earth of which the Heavenly Jerusalem would be the focal point. Literary references vary in their degree of sublimity. Dante, who refers to Jerusalem as the centre of the world (*Purg.* ii, 3) at the antipodes of the mount of Purgatory (*Purg.* iv, xxiii), also (*Par.* xix) uses it as a symbol for heaven:

> E quella pia che guido le penne
> delle mie ali a cosi alto volo,
> alla riposta cosi mi prevenne:
> 'La Chiesa militante alcun figliolo
> non ha con piu speranza, com's scritto
> nel sol che raggia tutto nostro stuolo:
> Pero li e conceduto che d'Egitto
> vegna in Ierusalemme, per vedere
> anzi che'l militar li sia prescritto . . .'

(And that compassionate one who directed the feathers of my wings to so high a flight anticipated my answer: 'The Church Militant has not a child more full of hope, as is written in the Sun that irradiates all our host; therefore it is granted him to come from Egypt to Jerusalem that he may see it before his warfare is accomplished . . .')

Milton, too, refers to the historical destiny of Jerusalem in *Paradise Lost* (Book xii), where Michael prophesies to Adam, and speaks of the descendants of Solomon:

> Such follow him, as shall be register'd
> Part good, part bad, of bad the longer scrowl,
> Whose foul Idolatries, and other faults
> Heapt to the popular sum, will so incense
> God, as to leave them, and expose this Land,
> This City, his Temple, and his holy Ark
> With all his sacred things, a scorn and prey
> To that proud City, whose high walls thou saw'st
> Left in confusion, Babylon thence called.

Shakespeare, finally, suggests

> So part we sadly in this troublous world
> To meet with joy in Sweet Jerusalem.
>
> *Henry VI*, iii

After the Renaissance, and with the renewed interest in the Scriptures resulting from the Reformation, the fantasy of Jerusalem, centre of redemption for all men, became even more firmly established. No other symbolism approximated in intensity that of the New Jerusalem throughout Western Europe. An immense number of hymnological references, stemming primarily from Bernard of Cluny's *Hora Novissima*—'Urbs Syon aurea, patria lactea, cive decora'—grew up to supplement the already large collections of screeds [*sic*] by Jewish, Christian and Moslem writers since the fall of Rome.

When, with the coming of science, human consciousness was split between the rational and imaginative faculties, it was almost inevitable that a poet and mystic such as Blake should challenge a rational century with the watchword of Jerusalem. The maze of his long 'prophetic books' is scarcely to be disentangled in its entirety even by the specialist, but the lyrics show us how Blake saw everyday life in London in the light of a deeper reality to which he often gave the name 'Jerusalem':

> I will give you the end of a golden string,
> Only wind it into a ball,
> It will lead you in at Heaven's gate
> Built in Jerusalem's wall.

In one of his leaps of intuition from the lower to the higher truth, Blake made Jerusalem symbolise the spirit, or, in his own words, the 'emanation' of the ideal man and woman, the ideal humanity in fact:

In the great Eternity every particular Form gives forth or Emanates
Its own peculiar Light, & the Form is the Divine Vision
And the Light is his Garment. This is Jerusalem in every Man,
A Tent & Tabernacle of Mutual Forgiveness, Male & Female
  Clothings.
And Jerusalem is called Liberty among the Children of Albion.

How did the dualistic conception of Jerusalem as an earthly and spiritual centre arise? Obviously, the concentration of Jewish national worship on the Temple and the 'city of David' led to the use of the adjective 'holy'; and there is a considerable body of Midrashic tradition on the subject. According to the Midrash, the Holy Rock, the first part of the world to be created, will be the first to be destroyed, and so the future re-creation will begin with Zion. To pray in Jerusalem was recognized as the equivalent of standing before the throne of God. The future Jerusalem would surpass the city's past glories, and all the peoples of the earth would dwell there. Hence the idea of Heavenly Jerusalem which has appealed to many even more forcefully than the words of biblical prophecy, conveying a message as universal as music. Gerald Massey's 'Jerusalem the Golden' was written in this spirit:

> Jerusalem the Golden! I toil on day by day;
>   Heart-sore each night with longing.
> I stretch my hands and pray,
>   That mid the leaves of healing
> My soul may find her nest,
>   Where the wicked cease from troubling
> And the weary are at rest!

Thus the image of Jerusalem has sometimes come to signify more at times than the Jerusalem of actuality from which it sprung—and which it has conquered.

Nor has Jerusalem lacked its scorners. Samuel Butler's *Note Books* contain this entry: 'The new Jerusalem, when it comes, will probably be found so far to resemble the old as to stone its prophets freely'. (Cf. 'New presbyter, old priest writ large.') While Havelock Ellis, in *Impressions and Comments*, wrote: 'Had there been a Lunatic Asylum in the suburbs of Jerusalem, Jesus Christ would infallibly have been shut up in it at the outset of his public career. That interview with Satan on a pinnacle of the Temple would alone have damned him, and everything that happened after could but have confirmed the diagnosis. The whole religious complexion of the modern world is due to the absence from Jerusalem of a Lunatic Asylum.'

While dealing with the Heavenly City it is worth pointing out that Jerusalem is also a source of Hell. The valley of Hinnom at whose mouth was situated Topheth, where Achaz and Manasseh set up the worship of Baal-Moloch, is the place of Gehenna, the New Testament name for the primitive concept of Hell, a place of spiritual punishment and torment. There had been fires there which apostate Jews caused their children to pass, to consecrate them to Moloch. 'Therefore behold the day cometh, saith the Lord that it shall not more be called the Valley of the son of Hinnom, but the valley of slaughter, for they shall bury in Topheth till there be no place. And the carcasses of the people shall be meat for the fowls of the heaven and for the beasts of the earth, and none shall frighten them away . . .' (Jer. vii., 31–33).

Louis Untermeyer (b. 1885)

JERUSALEM DELIVERED

(King David Hotel, Jerusalem, offers Tea Dances, Wednesday and Saturday,
Aperitif Concerts every Sunday, and Cocktail Parties in the Winter Garden.
Advert in the Palestine News.)

Miriam, strike your cymbal,
Young David, add your voice;
Once more the tribes are nimble,
Once more the Jews rejoice.

Beneath the flowering mango
Where peace and perfume frip,
Solomon does the Tango
And Sheba shakes a hip.

Rebekah trots with Aaron,
Deborah treads the earth,
Fresh as the Rose of Sharon
With evening gowns by Worth.

Susannah meets the Elders
With an increased regard;
Pounds, dollars, marks and guilders
Receive their due reward.

Jerusalem the Golden,
With milk and honey blest,
Revive the rapt and olden
Ardour within each breast;

Add Gilead to Gomorrah;
Fling torches through the dark;
Dancing before the Torah,
With cocktails at the Ark!

Modern American Poetry, New York, 1936

Philo Judaeus (1st century)

THE CITY OF GOD

Do not seek for the City of God on earth, for it is not built of wood or
stone; but seek it in the soul of man who is at peace with himself and is
a lover of true wisdom.

If a man practises ablutions of the body, but defiles his mind—if he
offers hecatombs, founds a temple, adorns a shrine, and does nothing for
making his soul beautiful—let him not be called religious. He has wandered far from real religion, mistaking ritual for holiness; attempting as
it were, to bribe the Incorruptible and to flatter Him whom none can
flatter. God welcomes the genuine service of a soul, the sacrifice of truth;
but from display of wealth He turns away.

Will any man with impure soul and with no intention to repent dare to
approach the Most High God? The grateful soul of the wise man is the
true altar of God.

Philonis Alexandrini Opera, translated from
the Greek by F. H. Colson, 1896

St Augustine (354-430)

MY HAPPY HOME

Jerusalem, my happy home,
    Name ever dear to me!
When shall my labours have an end,
    In joy, and peace, and thee?

When shall these eyes thy heaven-built walls
    And pearly gates behold,
Thy bulwarks with salvation strong,
    And streets of shining gold?

There happier bowers than Eden's bloom,
    Nor sin nor sorrow know:
Blest seats, through rude and stormy scenes
    I onward press to you.

211

Why should I shrink from pain and woe,
  Or feel at death dismay?
I've Canaan's goodly land in view,
  And realms of endless day.

Apostles, martyrs, prophets there
  Around my Saviour stand;
And soon my friends in Christ below
  Will join the glorious band.

Jerusalem, my happy home,
  My soul still pants for thee!
Then shall my labours have an end,
  When I thy joys shall see.

Presumably translated by James Montgomery

Saint John Damascene[1] (8th century)

ODE IX

Thou New Jerusalem, arise and shine!
The glory of the Lord on thee hath risen!
Sion, exult! rejoice with joy divine,
Mother of God! Thy Son hath burst His prison.

O Heavenly Voice! O word of purest love!
'Lo! I am with you always to the end!'
This is the anchor, steadfast from above,
The golden anchor, whence our hopes depend.

O Christ, our Pascha! greatest, holiest, best!
God's Word and Wisdom and effectual Might!
Thy fuller, lovelier presence manifest,
In that eternal realm, that knows no night.

Hymns of the Eastern Church, 1862,
translated from the Greek by J. M. Neale

[1] Saint John Damascene was the last but one of the Fathers of the Eastern Church, and the greatest of her poets.

Hildebert of Tours (1051–1134)

ME RECEPTET SION ILLA

Mine be Sion's habitation,
Sion, David's sure foundation:
Formed of old by light's Creator,
Reached by Him, the Mediator:

Peace dwelleth uninvaded,
Spring perpetual, light unfaded:
Odours rise with airy lightness,
Harpers strike their harps of brightness;

None one sigh for pleasure sendeth;
None can err, and none offendeth;
Home celestial! Home eternal!
Home upreared by Power Supernal!
Grant me, Saviour, with Thy Blessed
Of Thy Rest to be possessed,
And amid the joys it bringeth,
Sing the song that none else singeth.

Translated from the Latin by J. M. Neale, 1851

Bernard of Morlaix (*circa* 1145)

JERUSALEM THE GOLDEN

1. Jerusalem the golden,
   With milk and honey blest,
   Beneath thy contemplation
   Sink heart and voice oppressed;
   I know not, O I know not,
   What joys await us there,
   What radiancy of glory,
   What bliss beyond compare!

2. They stand, those halls of Zion,
   All Jubilant with song,
   And bright with many an angel,
   And all the martyr throng;
   The Prince is ever in them,
   The daylight is serene;
   The pastures of the blessed
   Are decked in glorious sheen.

3. There is the throne of David;
   And there, from care released,
   The shout of them that triumph,
   The song of them that feast;
   And they, who with their Leader,
   Have conquered in the fight,
   Forever and forever
   Are clad in robes of white.

4. O sweet and blessed country,
   The home of God's elect!
   O sweet and blessed country
   That eager hearts expect!
   Jesus, in mercy bring us
   To that dear land of rest,
   Who art, with God the Father
   And Spirit, ever blest!

Translated from the Latin by J. M. Neale, 1851

Peter Abelard (1079–1142)

O QUANTA QUALIA SUNT ILLA SABBATA

O what their joy and their glory must be—
Those endless Sabbaths the blessed ones see!
Crown for the valiant; to weary ones rest:
God shall be all, and in all ever blest.

What are the Monarch, His court, and his throne?
What are the peace and the joy that they own?
Tell us, ye blest ones, that in it have share,
If what ye feel ye can fully declare.

Truly 'Jerusalem' name we that shore,
'Vision of Peace' that brings joy evermore;
Wish and fulfilment can severed be never;
Nor the thing prayed for come short of the prayer.

We, where no trouble distraction can bring,
Safely the anthems of Sion shall sing:
While for Thy grace, Lord, their voices of praise
Thy blessed people shall evermore raise.

There dawns no Sabbath—no Sabbath is over;
Those Sabbath-keepers have one, and no more;
One and unending is that triumph-song
Which to the angels and us shall belong.

Now in the meanwhile, with hearts raised on high,
We for that country must yearn and must sigh:
Seeking Jerusalem, dear native land,
Through our long exile on Babylon's strand.

Low before Him with our praises we fall,
Of Whom, and *in* Whom, and *through* Whom are all:
Of Whom—the Father, and in Whom—the Son:
Through Whom—the Spirit, with These ever One.
                                        Amen.

*From a twelfth-century MS. discovered in the Royal Library at Brussels, probably
part of a collection of hymns which Abelard prepared for the use of the Abbey of the
Paraclete of which Heloise was abbess.*

Milton (1608-1674)

SATAN AND CHRIST OVER JERUSALEM

So saying he caught him up, and without wing
Of *Hippegrif* bore through the air sublime
Over the Wilderness and o'er the Plain;
Till underneath then fair *Jerusalem*,
The holy City lifted high her Towers,
And higher yet the glorious Temple rear'd
Her pile, far off appearing like a Mount
Of Alabaster, top't with golden Spires:
There on the highest Pinnacle he set
The Son of God . . .

Paradise Regain'd, Book IV

Giles Fletcher (1585-1623)

THE HEAVENLY JERUSALEM

Here may the band, that now in triumph shines,
And that (before they were invested thus)
In earthly bodies carried heavenly minds,
Pitched round about in order glorious,
Their sunny tents, and houses luminous,
　　All their eternal day in songs employing,
　　　Joying their end, without end of their joying,
While their almighty prince destruction is destroying.

About the holy City rolls a flood
Of molten crystal, like a sea of glass,
On which weak stream a strong foundation stood,
Of living diamonds the building was,
That all things else, besides itself, did pass.
　　Her streets, instead of stones, the stars did pave,
　　　And little pearls, for dust, it seem'd to have,
On which soft-streaming manna, like pure snow, did wave.

In mid'st of this City celestial,
Where the eternal temple should have rose,
Lighten'd th' idea beatifical:
End, and beginning of each thing that grows,
Whose self no end, nor yet beginning knows,
  That hath no eyes to see, nor ears to hear,
  Yet sees, and hears, and is all eye, all ear,
That nowhere is contain'd, and yet is everywhere.

Had I a voice of steel to tune my song,
Were every verse as smoothly filed as glass,
And every member turned to a tongue,
And every tongue were made of sounding brass,
Yet all that skill, and all this strength, alas,
  Should it presume to gild, were misadvis'd,
  The place, where David hath new songs devis'd,
As in his burning throne he sits emparadis'd.

Christ's Triumph after Death, 1610

John Bunyan (1628–1688)

THE NEW JERUSALEM

Blessed is he whose lot it will be to see this holy city descending and
lighting upon the place that shall be prepared for her situation and rest!
Then will be a golden world: wickedness shall then be ashamed, especially
that which persecutes the church. Holiness, goodness and truth, shall
then, with great boldness, countenance, and reverence, walk upon the
face of all the earth. It will be then always summer, always sunshine,
always pleasant, green, fruitful, and beautiful to the sons of God. 'And
Judah shall dwell for ever, and Jerusalem from generation to generation.'
Joel iii. 18, 20. 'And the name of the city from *that* day *shall* be, The Lord
is there.' Eze. xlviii. 35. 'O blessedness.'

The holy city, or New Jerusalem, London, 1665

Anonymous

HYMN AT EVENSONG

Hierusalem, whose Heav'nly Mien
Betrays the Peace that reigns within;
Whose quarries living Rocks supply
To build and raise the Tow'rs so high,
Heav'n's brightest Angels crown the Pile,
And God does on the Labours smile.

O *Sion's Daughter* well betroth'd.
With all thy Easter's Glory cloth'd.
In all the Spouses Graces dress'd.
In thee, the Spouse himself is bless'd;
Thou beauteous Queen of Heav'nly Love,
Whom Christ espouses from above.

Thy Orient Gates with Pearl array'd,
Stand all ways open and display'd.
For all who thither drawn with Love,
Have nobly fixt their hearts above:
Such as here thought it high Reward
To suffer with their Suffr'ing Lord.

Thus hardest Marbles, toughest Oaks,
Polish'd and shap'd by dint of Streaks,
The skilful Artist's able Hand
Makes fit to take their Place and stand
On highest Pinacles to shine
O'er all the Edifice divine.

To thee, most High, our Voice we raise
To thee, most High, in all thy Ways,
We, both the Father and the Son,
And Paraclete adore in One:
Whilst endless Anthems sound the Fame,
And loud Hosana's echo 'to thy Name.

Primer, 1706

Christopher Smart (1721-1770)

PEACE

I

The Mount of Olives was thy seat,
  O Angel, heav'nly fair;
And thou, sweet Peace, didst often meet
  Thy Prince and Saviour there.

II

But now abroad condemn'd to roam,
  From Salem lov'd and bless'd;
A quiet conscience is thine home,
  In every faithful breast.

III

Thou didst Augustus first inspire,
  That bloody war should cease;
And to Melchisedec retire,
  The Sov'reign of our peace.

IV

O come unto the Church repair,
  And her defects review;
Of old thou plantedst olives there,
  Which to redundance grew.

V

Sustains the pillars of the state,
  Be health and wealth conjoin'd;
And in each house thy turtles mate,
  To multiply mankind.

Hymns for the Amusement of Children, 1770

PROLOGUE TO 'A PILGRIMAGE TO THE HEAVENLY JERUSALEM' BY A POOR CLARE

BRIEF RULES FOR THE PILGRIMS WHO TEND TO THE HEAVENLY JERUSALEM

1. First, they must endeavour to be deaf, dumb, and blind to all that does not concern them; they must love silence, recollection, and prayer, and practise it as much as their employments will permit them.

2. They must have a great love, tenderness, and compassion for their neighbours.

3. They must suffer injuries in silence, with patience, and without reply.

4. They must love holy poverty, practise humility, and render themselves exemplary in holy obedience, and in the mortification of their senses.

5. Finally, they must look upon themselves as pilgrims and strangers in the world, and sigh without intermission for the happy hour that will finish their exile.

PRAYER:

May the desire of the heavenly Jerusalem grow and be strong in our hearts, that we be not ever tossed on the streams of Babylon of this world of confusion; but that our captivity may pass away, and our everlasting happiness may arrive, where we shall never cease singing the songs of Sion with Christ our Lord.   Amen.

ASPIRATION:

Most loving Jesus, may the desire of the heavenly Jerusalem grow and be strong in our hearts.

From an ancient MS. belonging to the Bridgettine Nuns of
Sion House, Spetisbury

Francis Turner Palgrave (1824-1897)

O THOU, NOT MADE WITH HANDS

Thou art where'er the proud
   In humbleness melts down;
Where self itself yields up;
   Where martyrs win their crown;
Where faithful souls possess
Themselves in perfect peace.

Where in life's common ways
   With cheerful feet we go;
Where in his steps we tread
   Who trod the way of woe;
Where he is in the heart,
City of God, thou art.

The English Hymnal, 1903

Samuel Johnson (1822-1882)

CITY OF GOD

City of God! how broad and far
   Outspread thy walls sublime;
The true thy chartered freemen are
   Of every age and clime . . .

How purely hath thy speech come down,
   From man's primeval youth!
How grandly hath thine empire grown
   Of freedom, love and truth.

Hymns of the Spirit, 1864

Thomas Hardy (1840–1928)

THE MODEL OF THE CITY

For a few weeks their work had gone on with a monotony which in itself was a delight to him. Then it happened that the children were to be taken to Christminster to see an itinerant exhibition, in the shape of a model of Jerusalem, to which schools were admitted at a penny a head in the interests of education. They marched along the road two and two, she beside her class with her simple cotton sunshade, her little thumb cocked up against its stem; and Phillotson behind in his long dangling coat, handling his walking-stick genteelly, in the musing mood which had come over him since her arrival. The afternoon was one of sun and dust, and when they entered the exhibition room few people were present but themselves.

The model of the ancient city stood in the middle of the apartment, and the proprietor, with a fine religious philanthropy written on his features, walked round it with a pointer in his hand, showing the young people the various quarters and places known to them by name from reading their Bibles; Mount Moriah, the Valley of Jehoshaphat, the City of Zion, the walls and the gates, outside one of which there was a large mound like a tumulus, and on the mound a little white cross. The spot, he said, was Calvary.

'I think,' said Sue to the schoolmaster, as she stood with him a little in the background, 'that this model, elaborate as it is, is a very imaginary production. How does anybody know that Jerusalem was like this in the time of Christ? I am sure this man doesn't.'

'It is made after the best conjectural maps, based on actual visits to the city as it now exists.'

'I fancy we have had enough of Jerusalem,' she said, 'considering we are not descended from the Jews. There was nothing first-rate about the place, or people, after all—as there was about Athens, Rome, Alexandria, and other old cities.'

'But, my dear girl, consider what it is to us!'

She was silent, for she was easily repressed; and then perceived behind the group of children clustered round the model a young man in a white flannel jacket, his form being bent so low in his intent inspection of the Valley of Jehoshaphat that he was almost hidden from view by the Mount of Olives. 'Look at your cousin Jude,' continued the schoolmaster. 'He doesn't think we have had enough of Jerusalem!'

'Ah—I didn't see him!' she cried in her quick light voice. 'Jude—how seriously you are going into it!'

Jude started up from his reverie, and saw her. 'O—Sue!' he said with a glad flush of embarrassment. 'These are your school-children, of course! I saw that schools were admitted in the afternoons, and thought you might come; but I got so deeply interested that I didn't remember where I was. How it carries one back, doesn't it? I could examine it for hours, but I have only a few minutes, unfortunately; for I am in the middle of a job out here.'

'Your cousin is so terribly clever that she criticizes it unmercifully,' said Phillotson, with good-humoured satire. 'She is quite sceptical as to its correctness.'

'No, Mr. Phillotson, I am not—altogether! I hate to be what is called a clever girl—there are too many of that sort now!' answered Sue sensitively. 'I only meant—I don't know what I meant—except that it was what you don't understand!'

Jude the Obscure, 1895

Margaret Jourdain (1876–1951)

CHRISTMINSTER

'It was Christminster, the fancied place he had likened to the new Jerusalem.'
Hardy's Jude the Obscure

The vapour shadowing hill and plain is rent,
    The trembling cloud brings forth the sun to sight
And through the drifts, the city eminent
    Stirs itself in transparency of light.
The earth dilates; like jewels newly set
    The fluttering needles of rejoicing spires,
Blue bubble of dome, and vane and parapet
    Spring from the shallows of smoke—Jerusalem
Whose walks are as of jasper, with the fires
    Of the twelve divers jewels set in them.

Poems, 1911

John Masefield (1874-1967)

THE SEEKERS

Friends and loves we have none, nor wealth nor blessed abode
But the hope of the City of God at the other end of the road.

Not for us are content, and quiet, and peace of mind,
For we go seeking a city that we shall never find.

There is no solace on earth for us—for such as we—
Who search for a hidden city that we shall never see.

Only the road and the dawn, the sun, the wind, and the rain,
And the watch-fire under stars, and sleep, and the road again.

We travel the dusty road till the light of the day is dim,
And sunset shows us spires away on the world's rim.

We travel from dawn to dusk, till the day is past and by,
Seeking the Holy City beyond the rim of the sky.

Friends and loves we have none, nor wealth, nor blest abode,
But the hope of the City of God at the other end of the road.

Collected Poems, 1923

Humbert Wolfe (1885-1940)

UNCELESTIAL CITY

Creator of the spirit, self-created,
    since all creation is only thought ungodded
by gradual matter, slowly separated
    from beauty that is for ever disembodied,

be near us when we build our city, indulge
    the builders' plan with starshine, turn the brick
with the courses of dawn, and let the sun divulge
    the secret of his gold arithmetic—

one among many. Be near us when we stumble
  through myriad shapes, wherewith, when thou art dim, age
muffles the streets of vision, and, when these crumble,
  let us remember of what they were the image.

Be near us when we fail, and, helpless, gaze on
  the turrets, and tall cathedrals, that we planned
to be the music of life in diapason,
  unravelling through silence, strand by strand.

When in the east the dawns we pass from wait red
  and angry, till our own creations fear us,
when love, that was the builder, turns to hatred
  of those for whom he builded, then be near us.

Be near us when the uncelestial city
  in stone and marble coldly stands apart
against the sky, with room for all save pity,
  possessing everything except its heart.

Creator of the spirit, when a king
  sent out the last crusade, he built for this
a city in the marshes, encompassing
  his dream with wall and tower and fortalice.

A year he wrought it, and every stone he laid
  was quarried in your westering islands, set
with mortar to catch the east in ambuscade,
  and what he built with vision is lovely yet.

But for his fleet the ecstasy, turned traitor,
  faded, and only the cry remains of them
across the evening sea, '*Veni, Creator!*' —
  only the cry and lost Jerusalem.

Send the crusaders, spirit, through sunset drawn
  along the western seamarks of thy will.
Be near us always, but most of all when dawn
  breaks, and we see the City on the hill.

Uncelestial City, 1930

X The City of the future

> *'Awake, awake; put on thy strength, O Zion;*
> *put on thy beautiful garments, O Jerusalem,*
> *the holy city. Shake thyself from the dust;*
> *arise and sit down, O Jerusalem.*
>
> Isaiah lii. 1, 2

> *'Yet that make mention of the Lord, keep no*
> *silence, and give Him no rest till He establish,*
> *and till He make Jerusalem a praise in the*
> *earth.'*
>
> Isaiah lxii

> *. . . and men shall thereto and there shall be*
> *no more extermination but Jerusalem shall*
> *dwell safely . . .*
>
> Zech. xiv. 1–11

The fate of the Holy City is still contested by strongly embittered and highly emotional factions. Inevitably, the real heart of the problem remains aside: how can the three great world concepts that Jerusalem has called forth be reconciled? Age-old incompatibilities lie behind the various religious doctrines, superstitions and prejudices. At the stage now reached by civilization, when its very survival is at stake, can man any longer afford to nourish such stubborn antagonisms?

Even if, in the past, it may have been possible to seek spiritual peace along widely divergent paths, surely the great challenge that now arises is to fashion a new religious syncretism. This can be achieved only if one is prepared to survey and judge the three faiths (each of which lays claim to a universal spiritual dominion) from the vantage-point of a still greater universality which would transcend all three. With each of them continuing to draw on the deep springs of its own tradition, they should at least strive, in their temporal activities, to attain contact and understanding on a common ground of some charity. For each can offer its own contribution: Judaism, its broad vision of humanity; Christianity, its supra-racial message striving towards universal communion; and Islam, a sense of human dignity and, at its best, of tolerance. In this higher universality, man may at last recognize the best and the worst of his fate.

It may of course be objected that, while so many divergences still exist within each of the three creeds, to aim at a higher form of reconciliation between them would seem chimerical. The short and only answer is that life itself is running out. In an age of ever-increasing interchange between people of all races, the time seems to have come for a universal religion, all-embracing yet tolerant of individualism, as the one implied in Lessing's *Nathan der Weise*; a religion enriched by the continuity of values contained in art, literature and the humanities. In the tragic impasse of our atomic era Jerusalem is perhaps the only place on earth to engender such a concept.

The unique, imperishable significance of the city is that, for different reasons, it has always been not only the scene of bloodshed, but also a state of the spirit and an inspiration: first, for Jews after their first Temple was destroyed, for Christians as it became identified with the Cross and the empty tomb, and for Islam since the building of the Dome of the Rock. It may yet dawn upon the lazy consciences of clumsy politicians and narrow-sighted theologians that the true meaning of the Holy City—still torn by the clash of dogmas, of rival denominations and of rituals—is the assertion of the fundamental unity of the spirit. Jerusalem, as the world's centre, bringing together the piercing vision of individual mystics and the divergent systems of organized religions would then indeed become the first city of the future.

Gotthold Ephraim Lessing (1729-1781)

NATHAN THE WISE

NATHAN

But, Sultan
Ere I trust myself completely to you,
Will you permit me to relate a narrative?

SALADIN

Why not? I've aye been partial to a tale well told.

NATHAN

In days of yore a man lived in the East,
Who owned a ring of marvellous worth,
Given to him by a hand beloved.
The stone was opal, and shed a hundred lovely rays,
But chiefly it possessed the secret power
To make the owner loved of God and man,
If he but wore it in this faith and confidence;
What wonder then that this man in the East
Ne'er from his finger took the ring,
And so arranged it should for ever with his house remain,
Namely thus:—He bequeathed it to
The most beloved of his sons,
Firmly prescribing that he in turn
Should leave it to the dearest of his sons;
And always thus the dearest, without respect to birth,
Became the head and chieftain of the house
By virtue of the ring alone.
The ring, descending thus from son to son,
Came to the father of three sons at last,
All three of whom obeyed him equally,
And all of whom he therefore loved alike.
From time to time indeed, now one seemed worthiest of the ring.
And now another, now the third,
Just as it happened one or other with him were alone,
And his o'erflowing heart was not divided with the other two;
And so to each one of the three he gave
The promise—in pious weakness done—
He should possess the wondrous ring.
This then went on long as it could;
But then at last it came to dying,

Which brings the father into sore perplexity.
It pains him much to practise such deceit
Upon two sons who rested so upon his word.
What can be done? In secret
He seeks out a skilful artist,
And from him orders yet two other rings.
Just to the pattern of his own.
And urges him to spare neither pains nor gold,
To make a perfect match.
The artist so succeeded in his task,
That, when he brought the jewels home,
The father even failed to tell which was the pattern ring.
Now, glad and joyous, he calls his sons—
But separately of course—gives each
A special blessing with his ring, and dies.
. . . Scarce was the father dead,
When each one with his ring appears
Claiming each the headship of the house.
Inspections, quarrelling, and complaints ensue;
But all in vain, the veritable ring
Was not distinguishable,—
    (after a pause, during which he expects the Sultan's answer.)
Almost as indistinguishable as to us,
Is now—the true religion.
. . . As said, the sons accused each other,
And each one swore before the judge
He has received his ring directly
From his father's hand—which was quite true—
And that, indeed, after having long his promise held,
To enjoy, eventually the ring's prerogative,
Which was no less the truth.
Each one insisted that it was impossible
His father could play false with him,
    . . . The judge said this: Produce your father here
At once, or I'll dismiss you from this court.
Think you I'm here but to solve riddles?
Or would you wait till the true ring itself will speak?
. . . The judge went further on to say:
If you will have my judgement, not my advice,
Then go, But my advice is this:
You take the matter as it stands.

If each one had his ring straight from his father.
So let each believe his ring the true one.
'Tis possible your father would no longer tolerate
The tyranny of this one ring in his family,
And surely loved you all and alike,
And that he would not two oppress
By favouring the third.
So said the modest judge.

SALADIN
God, oh God—

NATHAN
Saladin, if now you feel yourself to be
That promised sage—

SALADIN
I dust? I nothing? O, God.—

NATHAN
What ails thee, Sultan?

SALADIN
Nathan, dear Nathan, your judge's thousand
Thousand years have not yet fled,
His judgement seat's not become mine.
Go, go; but be my friend.

NATHAN
And Saladin had nothing more to say?

SALADIN
Nothing.

> Act III, Scene VII, translated from the
> German by William Tacks, Glasgow, 1894

Theodor Herzl (1860–1904)

THE JERUSALEM OF MY DREAMS

I want to open out to those scorned ones a country which is *theirs*; where, in full freedom, and thanks to freedom, their qualities can find scope for development, while at the same time the vices and defects which ages of persecution and ostracism have developed in, the Jews will be diminished to free them finally of their moral squalor; and succeed in bringing into play their very real and intellectual and moral gifts, so that my people, in a word, may no longer be '*les sales juifs*' but the '*peuple lumière*', which they can be.

The New Jerusalem, which I see in my dreams, the reborn, rejuvenated and very living Israel which is in my mind, appears to me in its minutest details, and I perceive it as the epitome, the extract, of all that civilization has spent centuries in achieving. And yet more: 'Pray, realise how countries, how cities, have always owed their origin to chance,' that they grew slowly, perfected themselves by a slow progression; and, lastly, that even in the fairest city there always exists, by the side of progress and modernity, vestiges more or less considerable, of vanished epochs: old quarters, picturesque but unhealthy, where often it is difficult to introduce modern improvements.

Over there it will be very different—that land which to-day seems dead, though merely sleeping, ready like *Jairus*' daughter, to rise from the grave and to take up again its place among the living. Everything remains to be done? Then, so much the better. We shall do everything. We shall select the best sites whereon to plant our cities; to build these we shall employ all the resources of modern science; we shall restore the value of the land, and our people will learn to cultivate that land; they will learn to exercise their faculties and their gifts of endurance, of industry and intelligence, in other pursuits than those to which they have been hitherto confined.

From Jerusalem, the Holy City, I would fain banish the traffickers and the uncleanliness which dishonour her. Without interference, and with reference for each stone, I would cleanse her and consecrate her to works of benevolence, build shelters for old men and little children, stimulate labours of intelligence, do anything that would preserve for her the character of self-communion and lofty grandeur. And only outside those walls would rise up the new city, the modern Jerusalem, dominated and protected by the majesty of the ancient walls. . . .

Old New-Land, 1902

Louis Golding (1895–1958)

THE UNIVERSITY

It was the day of the unveiling by Lord Allenby of the great cemetery upon Mount Scopus. When the monument was unveiled and the crowd dispersed, I turned from the youthful dead to the youthful living, from the cemetery to the Hebrew University, farther along the flank of Mount Scopus. I remembered a day in Spring a year ago, when I had climbed another and a greener hill, and looked upon a mellower University. I had wandered out of Oxford by way of Cumnor Hill, and turned on my traces and looked down over woods and willowy meadows towards the tall, grey towers.

A year ago I had not dreamed that my fate should find me here in a score of years. Here now, not in mere fantasy, I stood upon Scopus. The professors and students were in their homes this day, this being the Sabbath. And I paced the small circuit of the buildings, looking between the growing walls by my side and the remote bastions of Moab, and meditated upon the deeds achieved, and upon the critics and the cynics, and those that had faith.

Bologna endured. Oxford endured. Had the dice been loaded against them, Naples or Cambridge would have sufficed to hold up the torch of learning. There was no danger that the culture of England or Italy would be extinguished for want of an altar where it might be tended. Israel, on the other hand, had waited so long that to wait longer would have been dangerous, to act at once was not only true policy but true religion.

It will not, therefore, prejudice the prospects of the Hebrew University that the whole of Jewish history in the Diaspora has been a conscious preparation for it. It might be said that all Jewry instituted itself a 'University' in the exact mediaeval sense of that term. The illustrious schools of Hillel and Shamai were foreshadowings of Scopus, and the academies of Jabneh and Tiberias; and Scopus has no easy task before it to resume the traditions of Sura and Nehardea in Babylonia. Yet not less than these, even in some senses more glorious, were the Yeshivehs of recent and more perilous centuries, from the tomb-like cellars in Spain to the crude huts in sequestered Russian villages. And if Scopus has high traditions to assume in purely Jewish learning, it has had doughty predecessors in secular scholarship. For during the middle ages of Jewish history, when Jew and Arab between them recreated upon the southern and western shores of the Mediterranean the glory that had passed with the classical world from the opposite shores, the Jewish academies were universities in the sense of Scopus—all knowledge was their province, divine, human, and infernal even.

I do not anticipate that the wilder sort of genius will be nourished by the university, for he is usually shy of institutions. But it will be remembered that if Oxford rejected Shelley, she retained Swinburne; and if Gauguin must needs betake himself to a South Sea island to express his genius, Cezanne, substantially a more frantic revolutionary, kept on painting demurely at home. We cannot but anticipate the establishment on Scopus of faculties in the arts and crafts. Sometimes precept stifles genius. Rather more frequently it does not. But there is much more decoration to be done, both in the direction of filling the air with goodly sounds and of covering bare walls with goodly pictures, than the necessarily restricted number of geniuses in a given generation is physically capable of executing.

It will be the duty of the University to interpret Judaism, in terms of its own self, not in terms borrowed from Frenchmen or Englishmen.

Is it too audacious to dream that Scopus might bring back again the two ancient splendours so long faded from those shores of the Mediterranean, the splendours of the Arabs who persist without splendour and the Greeks who are dead? It was the Jews and the Arabs, in the earlier Dark Ages—when Europe was as distracted by the wars of creed as she is to-day distracted by the wars of commerce—it was the Jews and Arabs who held the torch high upon the northern littoral of Africa and illumined the darkness of the plateaux of Spain. What a sodality might be restored between Jews and Arabs, housed in intricate philosophies and shadowy courts, taking equal delight in the fretting of logic and cedar-wood, the interweaving of rhymes and embroideries.

But northward shone a splendour more august than this, where the acres of scarlet anemones sweep from Delphi towards the sword-thrust of the Gulf of Corinth, where the tawny ruin of Sunium arrests the Aegean wind. Yet the Jews who gather upon Mount Scopus have returned from an Odyssey more heart-breaking and perilous than ever the worshippers at Delphi or Sunium engaged on, and out of their wars against gods and men might extract an ore to be fashioned into shapes not less grand than Prometheus or the Parthenon.

Those Ancient Lands, being a journey to Palestine, 1928

Michael Harari (b. 1928)

JERUSALEM SONNET

I call myself an internationalist,
I've tangled up in love with many places
And sticking to each place that I have kissed
Is one of my innumerable faces.
But where this white Mesanna shouts all day
Inside the God-exploded roofless sky—
Stone houses white as a free Saturday
And stones like my own flesh that make me cry.

Where pedlars are enthroned like kings upon
The doorsteps with the Bible on their knee
And night is tall as consolation and
Plays the accordion with a starry hand:
Jerusalem is all the world to me
And all the world to me is Babylon.

David Lutyens (b. 1929)

THE SECOND COMING

Beside the tomb where the Messiah lay
The great white stone was rolled away;
Beside the tomb three soldiers sat;
They chewed their cud, and snored and spat.

And where the soldiers sat and spat,
Armies tramped, the worm and rat;
The Syrian and the Coptic Priest,
The bully and the mail-clad beast.

Each sect claimed its own corner,
Stabbed heretics, and every mourner
Of dead Christ who dared to mourn in his own way
Was called a heretic and showed away.

235

There was the sallow Russian Priest,
His face as puffed and pale as yeast;
His garments made him seem a bat
From his winged coat to his peaked hat.

Then suddenly the confused tongues
Turned to a single uproar; the lungs
Were pierced by a great cry,
'What is that mushroom in the sky?'

Suddenly babbling tongues were still;
A single hush fell on them all:
'It is the Second Coming,' they cried.
'It is man's Doom,' the sky replied.

A solitary tower of fire,
Above the city higher, higher,
With golden fist filled up the sky;
'Jerusalem,' was what it wrote on high.

THE NEW JERUSALEM

But in the last days it shall come to pass, that the mountain of the house of the Lord shall be established in the top of the mountains, and it shall be exalted above the hills; and people shall flow into it.

And many nations shall come, and say, Come, and let us go up to the mountain of the Lord, and to the house of the God of Jacob; and he will teach us of his ways, and he will walk in his paths; for the law shall go forth of Zion, and the word of the Lord from Jerusalem.

And he shall judge among many people, and rebuke strong nations afar off; and they shall beat their swords into ploughshares, and their spears into pruning hooks: nation shall not lift up a sword against nation, neither shall they learn war any more.

But they shall sit every man under his vine and under his fig tree; and none shall make them afraid: for the mouth of the Lord of hosts hath spoken it.

Micah iv. 1–4

TO PLEASE GOD

Jerusalem was a ploughed field, and the ground on which the Temple now stands the joint inheritance of two brothers; one of these was married, and had several children, the other lived a bachelor. They cultivated in common the field which had devolved on them in right of their mother. At harvest time the two brothers bound up their sheaves, and made them of two equal stacks, which they left upon the field. During the night a good thought presented itself to the one who was not married: 'My brother', said he to himself, 'has a wife and children to maintain; it is not just that our shares should be equal; let me then take a few sheaves from my stack, and secretly add them to his; he will not perceive it, and therefore cannot refuse them.' This project the young man immediately executed. The same night the elder awoke, and said to his wife, 'My brother is young, and lives alone, without a companion to assist him in his labours, and console him under his fatigues; it is not just that we should take from the field as many sheaves as he does; let us get up, and secretly go and carry a certain number of sheaves to his stack; he will not find it out to-morrow, and therefore cannot refuse them', and they did so accordingly. The next day both brothers went to the field, and each was much surprised to find the two stacks alike; neither being able, in his own mind, to account for the prodigy. They pursued the same course for several successive nights; but as each carried to his brother's stack the same number of sheaves, the stacks still remained equal, till one night both determined to stand sentinel to elucidate the mystery; they met, each bearing the sheaves destined for his brother's stack.

'Now the spot where so beautiful a thought at once occurred to, and was so perseveringly acted upon, by two men, must be a place agreeable to God; and the two men blessed it, and chose it whereon to build a house to his name.'

Arabian Legend

Isaiah

LIGHT EVERLASTING

Arise, shine, for thy light is come
And the glory of the Lord is risen upon thee.

Lift up thine eyes round about, and see:
Thy all are gathered together, and come to thee;
Thy sons come from far,

And thy daughters are borne on the side.
Then thou shalt see and be radiant,
And thy heart shall throb and be enlarged.

Whereas thou hast been forsaken and hated,
So that no man passed through thee,
I will make thee an eternal excellency,
A joy of many generations.

Thy sun shall no more go down,
Neither shall thy moon withdraw itself,
For the Lord shall be thine everlasting light,
And the days of thy mourning shall be ended.

lx. 4–5, 15, 20

Israel Zangwill (1864–1926)

MOSES AND JESUS

In dream I saw two Jews that met by chance,
One old, stern-eyed, deep-browed, yet garlanded
With living light of love around his head.
The other young, with sweet, seraphic glance.
Around went on the town's satanic dance,
Hunger a-piping while at heart he bled,
Shalom Aleichem mournfully each said,
Nor eyed the other straight, and looked askance.
Sudden from Church outrolled an organ hymn,
From synagogue a loudly chaunted air,
Each with its Prophet's high acclaim instinct.
Then for the first time met their eyes, swift-linked
In one strange, silent, piteous gaze, and dim
With bitter tears of agonized despair.

From *Blind Children*, 1903

AND HERE WILL I MAKE AN END

And here will I make an end.

And if I have done well, and as is fitting the story, it is
that which I desired; but if slenderly and meanly, it is
that which I could attain unto.

For as it is hurtful to drink wine or water alone; and as
wine mingled with water is pleasant, and delighteth the taste;
even so, speech finely framed delighteth the ears of them that
read the story.

And here shall be an end.

2 Maccabees xv. 37–39

ACKNOWLEDGEMENTS

The Editor wishes to thank the following publishers, authors and literary executors who have permitted the use of copyright material:
Mr. Stil Apelgren, Finland, for the poem *The disbeliever at the Wailing Wall* by Arvid Mörne; Mrs. Shaffer and Messrs. Macdonald for a passage from *The Nazarene* by Sholem Asch; Dr. I. Bein, Jerusalem, for the text from Theodor Herzl *Altneuland*; Miss Ivy Compton Burnett for the poem *Christminster* by Margaret Jourdain; the Martin Buber Estate, Jerusalem, for the text *Balshem at Jerusalem*; Messrs. Jonathan Cape and Mrs. Mary Gill for three passages from Eric Gill's *Letters* and *Autobiography*; the Columbia University Press, Professor Merton Jerome Hubert, Professor John La Monte and Professor Martha Evelyn McGinthy for two extracts from Ambroise's *Estoire de la guerre sainte* and Fulcher's *Chronicle of the First Crusade*; Messrs. Cassell, Mr. Robert Graves and Mrs. Joshua Podro for a fragment from *The Nazarene Gospel Restored* and an extract from Hilaire Belloc's *The World's Debate;* Messrs. Chatto and Windus and Mrs. Annie Winnick for a poem by Isaac Rosenberg; Dr. Chazar, Mr. I. M. Lask, Jerusalem, and ACUM for the translation rights of the modern Hebrew poets Chaim Bialik, Jacob Kamzon, Jehuda Carni, Abraham Schlonsky; Miss Babette Deutsch for *Psalm 1933*; Mrs. T. S. Eliot and Messrs. Faber and Faber for a passage from *The Rock*; Mr. G. S. Fraser and Sir John Waller for the poem *Saturday Evening in Jerusalem* by Keith Douglas; Messrs. Ginn and Co., Boston, for the passages from Cynewulf's *Christ*; Mrs. Louis Golding for *The scope for Scopus*; Messrs. Victor Gollancz, Miss Anne Wolfe and Mme Edmond Fleg, Paris, for *Faith and Hope* and *Uncelestial City*; Mr. Zev Vilnay for two texts from his *Legends of Palestine*; The Society of Authors for the poem *The Seekers* by the late Poet Laureate; Messrs. Macmillan for a page from *Jude the Obscure* by Thomas Hardy; A. P. Watt & Son for a page from *A History of the World* by H. G. Wells; Simon & Schuster Inc., New York for *A Report on Israel* by Irwin Shaw. Personal acknowledgements are due to the Librarian of the Vatican; the Arabic Department of the Hebrew University, Jerusalem; the Director of the British Council in the old part of the Holy City; the Director of the Ecole St. Etienne; to Dorothy and Ruth Partington for valuable assistance during the various stages of research and last but not least to the Reading Room of the British Museum and to the learned staff of the London Library.

To many other people and sources of information thanks should also have been expressed. Every possible effort has been made to trace owners of copyright material. If, however, some material has been used without acknowledgement it is in error and the Editor here makes his sincere apologies.

SELECTED BIBLIOGRAPHY

The Catholic Encyclopaedia, ed. Charles Herbermann, N.Y., 1911
Dictionnaire de la Bible, publié sous la direction de Louis Pirot, Paris, 1928
The New Schaff-Herzog Encyclopaedia of Religious Knowledge, N.Y., 1908-12
The Encyclopaedia of Islam, Luzac, London, 1913
The Palestine Exploration Quarterly, London
Abel, F. M.: *Géographie de la Palestine*, 2 vol., Paris, 1933-38
Albright, W. F.: *The Archaeology of Palestine and the Bible*, N.Y., 1935
Diringer, David: *Le Iscrizioni antico-ebraichi Palestinense*, Florence, 1934
Gaster, Moses: *The Samaritans*, Oxford, 1926
Simons, Dr. J.: *Jerusalem in the Old Testament*, Leyden, 1952
Bonsirven, J.: *Exégèse rabbinique et exégèse palestinienne*, Paris, 1939
Montgomery, James A.: *Arabia and the Bible*, Univ. of Pennsylvania Press, 1934
Vaccari, A.: *Libri Poetici della Biblia*, Rome, 1925
Marmardji, P. A.: *Textes Géographiques Arabes sur la Palestine*, Paris, 1951

CONTENTS

DOMINI TOTIVSQ, SACRI TEMPLI EXEMPLVM EX ANTIQ

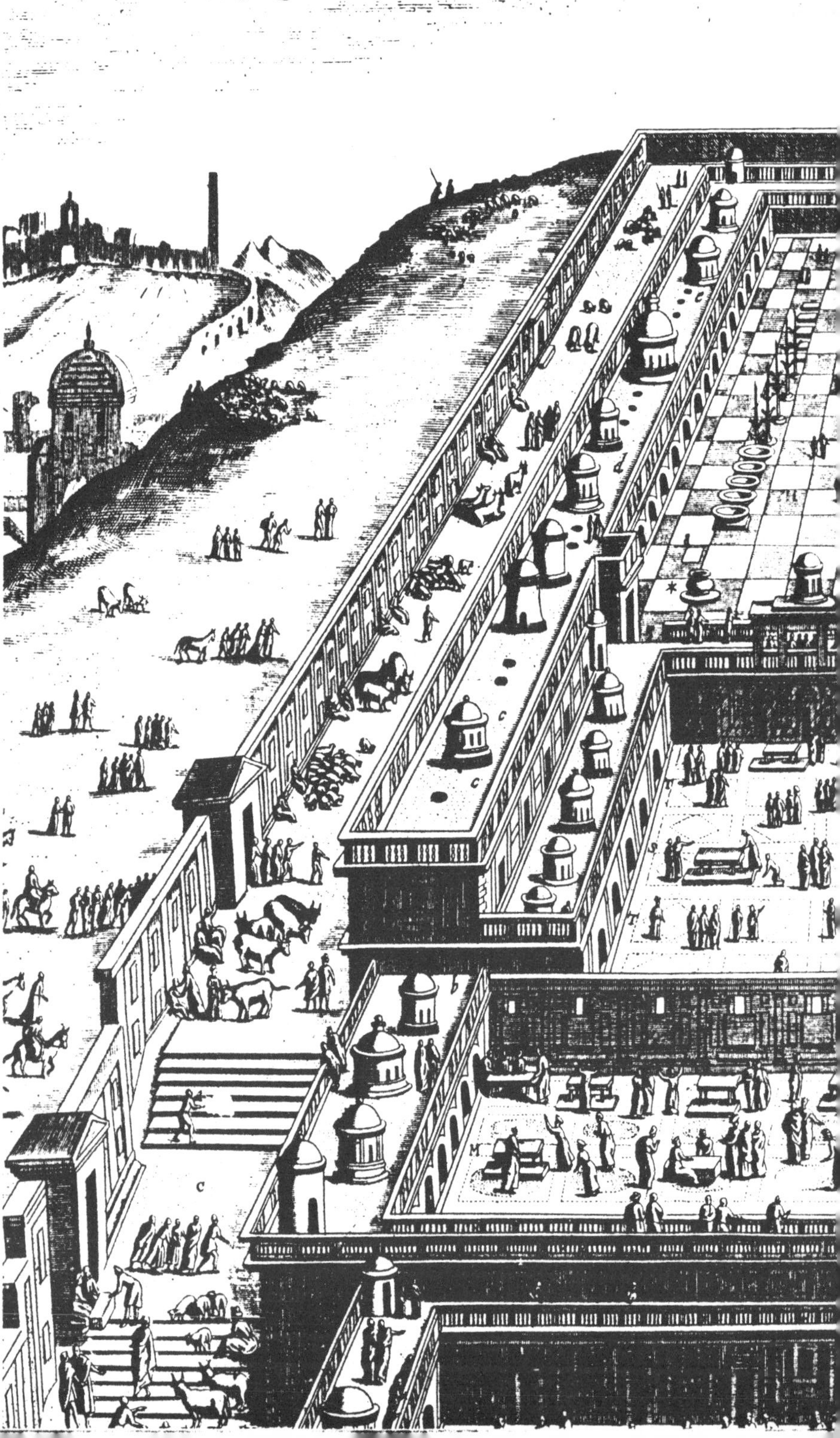